The Illusion of
Public Opinion

The Illusion of Public Opinion

Fact and Artifact in American Public Opinion Polls

George F. Bishop

ROWMAN & LITTLEFIELD PUBLISHERS, INC.
Lanham • Boulder • New York • Toronto • Oxford

ROWMAN & LITTLEFIELD PUBLISHERS, INC.

Published in the United States of America
by Rowman & Littlefield Publishers, Inc.
A wholly owned subsidiary of The Rowman & Littlefield Publishing Group, Inc.
4501 Forbes Boulevard, Suite 200, Lanham, MD 20706
www.rowmanlittlefield.com

P.O. Box 317, Oxford OX2 9RU, UK

British Library Cataloguing in Publication Information Available

Library of Congress Cataloging-in-Publication Data

Bishop, George F.
   The illusion of public opinion : fact and artifact in American public
opinion polls / George F. Bishop.
      p.   cm.
   Includes bibliographical references and index.
   ISBN 0-7425-1644-X (cloth : alk. paper)—ISBN 0-7425-1645-8 (pbk. :
alk. paper)
   1. Public opinion—United States.   2. Public opinion polls.   I. Title.
HN90.P8B57 2004
303.3'8'0973—dc22   2004004906

Printed in the United States of America

♾ ™ The paper used in this publication meets the minimum requirements of American
National Standard for Information Sciences—Permanence of Paper for Printed Library
Materials, ANSI/NISO Z39.48-1992.

To my two biggest supporters
Pama and Kristina

We are inevitably encapsulated in some paradigm of presuppositions, inexplicit or explicit.

—Donald T. Campbell, *Methodology and Epistemology for Social Science*

Contents

Tables, Figures, and Boxes

TABLES

FIGURES

BOXES

Preface

"Americans Favor U.S. Peacekeeping Force in Liberia."[1] So said the press release from the Gallup News Service (July 11, 2003). The question asked by the Gallup Organization was fairly typical in form; it read, "Would you favor or oppose the presence of U.S. ground troops, along with troops from other countries, in an international peacekeeping force in Liberia?" A solid majority (57 percent) favored the idea; just 36 percent opposed it, and only 7 percent volunteered they had "no opinion." The small percentage with "no opinion" seemed particularly surprising since only 10 percent of the respondents had said, in response to a prior question, that they were following the news about the situation in the African country of Liberia "very closely." But however carefully the Gallup analysts qualified and interpreted their findings (see Moore 2003), the headline that became public opinion in the mass media was that Americans favored the idea of a U.S. peacekeeping force in Liberia. Though they had not followed the matter too closely, the great majority of Americans had evidently formed an opinion on the issue. That at least is how it appeared.

The same opinionated public seemed to exist in an ABC News/*Washington Post* poll conducted at about the same time (July 9–10, 2003), but in this case the majority opposed sending troops to Liberia, most likely because the question was worded somewhat differently. It read, "Would you support or oppose sending 2000 U.S. troops to the African nation of Liberia as part of an international force to help enforce a cease-fire in the civil war there?" When the question was asked this way, just 41 percent supported our involvement in Liberia, 51 percent were opposed, and the rest of the respondents (8 percent) had "no opinion" (www.pollingreport.com/liberia). An

NBC News/*Wall Street Journal* poll conducted just two weeks later (July 26–28, 2003), however, indicated that the American public could be readily talked into sending soldiers to Liberia if the question gave them a brief education and persuasive argument. It read, "The West African nation of Liberia, which was founded by former U.S. (United States) slaves, has recently experienced growing poverty and civil war. The United Nations wants to negotiate a ceasefire in this war and send armed peacekeepers to enforce it. Would you approve or disapprove of sending a thousand American soldiers to Liberia as part of a UN peacekeeping force?" When the questions was asked this way, a substantial majority (58 percent) approved of sending troops, 35 percent disapproved, and the rest (7 percent) said "not sure" or "it depends." Though it might not know much about Liberia, the American public appeared to be paying close attention to the wording of the questions.

Just how sensitive respondents were to the wording of the questions became clear from a *Time*/CNN poll on the Liberian situation conducted by Harris Interactive just one week later (July 16–17, 2003). The question, which presumed the respondent knew something about the topic, was asked in one of two ways. In form A the question read, "*As you may know*, the U.S. has been asked to contribute military troops to an international peacekeeping force to deal with the situation in Liberia. Do you favor or oppose sending about a *hundred* troops into Liberia *for a few months or less*?" (emphasis added). In form B it read, "*As you may know*, the U.S. has been asked to contribute military troops to an international peacekeeping force to deal with the situation in Liberia. Do you favor or oppose sending about a *thousand* troops into Liberia *for a year or more*?" (emphasis added). Not surprisingly perhaps to inveterate poll watchers, the change in wording made a noticeable difference in the results. Given the commitment of a small number of troops for a very limited amount of time in form A, a borderline majority (50 percent) was opposed to the peacekeeping action. But when the ante was upped in form B to a thousand troops for a year or more, a solid majority opposed any such action, only 35 percent favored it, and the rest (8 percent) were "not sure" (www.pollingreport.com/liberia). Americans thus seemed tuned in to the nuances of what our policy commitments in Liberia should be.

Or were they? I would contend that this impression was highly misleading in that it suggested the American public knew enough about the situation in Liberia to have formed an opinion. At the time these polls were conducted (July 2003), most Americans probably could not have located Liberia on a world map, nor could they have distinguished it from Nigeria or many other African nations—or for that matter perhaps from an entirely fictitious one (see chapter 2). Indeed, two weeks after the initial Gallup poll had been conducted on the situation in Liberia (July 25–27, 2003), only 13 percent said they had followed the news about the situation in Liberia "very closely"; one-third (33 percent) indicated that they had followed it "somewhat closely" (whatever that meant); and over half (54 percent) admitted they had followed it "not too closely" or "not at all." If so many Americans, by their own admission, were not very up on what was going on in Liberia, on what, then, were they basing their opinions? Most likely, as the cautionary tales in chapter 2 would suggest, they picked up on cues from words and phrases in the question to interpret what it might be about (e.g., American military involvement overseas or a new military commitment by President George W. Bush) and then fell back on their general attitudes toward that constructed psychological object to answer the question. The opinions respondents manufacture on the spot in reaction to such questions are no doubt real, psychologically speaking, insofar as they are based on underlying dispositions toward the mentally constructed object, but when aggregated into the mass we call "public opinion" in the press, they are often illusory with respect to the specific substance of the policy issue that the questions were designed to measure. And if different respondents interpret such frequently ambiguous questions in different ways, and in other ways at different times (see chapters 5 and 6), what unlike psychological objects are being aggregated together when we report findings in the press as if they represented the American public's opinion? This becomes painfully clear when we look closely at public opinion on controversial policy issues such as the teaching of creationism and "intelligent design" in American public schools (see chapter 7). Polls on such matters frequently give a rather spurious impression of what the questions are actually measuring and may in fact measure, as sociologist Howard Schuman (1998) has put it, something partly or entirely different from what was intended.

In fairness, it should be said at the outset that most professional pollsters today do their very best to develop survey questions that measure what people actually think about various issues and problems in American society. They generally do an extremely good job in asking questions that accurately predict the outcome of most elections, and for good reason (see chapter 1). Furthermore, premier polling organizations, such as Gallup (and its partners CNN and *USA Today*), CBS News/*New York Times*, ABC News/*Washington Post*, NBC News/*Wall Street Journal*, and the Pew Research Center for the People and the Press, often experiment with the wording and sequence of the questions they ask because these survey organizations are quite sensitive to the consequences of such variations and typically report them in their press releases. Some organizations experiment as well with the use of filter or quasi-filter questions to screen out respondents who may not have thought enough about an issue to have formed an opinion, though this is far from routine practice in public opinion polling today (see, e.g., the practices of the CBS News/*New York Times* polls). Most of them have become quite aware as well of the sizable and ever-growing cognitive-psychological research litera-ture on the design of survey questions and questionnaires. And, by and large, they are practitioners of the best practices in the field.

All that said, I would contend nonetheless that polls today often create a misleading illusion of public opinion as a result of the ambiguous way in which survey questions are worded and the way in which poll results are reported and interpreted in the mass media. With evidence from a variety of data sources, I will illustrate how polls reported in the press frequently give the spurious impression that a definitive public opinion exists on numerous political and social issues when there is, in fact, widespread public ignorance and poorly informed opinions on such issues at best. I will also present a number of cautionary tales from the worlds of polling and political science of illusory changes in well-known indicators of American political attitudes and public opinion.

My analysis of the pitfalls of asking survey questions and interpreting poll results will presumably lead the reader to a more skeptical appreciation of the art and science of public opinion polling as it is practiced today. The intended audience is not the survey methodologist or cognitive social psy-chologist who is well aware of such pitfalls and the voluminous technical and theoretical literature on the psychology of responses to survey questions. Instead, the book speaks much more to the educated consumers, gatekeepers, and producers of public opinion polls: graduate and undergraduate students, the educated lay public, journalists, political scientists, policy makers, politi-cians, and, of course, the ultimate practitioners and producers themselves, the pollsters. It strives to strike a balance between a readily understandable quantitative analysis of survey data and an interpretive critique of the state of public opinion polling in the United States today.

THE THESIS AND PLAN OF THE BOOK

The chapters that follow track the thesis that a fair amount of what passes as "public opinion" in mass media polls today represents an illusion, an artifact of measurement created by the way in which survey questions are designed and administered to respondents, who often construct their opinions on the spot in response to the frequently vague and ambiguous questions presented to them. Chapter 1 begins with an overview of the elusive concept of public opinion and the enduring controversies in the field about its reality, mea-surement, and utility. I then present the conceptual underpinnings for understanding how polls frequently generate spurious impressions of public opinion, identifying several key problems: (1) widespread public ignorance about public affairs, (2) the inherent vagueness and ambiguity of the language used in most survey questions, and (3) the unpredictable influence of variations in question form, wording, and context. Chapter 2 raises the theme of illusion in its most conspicuous form: the well-documented disposition of many survey respondents to offer opinions on topics they know little or nothing about and even to give responses to totally ambiguous questions about fictitious public affairs issues. Drawing upon the ever-growing literature on "split-ballot" experiments in public opinion and survey research, chapter 3 demonstrates how the form in which the question is asked (e.g., open versus closed), the way in which it is worded and interpreted, and the order in which the question and the response alternatives are presented contribute to the construction of public opinion.

Chapter 4 follows the thesis into the mainstream of political science. First, we revisit a classic controversy over whether the evidence of a "changing American voter" was just an illusion and merely an artifact of a change in the form of the questions used by the University of Michigan Survey Research Center to measure political attitudes in its National Election Studies (NES). We then take a look at other apparent changes in well-established political indicators in the NES that turn out, upon more rigorous examination, to be artifacts of changes in the order and context in which the questions were asked, raising the larger issue of whether these methodological episodes represent but the tip of a much larger iceberg of incomparable survey measures. Pursuing the same theme of illusory changes, chapter 5 returns the focus to the contemporary world of public opinion polling, showing how a number of apparently dramatic changes in American public opinion following the events of September 11, 2001, resulted from an unintended artifact of measurement: changes in the meaning and interpretation of standard survey questions. Chapter 6 takes the artifact theme a step further, looking closely at the troublesome ambiguities of measurement that arise when pollsters and survey researchers try to monitor changes in political attitudes and public opinion over time. We venture once again into the mainstream of political science and consider examples of ambiguities that plague the measurement of well-established concepts such as political ideology, party identification, and trust in government. Here I introduce a rival theory of the survey response that challenges the dominant axiomatic model in contemporary political science and has significant practical implications for the measurement and understanding of public opinion. In chapter 7 we focus on some telling case histories of illusion from another angle: how spurious and misleading impressions of public opinion can be manufactured in the mass media by various means. Examples of such manufactured impressions include the totally unfounded claims of public support for the Contract with America; the unintended consequences of asking poorly worded questions about public opinion on the reality of the Holocaust; the misunderstanding of public approval for President Bill Clinton during the Lewinsky scandal and impeachment episodes; and the highly misleading polls on public support for teaching creationism and "intelligent design" in American public schools.

The theme of illusion surfaces in yet another guise in chapter 8, where I take on the widespread, erroneous belief that we can actually learn about the causal influences on survey respondents' opinions and behavior by simply asking them why. Using data from exit poll experiments as an example, I illustrate how easily the illusion of causality can be generated by the form and sequence in which questions are asked about what exactly influenced the respondent's voting decision. In chapter 9 the bill for critical damages comes due, and I make a case for how to improve the measurement of public opinion, revisiting George Gallup's classic "quintamensional" plan for question design, Howard Schuman's much neglected random probe technique, and Daniel Yankelovich's "mushiness index." The chapter concludes with a call for the application of the techniques of cognitive laboratory testing to many well-established measures of public opinion and for the routine breakdown of poll results by levels of knowledge, attention, or awareness. But I make these recommendations with the clear recognition of the practical problem of pleasing the mass media, which typically demand definitive conclusions about public opinion, and the powerful disincentives for pollsters to change their practices in measuring and reporting opinions in the absence of anything like the Wednesday morning reality check that generally follows their predictions of the outcome of an election. It's not all just an illusion, but validating the reality of "public opinion" poses a problem of a whole other order of difficulty than validating the vote. Political scientist V. O. Key was right: Measuring public opinion is a task not unlike coming to grips with the Holy Ghost.

CREDITS

Portions of chapter 5 and figures 5.1 and 5.2 were adapted from my previous article "Illusion of Change: Sometimes It's Not the Same Old Question," which appeared in *Public Perspective* 13 (May/June 2002): 38–41. Portions of chapter 7 were adapted from my article "'Intelligent Design': Illusions of an Informed Public," *Public Perspective* 14 (May/June 2003): 5–7.

ACKNOWLEDGMENTS

First and foremost, I owe thanks to my present and former students and colleagues, who, willingly or unwillingly, have served as a sounding board over the years for many of the ideas, insights, and hypotheses presented in this volume. In particular I want to thank Robert Oldendick, Andrew Smith, Bonnie Fisher, and the late David Resnick for the time they took on numerous occasions to listen to whatever had popped into my mind about the nuances of asking questions in public opinion surveys. Their insightful reactions and comments on my countless theoretical ramblings, as well as their collaborative efforts, are greatly appreciated. I also want to thank my current colleague and Ohio pollster, Eric Rademacher, who read this manuscript carefully and provided many useful comments and suggestions for revisions. While I haven't heeded all of his good advice, I am grateful nonetheless and will probably wish I had taken more of it to heart and paper. My good friend and colleague B. J. Jabbari should be singled out as well for his priceless collaboration on part of the research presented here and for his superb assistance in analyzing the data and constructing the figures, charts, and artwork throughout this volume. I don't know how I could have gotten it all done in time without him.

My editor at Rowman & Littlefield, Jennifer Knerr, should be acknowledged as well for giving me the opportunity to carry out this book project when it was still very much in its infancy. So too should the initial reviewer of the prospectus for this book for Rowman & Littlefield, Herbert Asher, be thanked for his enthusiastic recognition and endorsement of the potential contribution of this volume to the field of public opinion and survey research. It comes as a high compliment from such an astute scholar of the practice of public opinion polling in the United States. Much the same gratitude goes to the anonymous reviewer of the final draft of this manuscript for Rowman & Littlefield, who not only valued what I had to offer the field, but also made several useful suggestions for revising the manuscript, including the opportunity to elaborate explicitly on my rival theory of the survey response (chapter 6). Nor should I forget to thank my production editor, Alden Perkins, who kept me on deadline, nullifying my worst instincts toward procrastination and perfectionism. Thanks too to my copyeditor, Jen Sorenson, who turned much of what I had written into more intelligible prose, and did so with a lucid comprehension of what it was I was trying to say.

Finally, I would like to acknowledge my own intellectual limitations in measuring and understanding the meaning of public opinion, as well as any errors in analyzing and interpreting the data presented in this volume. Any mistakes are mine and mine alone. And last, but not least, I fully recognize that I am just as much a prisoner of my own presuppositions as anyone else.

NOTE

1. The polling data and findings on American public opinion cited here and throughout the book were, except as otherwise noted, compiled from the following sources: the Roper Center for Public Opinion Research's online Public Opinion Location Library (POLL) at the University of Connecticut (www.ropercenter.uconn.edu/), the Polling Report (www.pollingreport.com), and the Gallup Organization's online polling data archive (brain.gallup.com) and its website (www.gallup.com).

1

The Elusiveness of "Public Opinion"

> To speak with precision of public opinion is a task not unlike coming to grips with the Holy Ghost.
>
> —V. O. Key Jr., *Public Opinion and Democracy*

ARTIFACTS, FICTIONS, AND ILLUSIONS

"Public opinion does not exist," declared the late French sociologist Pierre Bourdieu (1979). In a trenchant, ideologically driven critique of public opinion polling, reminiscent of Herbert Blumer's broadside (1948a), Bourdieu argues that opinion polls in modern society largely serve the interests of political and journalistic elites, and that perhaps their most important function is "to impose the illusion that a public opinion exists, and that it is simply the sum of a number of individual opinions" (125). Blumer (1948b) regarded as "an untenable fiction" the whole idea of public opinion as just an aggregate of individual opinions. Similarly, Bourdieu describes the typical presentation of "public opinion" press releases in the mass media as "a pure and simple *artefact* whose function is to conceal the fact that the state of opinion at any given moment is a system of forces, of tensions, and that there is nothing more inadequate than a percentage to represent the state of opinion" (125).

"Public opinion," as it is presented in the modern press, occurs as an *artefact* for Bourdieu, not only because it conceals underlying political forces and dynamics, but also because, in his view, the whole enterprise of modern opinion polling rests on a rather shaky foundation of false assumptions. To begin with, he believed the practice of polling mistakenly assumes that everyone is politically and intellectually competent enough to interpret the questions the way pollsters and journalists do, and that all people must have an opinion on such matters. The common practice of minimizing, eliminating,

1

or simply ignoring "don't know" or "no opinion" responses not only reinforces the illusion that everyone or nearly everyone has an opinion on the
issues of the day, but also, for Bourdieu, becomes an inherently political act
because such "no replies," as he calls them, were at the time of his critique
(early 1970s) generally more common among women than among men and,
as in most public opinion polls today, significantly greater in frequency
among the less well educated than among the better educated. Proof positive,
he would say, that the politically less powerful do not comprehend the poll
questions being asked in the same way that journalistic and political elites
do.

Echoing Blumer's earlier critique (1948a, 1948b), Bourdieu attacks too
what he considers pollsters' implicit fallacy that "all opinions have the same
value" and should therefore be equally weighted when pollsters present the
statistical results of their polls to the public and to the powers that be. For
Bourdieu, as for Blumer, nothing could be further from the truth of how
diverse groups come to influence the decisions of administrators, legislators,
and policy makers in a complex society. Some interest groups and opinions
will always count more than others, they would say. But the false impression
that all opinions are equal arises, Bourdieu contends, because of the artifici-
ality of the isolated survey-interviewing situation in which opinions are typically measured, as compared to the real-life situations in which they are
formed and expressed. And no doubt Blumer, who stressed the clash of com-
peting groups in the formation and expression of public opinion, would have
agreed as well with Bourdieu's summation of the problem when he says:

> The important thing is that the opinion survey treats public opinion like the simple
> sum of individual opinions gathered in an isolated situation where the individual
> furtively expresses an isolated opinion. In real situations opinions are forces and
> relations of opinions are conflicts of forces. Taking a position on any particular
> problem means choosing between real groups, which leads us to see that the second
> postulate, the assumption that all opinions are equal, is totally unfounded. (128)

Not only that, but opinion polling rests as well on what he regards as an
equally false assumption: that merely asking a question about an issue implies
there is a consensus among the public that the issue is an important one to
ask about. But for Bourdieu, many, if not most, of the questions asked in
opinion polls reflect the interests of political and journalistic elites rather
than the real day-to-day concerns of common citizens. They ask about
abstract policies rather than the concrete realities of everyday life. And pollsters, who run in the same elite circles, often further these powerful political
interests, creating a false "consensus effect" by regularly putting such policy

issues in their polling-question agendas. The basic effect of opinion polling for Bourdieu, then, is that it creates the illusion "that a unanimous public opinion exists in order to legitimate a policy, and strengthen the relations of force upon which it is based or make it possible" (125). Limor Peer (1992), following Michel Foucault's critique of knowledge and power in social institutions, argues similarly that the practice of modern opinion polling as an institution is a "disciplinary mechanism which creates a 'public that has opinions,'" and that "the consequences of this process include the exercise of power, surveillance and control." Taking the view that public opinion polling today is part of a larger trend toward the "increasing rationalization of public opinion," Herbst (1993, 166) too believes that polls often exert political control in democratic societies by creating "the illusion that the public has already spoken in a definitive manner."

One does not, of course, have to share Bourdieu's Marxist critique of the power dialectics that underlie opinion polling, Foucault's (1979, 1980) "disciplinary power" perspective, Ginsberg's (1986) claim about how polls lead to "the domestication of mass beliefs," or Habermasian theories about how the rise of scientific opinion polling may have contributed to the "collapse of the public sphere" (Beniger 1992; Goodnight 1992) to agree that the question-asking agenda of most pollsters is hardly set by the typically unorganized interests of average citizens. If anything, it is the topics the mass media choose to cover in forums like the *New York Times*, the *Washington Post*, and the *Wall Street Journal* that largely set the mirrorlike agenda for the questions pollsters ask (e.g., see Dearing 1989; see also Gollin 1987). Nor does one have to fully share the critique of Bourdieu and other social critics to ask what sets the agenda for these mass media, beyond obvious events such as those of 9/11, if not what journalism critic Michael Kelly (cited in Rosen 1999, 207) calls "the shared assumptions of the nation's professional political class: the 'pollsters, news media consultants, campaign strategists, advertising producers, political scientists, reporters, columnists, commentators.'" Likewise, one need not share Bourdieu's cynicism to ask as Susan Herbst does, in her discussion of his critique (1992, 222), whether what passes as "public opinion" in the press is just a reification and "projection of what political elites and journalists think about." "Public opinion" thus does not exist for Bourdieu, except as an *artefact* produced by the public opinion polling industry. Polls, as Blumer might have put it, are in the business of aggregating and manufacturing "mass opinion."

Springing from similar intellectual soil, Susan Herbst, one of Blumer's theoretical descendants, talks about public opinion as a "socially constructed" reality created by our shared model of democracy in contemporary society, the methodologies and technologies of opinion measurement (e.g., polls), the rhetoric of political leaders and policy makers, and the journalistic reporting and interpretation of polls and public opinion in the mass media (Herbst 1998). For Herbst, public opinion as a social construct ultimately becomes conflated with the media and intimately connected with the postmodernist cultural critique. From the critical constructivist perspective (Lewis 2001), opinion polls are not to be regarded as "scientific" instruments, but rather as a cultural form bound up with news production in the mass media and thus laden with political ideology. And from there it is but a short step to the postmodernist view that there is no such thing as "public opinion," but rather various mental constructions of it from different points of view, all of which are equally "true"—making it more elusive than ever for modern polling empiricists. Looked at from a quantum philosophy of science perspective—the Heisenberg uncertainty principle—this may all be much ado about nothing since public opinion, or anything else in the universe for that matter, does not exist apart from the act of measurement. And, as sociologist Earl Babbie (1986) aptly reminds us in his essay "Concepts, Indicators, and Reality," concepts like "public opinion" are fundamentally figments of our imagination, distinctions that are more or less useful for scientific research but often in danger of reification.

Bourdieu, of course, was neither the first nor the last critic to treat public opinion as a fiction or an illusion. Beginning with classical democratic theorists, such as Bentham, Bryce, Locke, and Rousseau, a long line of critical theorists and social scientists have wrestled with the meaning and reality of the elusive concept of public opinion (see Noelle-Neumann 1993 for an excellent, extensive review of the numerous conceptualizations; also see Splichal 1999, especially chapters 1–3, for an insightful, historical critique of the concept in the twentieth century). In the prepolling era, Walter Lippmann (1922, 1925) anticipated many later critics and theorists, including Bourdieu, when he talked about the political ignorance and incompetence of the average citizen, the "phantom public," and about how "public opinion" was essentially a self-serving, rhetorical construction created by elites who dominated the discourse of democratic society. For Lippmann, as for many critics who would follow, the informed and politically competent citizens of traditional democratic theory simply did not exist—not because most people were innately incapable of understanding the world of politics and public affairs, but rather because they just did not have the time or energy to invest in learning about issues, policies, and other political matters that were remote from the practical concerns of their daily lives. As Lippmann saw it, traditional theory, which "identified the functioning of government with the will of the people," identified it with "a fiction" (Lippmann 1925, 61). For such theory "rests upon the belief that there is a public which directs the course of events. I hold that this public is a mere phantom. It is an abstraction" (67).

Floyd Allport, a prominent social and political psychologist at Syracuse University, made an even more compelling argument for regarding the concept of public opinion as a fiction. Using his inaugural article of the *Public Opinion Quarterly*, "Toward a Science of Public Opinion," as a platform, Allport (1937) debunked various metaphorical and fictional uses of the term: personifications such as the "voice of public opinion" and the "public conscience"; group fallacies exemplified by statements such as "the public wants so and so" or "the country voted dry"; and other fallacies of partial inclusion in using the term "public," as, for example, when those who share a common interest are referred to as a type of "public." Much ahead of his time, Allport also singled out what he called the "journalistic fallacy" or the tendency to confuse public opinion with "the public presentation of opinion." This, he explains, is the "illusion that the item one sees in print as 'public opinion,' or which one hears in speeches or radio broadcasts as 'public information' or 'public sentiment,' really has this character of widespread importance and endorsement" (Allport 1937, 12). For Allport, the psychologist, opinions were just instances of individual behaviors, verbalizations about some person, object, or situation that could be aggregated statistically. All the other ideas about public opinion represented just old wine in new bottles, variations of the "group-mind" fallacy that he thought he had dispensed with in a much earlier critique (Allport 1924). But the "ghost" of such group concepts, as he remarked, has always been difficult to put to rest, as witnessed once more in the theorizing of contemporary political scientists about changes in the "public mood" (Stimson 1999), shifts in "macropartisanship" (MacKuen, Erickson, and Stimson 1989), and the collective wisdom of "the rational public" (Page and Shapiro 1992). Allport, for one, would not be surprised to see such fictions revived.

Allport's inaugural address to the field of public opinion research proved to be equally prophetic. Together with the rise of opinion polling in the 1930s and George Gallup's gospel about polls as "the pulse of democracy" and "the voice of the people" (Gallup and Rae 1940), Allport's conceptualization of public opinion as an aggregation of individual opinions rapidly became the dominant paradigm of inquiry. As the former editor of *Public Opinion Quarterly*, Vincent Price (1992), observed in his overview of the sociological versus individualistic, social-psychological conceptions of public opinion that have preoccupied the field, the aggregate model provided a much simpler and more practical way to study public opinion than did the more empirically elusive notions of the concept put forth by scholars such as Blumer and his followers. Reviewing the history of the public opinion concept for the fiftieth-anniversary issue of *Public Opinion Quarterly*, Philip Converse (1987) argues that the pollsters' practical definition, not Blumer's, has prevailed: "What the firm establishment of a public opinion polling industry has done is to homogenize the definition and to stabilize it for the foreseeable future" (S13). So ingrained has this definition become, Converse would say, that today we almost invariably think of public opinion as whatever public opinion polls "try to measure" or, as he puts it, "what they measure with modest error" (P. Converse 1987, S14). Or, as Converse's fellow political scientist, Benjamin Ginsberg (1986, 60), said at nearly the same time, "Poll results and public opinion are terms that are [now] used almost synonymously."

But equating public opinion with whatever opinion polls measure, plus or minus some margin of error, has not, in the eyes of many critics, made it any less elusive. Commenting on the uncritical practice of much modern opinion polling, a prominent mass media and public opinion analyst, Leo Bogart (1972), observes that by repeatedly reducing the meaning of public opinion to the static measurements of the survey interview, the analyst falls victim to an illusion: "Once this is done, and done over and over again, it is easy to succumb to the illusion that the measurements represent reality rather than a distorted, dim, approximate reflection of a reality that alters its shape when seen from different angles" (15). Though skeptical of what surveys can tell us—much more about the public's ignorance than about its opinion, he would say—Bogart subscribes to the modernist view that there is a public opinion out there, but polls do not do a very good job of capturing it: "There is a vast difference between the reality of public opinion and the polls that measure shadows cast, as in Plato's myth, upon the wall of the cave" (Bogart 1972, 17). Equating public opinion with whatever polls try to measure frequently creates what he thinks is another insidious fiction about the intensity and polarization of public opinion (e.g., "Americans *divided*, says Gallup poll"): "Because of the identification of public opinion with the measurement of surveys, the illusion is easily conveyed of a public which is 'opinionated'—which is committed to strongly held views (Bogart 1972, 20)." For Bogart, as for other like-minded critics of what opinion polls often measure, the real problem is whether respondents know anything at all about the public affairs issues that pollsters typically ask them. As he puts it, "The first question a pollster should ask is: 'Have you thought about this at all? Do you *have* an opinion?'" (Bogart 1972, 101).

Bogart's critique of the polling enterprise has since found strong allies in the public journalism and deliberative polling movements. Reflecting on the overdependence of traditional journalists on polls, civic journalism protagonist, Jay Rosen (1999, 70), bemoans the current state of affairs: "Today the polls offer the impression of a fully formed public on virtually any issue: publish a poll and 'public opinion' springs magically to life." For critics of traditional journalism the ordinary poll only scratches the surface of public opinion; "true" public opinion, they contend, can only come about through deliberative community discussions enabling citizens to reach what Yankelovich (1991) calls an informed state of "public judgment." Civic journalist Cole Campbell argues that newspaper editors "have an obligation to 'depict reality' in their news coverage" (interviewed in Warren 2001, 188). But ordinary polls, as Campbell sees it, "cannot deliver this reality because they . . . only tend to measure 'off of the top of the mind opinion' . . . public opinion realities . . . are much more likely to be generated in community conversations in which people . . . reach informed 'best public judgments' about the issues and what to do" (Warren 2001, 188). Responding to many of the same concerns about polls based on public ignorance and the need for policy makers to heed an ideally well-informed public opinion on the issues of the day, democratic theorist James Fishkin (1992, 1995) makes a case for experimenting with what he calls a "deliberative public opinion poll":

> An ordinary poll models what the electorate thinks, given how little it knows. A deliberative opinion poll models what the electorate *would* think, if, hypothetically, it could be immersed in intensive deliberative processes. The point of a deliberative opinion poll is prescriptive, not predictive. It has a recommending force, telling us what the entire mass public would think about some policy issue or some candidates if it could be given an opportunity for extensive reflection and access to information. (Fishkin 1992, 81)

Not for the first time have the polling and journalism communities heard such concerns about the problem of ordinary polls based on public ignorance. Criticisms of polling and the misleading impressions of public opinion it generates merely reiterate a long-standing complaint about the failure of the polls to emphasize the vast amount of public ignorance that masquerades as "public opinion." In his scathing critique of pollsters, Lindsay Rogers (1949), one of George Gallup's sharpest adversaries, voiced many of the same concerns. His chapter 13, as he describes in the chapter's preface, "Notes that the Pollsters have disclosed that large Segments of the Electorate confess ignorance of many Political Questions, and asks why the Pollsters ignore this when they announce the results of Polls" (Rogers 1949, 139). So too did one of the pioneering pollsters, Elmo Roper (1942), worry about the issue in his essay for *Fortune* magazine, "So the Blind Shall Not Lead" (cited in Rogers 1949, 144): "I think the emphasis in public-opinion research has been largely misplaced. I believe its first duty is to explore the areas of public ignorance." Many years later his son, Burns W. "Bud" Roper (1983, 307–308), in his presidential address to the American Association for Public Opinion

Research, "Some Things That Concern Me," revisited his father's research agenda on public ignorance of public policy when he talked about the lack of Americans' knowledge of the MX missile proposal then being considered in Congress: "Should we be measuring and reporting public opinion on a subject that so few people feel informed about? Should public opinion like this—if it can be called public opinion—play a role in policy formation on a subject like this?" Or, as more than a few investigators have believed since the early days of public opinion polling, should uninformed respondents be filtered out or at least separated from those with more informed opinions in the analysis and reporting of poll results? Passionately committed though he was to the use of opinion polls as an instrument for measuring "the will of the people," George Gallup (1947) nonetheless recognized the problem of public ignorance in the polls he conducted and developed a practical solution to what would eventually become known as "the problem of nonattitudes" (Asher 2001; P. Converse 1970; chapter 2): something he dubbed "the quint-amensional plan of question design"—a greatly neglected technique in the modern practice of survey research (cf. chapter 9).

Far from an isolated example, Roper's illustration of the illusions of public opinion generated by polls on the MX missile issue represents an all too common occurrence in contemporary survey research. As I will argue, such illusions have become more ubiquitous than ever, not only because of the obvious proliferation of "pseudopolls" in the mass media—especially now on the Internet—that give the false impression of a public that has opinions on nearly every topic under the sun, but also largely because of several chronic problems in the practice of asking survey questions about public opinion. These include (1) widespread public ignorance of public affairs, (2) the inherent vagueness of the language used in most survey questions, and (3) the unpredictable influence of variations in question form, wording, and context—all of which may also interact with differences in methods of collecting survey data (see, e.g., Bishop and Smith 2001; Sudman, Bradburn, and Schwarz 1996, chap. 6). Figure 1.1 presents a summary diagram of the elements involved in generating what I call illusions of public opinion. Here I provide an overview of these problems, the details of which are described and explicated in the chapters that follow.

THE PROBLEM OF PUBLIC IGNORANCE

Public ignorance of public affairs, as Bogart (1972) and many others have warned us, has become probably the most conspicuous of these problems.

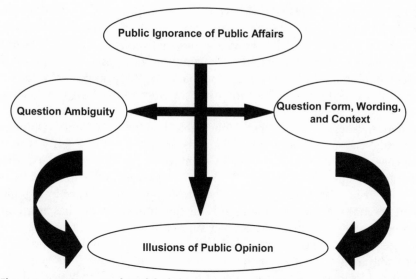

Figure 1.1   A Conceptual Model of Elements Generating Illusions of Public Opinion

Despite a pile of evidence showing the American public to be inattentive and uninformed about many aspects of politics and public affairs (Bennett 1996; Delli Carpini and Keeter 1996; Morin 1995), national and regional polls frequently fail to screen out respondents who know little or nothing about the subjects of the questions they ask. Instead of asking filter and knowledge questions that separate the informed from the uninformed, as exemplified in Gallup's classic quintamensional plan, many national and regional polls today deliberately discourage "don't know" (DK) responses and other forms of "no opinion" by constraining respondents to choose from a fixed set of categories (cf. Schuman and Presser 1981). And if respondents do volunteer a DK response, survey interviewers will frequently get them to give an opinion by using a follow-up probe such as "Would you say you *lean* toward one side or the other?" "Would you say you are *closer to* one side or the other?" "If you *had to choose*, would you say you favor one side or the other?" Respondents thus get the message that they should give an opinion even if they don't know very much about the topic.

Not only that, but polling organizations frequently encourage respondents to answer questions by presuming they are familiar with the topic. Survey questions of this kind often begin by saying to the respondent, "As you may know . . ." "As you may have heard . . ." "From what you have heard or read . . ." "Given what you have heard . . ." As the examples in table 1.1 illustrate, such leading assumptions about what respondents know can range from the trivial and obscure (passages about the end of the world in the Book of Revelations) to the very complex (what respondents presumably know about federal judiciary nominations). Pollsters generally defend these practices by saying they are just a way to find out how respondents would think about the issue or topic if they did know more about it. In a provocative essay titled "The Unbearable Lightness of Public Opinion Polls," *New York Times* writer Adam Clymer (2001) cites a fairly typical defense of this common practice by Democratic pollster Peter Hart, who designs the questions for the NBC/*Wall Street Journal* poll with Republican Robert Teeter. Hart, according to Clymer, supports the practice by arguing that "even if the poll question itself is the first thing someone has heard on a subject, it at least shows the potency various arguments will have once the subject becomes part of a public dialogue." But as Hart and most pollsters probably realize, in the absence of such lead-in phrases ("As you may know . . ."), significant percentages of respondents would volunteer "don't know" responses. Furthermore, as a number of well-designed experiments suggest (Bishop, Oldendick, and Tuchfarber 1983, 1984; Schuman and Presser 1981; chapter 2), even more sizable percentages would end up not giving an opinion at all if they were explicitly asked filter questions such as "Do you have an opinion on this or not?" or "Have you thought much about this issue?" Or, to take a page from Gallup's (1947) classic quintamensional plan for measuring public awareness, "Have you heard or read anything about [the issue at hand]?"

Consider the examples in table 1.1. How likely is it that even a majority of Americans would know (without being told), for example, that the Bush administration had decided to allow federal grants to be used to renovate churches and religious sites that are designated historic landmarks? That the terrorist attacks in Saudi Arabia and Morocco had been explicitly linked to Osama bin Laden's al Qaeda organization? How many would know about the U.S. bishops' newly adopted policy on dealing with the issue of sexual abuse of children by priests? Or how the current judicial review nomination process is working at the federal level? What percentage of American adults under the age of forty would even know who pardoned Richard Nixon, and for what? Or what the Book of Revelations is possibly about? In each of these instances a majority of respondents were most likely induced into manufacturing an opinion "off the top of their heads" from the educational preface provided by the question (cf. Zaller 1992, chap. 2). In the absence of the suggestion about *information available to the FBI* prior to September 11, how plausible is it that only 2 percent of

Table 1.1. Survey Questions with Leading Knowledge and Opinion Presumptions

Gallup, CNN, *USA Today* (May 30–June 1, 2003, national adult, N = 1,019)

"As you may know, President (George W. Bush) is meeting next week (June 2003) with leaders of Israel and the Palestinians. Do you think those meetings and other diplomatic efforts during Bush's first term in office will—or will not—produce real significant progress toward a lasting peace between Israel and the Palestinians?"

Yes, will	35%
No, will not	59
No opinion	6

Quinnipiac University Polling Institute (June 4–9, 2003, national sample, N = 1,015)

"As you may know, the Bush administration recently decided to allow federal grants to be used to renovate churches and religious sites that are designated historic landmarks. Do you approve or disapprove of this decision?"

Approve	70%
Disapprove	22
DK/no answer	8

CBS News (January 4–6, 2003, national adult, N = 902)

"As you may know, North Korea has resumed its production of nuclear weapons. What do you think the United States should do with respect to North Korea—use military force in some way or try to find a diplomatic solution?"

Use military force	6%
Find diplomatic solution	91
Both (volunteered)	3
DK/no answer	1

Gallup, CNN, *USA Today* (May 19–21, 2003, national sample, N = 1,014)

"As you may know, in recent weeks (May 2003) there have been terrorist attacks in Saudi Arabia and Morocco, which have been linked to Osama bin Laden's terrorist organization known as al Qaeda. How much do you blame the Bush administration for these attacks—a great deal, a moderate amount, not much, or not at all?"

Great deal	8%
Moderate amount	19
Not much	26
Not at all	45
No opinion	2

NBC News, *Wall Street Journal* (May 17–19, 2003, national sample, N = 1,000)

"As you may know, people become federal judges by being nominated by the president and then being approved by a majority of the Senate. Now let me read you two views about this process, and please tell me which one you agree with more. Statement A: The current judicial nomination review process is working well, because most nominees are approved. Statement B: The current judicial nomination review process is not working well, because opponents in the Senate hold up too many nominees."

Statement A: process works	42%
Statement B: rules not working well	46
Not sure	12

Newsweek, Princeton Survey Research Associates (July 18–19, 2002, national adult, N = 1,004)

"As you may know, George W. Bush and Dick Cheney are both former business executives who still have close ties to business leaders. Which one of the following statements comes closer to your own views on how their past business experience and connections affects their handling of the recent corporate scandals? It makes them better able to deal with the scandals and develop policies to reduce corporate wrongdoing. It makes them less likely to propose and support the kinds of policies needed to deal with the scandals and reduce corporate wrongdoing."

Makes them better able to deal with it	50%
Makes them less likely to propose policies	42
Don't know	8

Washington Post (June 16–17, 2003, national adult, N = 1,004)

"As you may have heard, U.S. (United States) bishops approved a policy on Friday (June 14, 2002) to deal with the issue of sexual abuse of children by priests. Under the new policy, a priest who has sexually abused a child cannot serve as a pastor or chaplain and is barred from all other public church duties. The policy does not require that this priest be automatically removed from the priesthood. Do you support or oppose this policy?"

Support	38%
Oppose	60
No opinion	3

ABC News (June 7–9, 2002, national adult, N = 1,004)

"As you may know, President Gerald Ford granted (Richard) Nixon a pardon from criminal charges arising out of Watergate. Do you think Ford did the right thing or wrong thing in granting Nixon a pardon?"

Right thing	59%
Wrong thing	32
No opinion	8

Time, CNN, Harris Interactive (June 19–20, 2002, national adult, N = 1,003)

"As you may know, the last book of the New Testament called the Book of Revelations contains passages which some people say predict how the world will end. Do you think the events described in the Book of Revelations will occur at some point in the future or don't you think so?"

Yes	59%
No	33
Not sure	8

Gallup, CNN, USA Today (April 10, 2003, national adult, N = 522)

"As you may know, the U.S. (United States) believes Iran, North Korea, and Syria are either providing assistance to terrorists or attempting to develop weapons of mass destruction. For each, please say if you think the U.S. should or should not go to war with that country. How about . . . North Korea?"

Yes, should	28%
No, should not	67
No opinion	5

Gallup (May 20–22, 2002, national adult, N = 1,002)

"As you may know, the (Bush) administration says that some general information was available to the FBI (Federal Bureau of Investigation) or White House officials before September 11 (2001), the date of the attacks on the World Trade Center and the Pentagon, concerning terrorist plans by Osama bin Laden, but that there was no specific information about the September 11 attacks in particular. Which comes closer to your view about the White House officials' actions in this situation—they did the best job they could with the information available to them or they could have done a better job handling this information?"

Did the best job	54%
Could have done better	44
No opinion	2

Gallup, CNN, *USA Today* (September 2–4, 2002, national adult, N = 1,003)

"As you may know, shortly after the September 11 (2001) terrorist attacks (on the World Trade Center and the Pentagon) President (George W.) Bush created the Office for Homeland Security. Now Bush is proposing that this office be combined with many existing government agencies to create a new cabinet-level department. Do you think Congress should—or should not—pass legislation to create a new cabinet-level Department of Homeland Security?"

Yes, should	60%
No, should not	29
No opinion	11

Source: Public Opinion Location Library (POLL), Roper Center for Public Opinion Research, University of Connecticut, available through Lexis-Nexis Academic Universe.

Americans would have "no opinion" on the question of how good a job the White House did with that information? The vast majority probably had no idea whatsoever about what White House officials might or might not have known prior to September 11. The opinions thus seem "manufactured out of whole cloth."

It would certainly not make good copy to report, again and again, that a majority, or perhaps a sizable plurality, of Americans have no opinion on issues and topics that have been the subject of daily discourse among political, academic, and journalistic elites and that have thus received significant media coverage in places like the *New York Times*, the *Washington Post*, and the *Wall Street Journal*. It would amount to saying that on many issues of the day, there is no public opinion to speak of—a distinct disincentive to many pollsters perhaps—though, as Bogart (1972) might say, it is their professional obligation to report it. And while there may well be "a fine line between public opinion and public ignorance," as Schuman and Presser (1981) have astutely observed, much of the modern practice of opinion polling blurs that distinction.

QUESTION AMBIGUITY

Just as problematic is the fog in public opinion created by the ambiguity of the language used in most survey questions. Ever since the inception of modern polling, survey researchers have struggled with the Achilles' heel of their measuring instrument: the frequently vague meaning of survey questions. Over half a century ago, Cantril and Fried (1944) called it an "important and neglected problem." Stanley Payne, who preaches the virtues of brevity, simplicity, and specificity in his classic work *The Art of Asking Questions* (1951), warns his fellow pollsters, "the penchant of many respondents for answering questions which have no meaning for them poses a major problem for public opinion researchers" (Payne 1950–1951, 687). Nearly thirty years later, Norman Nie and his colleagues (Nie, Verba, and Petrocik 1976, 1979, 11) wrestled with the same problem in another guise when they described the vicissitudes of understanding "the changing American voter": "Even if the same question is asked at two different times, is it really the same question? The fact that times change may mean that the meaning of the question undergoes change." Writing on the future of public opinion research in the fiftieth-anniversary issue of *Public Opinion Quarterly*, sociologist James Davis (1987) lists first among the three biggest problems facing the field "Validity: What do the questions mean? We know respondents answer reliably and carefully, but we do not really know what they mean when they tell us about 'communism' or 'happiness' or 'performance on domestic issues.'" Summarizing a body of research on measurement errors associated with the meaning of survey questions (cf. Belson 1981; Bradburn and Miles 1979; Ferber 1956; see also Fee 1981; Fowler 1992; T. Smith 1989; Turner 1984), survey methodologist Robert Groves (1989, 450) puts the issue more precisely when he talks about language as the medium of survey measurement: "Although the language of the survey questions can be standardized, there is no guarantee that the meaning assigned to the questions is constant over respondents" (cf. Suchman and Jordan 1992). As Fowler (1992, 218) reminds us at the outset of his research on the measurement effects of ambiguous survey questions: "It has been axiomatic at least since Stanley Payne in 1951 wrote his classic book, *The Art of Asking Questions*, that survey questions should be clear. Ideally, they should mean the same thing to all respondents, and they should mean the same thing to respondents as to the researcher, the person who will interpret the answers."

Cognitive psychologists Herbert Clark and Michael Schober (1992, 27) probably identify the heart of the theoretical problem best in their discussion of how respondents answer vaguely worded survey questions in idiosyncratic ways: "Respondents . . . make the interpretability presumption: 'each question means what it is obvious to me here now that it means.'" If it is true that respondents interpret questions like this, their doing so violates a cardinal assumption in survey measurement: that the question should mean the *same thing* to all respondents. And if this assumption cannot be made, then valid comparisons across respondents become extremely difficult, if not impossible. Aggregating individual responses to a question to summarize public opinion on a given topic thus becomes a questionable, if not meaningless, exercise.

Consider as prime examples of the problem the following presidential approval questions asked in one form or another by virtually every national and regional poll in America: "Do you approve or disapprove of the way George W. Bush is handling his job as president?" (Gallup). "How would you rate the overall job President George W. Bush is doing as president: excellent, pretty good, only fair, or poor?" (Harris). Amorphous in meaning and highly ambiguous in what they refer to, each of these questions will almost certainly mean different things to different respondents. What does "handling his job as president" mean? For some respondents it may mean mostly how he's handling some current international crisis; for others it may refer to how he's dealing with various economic matters; and for still others, how he's providing moral leadership for the country; and so forth. For that matter, what does it mean to say you "approve" or "disapprove" of the way he's handling his job? Similarly, what is the meaning of such vague quantifiers in the Harris question on presidential approval as "excellent," "pretty good," "only fair," and "poor"? Given the implicit presumption that they have an opinion (the opinion presumption), most respondents will answer these questions by making the interpretability presumption: How he's handling his job as president *means what it is obvious to me here now that it means.* And that will likely be different things for different respondents, which is just another way of saying they are answering different questions. Theoretically speaking, it is as if the wording of the question itself had been changed for different respondents. The comparability issue is identical.

The same goes for the other equally vague measures of American public opinion that have become the stock and trade of so many polls today. "Do you think things in this country are generally going in the right direction or do you feel things have gotten pretty seriously off on the wrong track?" (ABC/*Washington Post*). "How much of the time do you think you can trust the government in Washington to do what is right: just about always, most of the time, or only some of the time?" (Gallup). "How would you rate the economic conditions in this country today—as very good, somewhat good, somewhat poor, or very poor?" (Gallup). "Do you think it will be best for the future of the country if we take an active part in world affairs, or if we stay out of world affairs?" (Gallup). "In your opinion which of the following will be the biggest threat to the country in the future—big business, big labor, or big government?" (Gallup). As Stanley Payne (1951, chap. 9) complained, unsuccessfully, about survey questions years ago, abstract concept words such as "right direction," "wrong track," "the government in Washington," "economic conditions in this country," "future of the country," "world affairs," "big business," "big labor," and "big government" are loaded with ambiguities (cf. Fee 1981 on "big government"). As a result, respondents may give different answers to questions using such terms, not because of genuine differences of opinion on the subject, but rather because they interpret the question differently. The typically sizable demographic differences between whites and African Americans, for example, in their approval ratings of President George W. Bush may reflect in large part a fundamental difference in how they interpret the meaning of "handling his job as president." So it goes too for the "gender gap" (Andersen 1997; Sapiro 2002), the "marriage gap" (Weisberg 1987; see also Connelly 2000), the "generation gap," and other sociodemographic gaps in public opinion. Some, perhaps much, of what appears to be a significant difference of opinion between various demographic categories of respondents may reflect simply differences in how they are interpreting the meaning of questions about abortion; affirmative action; government spending on health care, welfare, foreign aid, and national defense; Social Security; Medicare; prescription drugs; cloning; and the like—a hypothesis that is readily testable. Such gaps, in other words, may be no more than an illusion, an artifact of measurement due to differences in the interpretation of survey questions that vary in ambiguity.

QUESTION FORM, WORDING, AND CONTEXT

The vagueness and ambiguity of most survey questions also gives rise to a closely related source of artifacts in the measurement of public opinion: differences due to the way questions are worded and the order and context in which they are asked. As a sizable and ever-growing research literature has demonstrated time and again (Schuman and Presser 1981; Bishop and Smith 2001; Sudman, Bradburn, and Schwarz 1996; Tourangeau, Rips, and Rasinski 2000), variations in question form, wording, and context frequently change how respondents interpret the meaning of survey questions, depending in part on the method of survey data collection (i.e., phone versus face-to-face versus self-administered by mail or the Internet). Indeed, as a general proposition, it can be argued that the greater the ambiguity of the subject matter of a question, the more likely that responses to it will be influenced by such question-design features and data-collection methods. And, conversely, the more familiar, specific, and concrete the subject of the question, the less susceptible responses are likely to be to these influences.

Consider a typical preelection question about a respondent's voting intention in the 2000 presidential campaign: "If the 2000 presidential election were being held today and the candidates were Al Gore, the Democrat, George W. Bush, the Republican, Pat Buchanan, the Reform Party candidate, and Ralph Nader, the Green Party candidate, would you vote for Al Gore, George W. Bush, Pat Buchanan, or Ralph Nader?" (CBS News, November 4–6, 2000). When other things are handled well (sampling, timing, turnout estimates, etc.), questions like this have proved to be highly accurate in predicting the outcome of modern presidential elections (see, e.g., Warren 2001, chap. 2). The preelection accuracy of such polls has in fact become the quintessential validation of the entire opinion polling enterprise. Unlike most survey questions in public opinion polls, however, voting preference questions have the virtues of specificity and concreteness and are virtually unambiguous for nearly all respondents. In the 2000 election campaign, the question about George W. Bush, the Republican, and Al Gore, the Democrat, and so on meant essentially the same thing to all respondents and the same thing each time it was asked. Not surprisingly then, there appears to be no evidence that variations in the wording of such voting preference questions make any significant difference in the accuracy of preelection polls (see Crespi 1988).

In contrast, as Crespi (1989) has observed, presidential popularity ratings, which are often regarded as an ongoing electoral referendum, have proven to be susceptible to whether the question is asked in a dichotomous form ("Do you approve or disapprove . . .") or in a rating scale format ("Would you say he's doing an excellent, pretty good, only fair, or a poor job?"). And so it is for many other survey questions that have proved sensitive to variations in question form, wording, and context; they are sensitive especially because they are often ambiguous and lead respondents to use such cues to interpret them in multiple ways (cf. James Davis, cited in Crespi 1989). Together with the effects of public ignorance of public affairs, it is this respondent reactivity to question vagueness and ambiguity, I will argue, that explains how the way in which survey questions are worded and the form and context in which they are asked can generate so many misleading impressions of public opinion. If, as Jean Converse (1987) has argued so persuasively in her history of the field, the survey instrument has become the equivalent of a social telescope for pollsters, then it is one that frequently generates the conceptual equivalent of an optical illusion.

2

Illusory Opinions on Public Affairs

The question of *what* people think about public issues is really secondary to the question of whether they think about them at all.

—Leo Bogart, *Silent Politics*

EARLY WARNINGS AND SYMPTOMS

Ever since Gallup and his peers began polling the nation in the 1930s, survey researchers have suspected that respondents will often express an opinion on an issue whether they know anything about it or not. In a facetiously titled essay, "How Do You Stand on Sin?" Sam Gill (1947), a marketing research director at Sherman & Marquette, Inc., tells the story of a poll with a question about an imaginary "Metallic Metals Act," on which 70 percent offered an opinion. While this poll war story, as Schuman and Presser (1981) have noted, is probably no more than an undocumented anecdote, it has become a classic example in the literature of meaningless responses to vague and ambiguous survey questions. In his influential book *The Art of Asking Questions* (1951) and in a prophetic essay in the *Public Opinion Quarterly*, "Thoughts about Meaningless Questions," Stanley Payne (1950–1951) used Gill's report to make the case that respondents will often answer survey questions that are meaningless to them if only to avoid looking ignorant and to satisfy what sociologists Riesman and Glazer (1948–1949) have identified as the social demand to "have an opinion."

Anticipating what other investigators would discover many years later, Payne (1950–1951) argued that if a question on a meaningless topic was asked in an apparently sensible manner in a plausible question context, it would be answered by a substantial number of respondents. He also predicted that the pattern of these responses would not necessarily be random because respondents would fall back on such predispositions as the tendency

19

to select the last-mentioned response alternative (what we now call a "recency effect"), to read meaning into the question on the basis of the similarity of one of its words or phrases to some other known word or expression (today's "imputed meaning hypothesis" [cf. T. Smith 1984]), to prefer the middle response category, and to cling to the familiar in making choices. All of this, he thought, would make it difficult, if not impossible, to separate random responses from meaningful replies to survey questions—an insight that would be rediscovered time and again. Payne's equally timeless solution to reducing the problem of meaningless survey questions and responses included, among other recommendations, avoiding questions with vague abstractions or ambiguous concept words, such as "world affairs," "big business," and "big government"; keeping questions short and simply worded, personally relevant to issues close to home, and specific and concrete; and, taking a page from Gallup's "quintamensional" practice of the time, he advocated using filter questions to screen out the politically uninformed.

Responding to essentially the same criticism that survey questions were often asked of respondents who had little or no knowledge of the issue being polled, Gallup (1947) developed an elaborate solution called "the quintamensional plan of question design." Based on five dimensions of opinion—hence the term "quintamensional"—the Gallup approach relied, first and foremost, on filter and knowledge questions designed to measure whether respondents had paid any attention to the issue. One of the filter questions Gallup found useful, particularly for legislative proposals, took the form: "Have you heard or read about the proposal to . . . ?" (Gallup 1947, 387). While some respondents might be able to guess what a given proposal might mean based on a familiar word or phrase in the question, Gallup believed that if someone had not even heard or read about the legislation, then he or she was hardly in a position to give an opinion on it. He believed as well that merely because a respondent said "yes" to the question on having heard or read about some bill before the Congress did not necessarily mean the respondent had actually read or heard anything about it. So he thought it was essential to follow up with additional knowledge questions to establish how familiar respondents were with the proposed legislation, asking respondents, for example, about the Taft-Hartley Act of that era: "What does it say about the closed shop?" "What does it provide about union political activities?" (Gallup 1947, 387). Asking them to give the arguments pro and con on the proposal before the Congress provided yet another indicator of how much they knew about it. In this way Gallup was able to determine whether respondents' opinions were based on "snap" judgments—what cognitive psychologists today call "top-of-the-head" responses—or on more substantial information about the issue. His technique thus made it possible to compare the opinions of those who were more knowledgeable with those who were less knowledgeable.

To the detriment of the polling field, Gallup's quintamensional approach to measuring public opinion never quite caught on, most likely because it was too expensive and impractical to convey such detailed results to a mass media audience. In the practical judgment of most pollsters, asking five or more questions about different dimensions of public opinion on a single issue consumes a lot of interviewing time, time that could probably be better spent asking questions on other topics that would result in more press releases and publicity for the polling organization. Curiously, the Gallup Organization itself pretty much abandoned the quintamensional technique not long after George Gallup published his seminal article in the *Public Opinion Quarterly*, though it has continued off and on over the years to use the basic filter question—"Have you heard or read about [the issue in question]?"—to measure public awareness of various and sundry issues in public affairs. Nor did other polling organizations heed Payne's early warnings about meaningless questions, pick up on Gallup's practice of screening out respondents who knew little or nothing about an issue, or pay much attention to Ferber's (1956) disturbing report in the mid-1950s on how respondents would often express opinions on issues about which they freely acknowledged they were uninformed or misinformed.

In his review of the literature on the linkage between knowledge and opinion, Tom Smith (1984, 219–220) gives a telling example of the fundamental problem still facing the field, using data from a national Gallup poll in the 1970s on the issue of balancing the federal budget:

> Gallup . . . finds that while 96 percent had an opinion on the importance of a balanced budget, 25 percent did not know whether the budget was balanced, 8 percent wrongly thought that it was balanced, 40 percent knew it was unbalanced but didn't know by how much, 25 percent knew it was unbalanced but overestimated or underestimated the amount by 15 percent or more, and 3 percent knew it was unbalanced and knew the approximate level of the deficit (plus or minus 15 percent).

To Smith this clearly suggests that many respondents were either "guessing" at their answers and inventing opinions on the spot or were so poorly informed about the issue that saying "don't know" would have been a more accurate response. Furthermore, and even more baffling, as Smith (1984) observes, Gallup found in the very same survey that those who were the least knowledgeable about whether the federal budget was balanced were, paradoxically, most likely to consider it to be an important issue! Such findings, however, have seemed to make little or no difference in the practice of public opinion polling. Indeed, ignoring or downplaying the problem became the standard practice in the polling profession. This practice would persist for many years, until a political social psychologist named Philip Converse at the University of Michigan's Center for Political Studies demonstrated that there was a disturbing source of error in public opinion and political attitude surveys: what he felicitously called "nonattitudes."

CONVERSE'S CRITIQUE

Converse's critical analysis of the "nonattitudes" problem became a seminal contribution to the field, generating controversy for years to come. In what are now regarded as two of the most influential essays in the study of American political behavior (P. Converse 1964, 1970), he made a compelling case that the opinions expressed by many respondents on numerous issues in public affairs represented random, inconsistent responses to questions asked by interviewers or, at best, feeble attempts on the part of respondents to conceal their ignorance and satisfy the demands of the situation by providing the interviewer with an opinion. Converse characterized their responses to most policy issues as a form of mental coin flipping based on little or no knowledge. In a word, they were not expressing any real attitudes on the issues but rather "nonattitudes." The bulk of the evidence for his argument came from analyzing interviews and reinterviews of respondents in the multiwave national election studies conducted by the Survey Research Center at the University of Michigan from 1956 to 1960. With a few simplifying assumptions, Converse found that he could explain most of the variation in respondents' answers from one interview to the next (two years apart) with a rudimentary "black-and-white" model comprising two types of respondents: those who had real and stable positions on the issue (the consistent) and those who had no real opinions on the issue and changed their answer from interview to interview based on random reactions to the question (the inconsistent). Though Converse identified another type of nonattitude—"self-confessed" no-opinion responses—it was his model of random responses to public opinion surveys, with all its negative implications for assumptions about the informed "rational voter" in classic democratic theory, that generated controversy for years to come, controversy that is as yet unresolved (see Kinder 1998; T. Smith 1984).

Converse's nonattitudes thesis inevitably drew more attention to the issue of whether people thought much about public affairs and their willingness to admit they had "no opinion." As another prominent public opinion analyst

(Bogart 1967) put it around the time of Converse's work: "The question of *what* people think about public issues is really secondary to whether they think about them at all. . . . The first question to ask is: 'Have you thought about this at all? Do you have an opinion?'" That was just the beginning of the field's worries. We now know from a number of carefully designed experimental studies that many respondents are reluctant to volunteer they do not have an opinion on an issue unless they are given an explicit opportunity to do so. Classic experiments by Schuman and Presser at Michigan (1981) and by my colleagues and me at Cincinnati (Bishop et al. 1980; Bishop, Oldendick, and Tuchfarber 1983) have convincingly shown that the percentage of respondents who are willing to give a "don't know" or "no opinion" response can be increased dramatically—typically by 20–30 percent on many public affairs topics—merely by asking respondents an explicit filter question, such as "Do you have an opinion on this or not?" or "Have you thought much about this issue?" That so many respondents are unwilling to admit they have no opinion in the absence of an explicit probe only confirms the suspicions of Bogart and Converse, and Gallup and Payne before them, that survey respondents will frequently manufacture opinions about issues on the spot, or as cognitive psychologists today would put it, off "the top of the head" (cf. Zaller and Feldman 1992).

We also know now that some people are significantly more likely than others to generate nonattitudes or "pseudo-opinions" (Bishop et al. 1980). Numerous investigations, for example, have told us that a respondent's level of education—a relatively good proxy for what he or she knows about politics and public affairs (Delli Carpini and Keeter, 1996)—is the single best predictor of his or her readiness to give a "don't know" or "no opinion" response (see, e.g., Faulkenberry and Mason 1978; Francis and Busch 1975; J. Converse 1976–1977; T. Smith 1984). As a general rule, the less well educated a respondent is, the more likely he or she is to have "no opinion" on a great variety of topics, especially on foreign affairs. Table 2.1 shows some selected examples on various topics from national opinion polls conducted during the past ten years. On the issue of government financing of presidential and congressional campaigns, for example, respondents with less than a high school education were nearly twelve times more likely to volunteer a "don't know" response than those with a postgraduate degree.

At the same time, other experimental studies have told us that less well educated respondents are, paradoxically perhaps, more likely to offer opinions on issues they couldn't possibly know anything about. In fact, they appear to be much more willing to answer questions about things that are totally fictitious.

Table 2.1.   No Opinion Responses by Education in Selected National Media Polls

ABC News (March 24–25, 1997, national adult, N = 752)
"I'm going to read a few statements and after each please tell me whether you tend to
agree or disagree with it, or if you have no opinion about the statement. . . . There's no
excuse for anti-Semitism, but much of the anti-Jewish feeling in this country today has been
brought on by Jews themselves. Do you agree or disagree?"

	Agree	Disagree	No opinion
<HS grad	24	46	30
HS grad	15	59	26
Some college	16	62	22
College grad	11	78	11
Postgrad	5	80	14

Gallup/CNN/*USA Today* (April 6–7, 1999, national adult, N = 1,055)
"If the current NATO (North Atlantic Treaty Organization) air and missile strikes are not
effective in achieving the United States' objectives in Kosovo, would you favor or oppose
President (Bill) Clinton sending US (United States) ground troops into the region along with
troops from other NATO countries?"

	Favor	Oppose	No opinion
<HS grad	40	44	16
HS grad	44	50	6
Some college	51	44	5
College grad	47	52	1
Postgrad	56	42	2

***Washington Post* (January 24–28, 1997, national adult, N = 1,007)**
"Would you favor or oppose the federal government financing presidential and congressional campaigns out of tax money, or don't you have an opinion on this?"

	Favor	Oppose	Don't know
<HS grad	13	64	23
HS grad	12	74	14
Some college	16	75	9
College grad	19	74	7
Postgrad	29	69	2

Gallup (February 26–28, 1999, national adult, N = 1,013)
"Would you favor or oppose placing the International Olympic Committee under the
oversight of a group such as the United Nations?"

	Favor	Oppose	No opinion
<HS grad	56	23	21
HS grad	46	44	10
Some college	44	49	7
College grad	43	54	2
Postgrad	40	53	7

Gallup (March 22, 1999, national adult, N = 1,025)
"Which of the following best describes your views of the relationship between China and the United States? Would you say China is an ally; friendly, but not an ally; unfriendly, but not an enemy; an enemy of the United States; or haven't you heard enough about that yet to say?"

	Ally/friendly	Enemy/unfriendly	*Haven't heard enough*
<HS grad	13	34	53
HS grad	29	27	44
Some college	28	40	33
College grad	37	49	14
Postgrad	47	43	10

OPINIONS ON FICTITIOUS ISSUES

If Converse thought a lot of nonattitudes were hidden among substantive responses to standard political attitude questions in the National Election Studies (T. Smith 1984), a lot more, we have learned, can be hidden in plain sight. Inspired in significant part by Converse's nonattitudes thesis, my colleagues and I (Bishop et al. 1980) demonstrated that about 30–40 percent of the adult respondents in surveys of the Cincinnati metropolitan area would offer an opinion on a totally nonexistent issue when asked about it in the following form: "Some people say that the 1975 Public Affairs Act should be repealed. Do you agree or disagree with this idea?" We also discovered that even when interviewers gave respondents in other experimental conditions an explicit opportunity to say they did not have an opinion on this nonexistent entity by asking them filter questions (such as "Do you have an opinion on this or not?" "Have you thought much about this issue?" or "Have you been interested enough in this to favor one side over the other?"), 7–10 percent would insist on saying "yes" and then indicate to the interviewer that they either agreed or disagreed that the Public Affairs Act should be repealed.

As often happens in scientific fields, around the same time, Schuman and Presser (1980) made a similar independent discovery. Exploring Converse's nonattitudes thesis from another angle, they found that between 25 percent and 30 percent of respondents in two different national surveys would, if asked without an explicit opportunity to say "don't know," offer opinions on highly obscure pieces of legislation in Congress unfamiliar to nearly all Americans—"the Agricultural Trade Act of 1978" and "the Monetary Control Bill of 1979." They also discovered, as had my colleagues and I, that roughly 7–10 percent of respondents to their surveys would say "yes" to a filtered version of the question ("Do you have an opinion on this issue?")

and then tell the interviewer that they either favored or opposed the proposed legislation. But contrary to the usual pattern of less well educated respondents being most likely to give a "don't know" or "no opinion" response, both my associates and I (Bishop et al. 1980) and Schuman and Presser (1980) found that it was the better educated who were more willing to admit they had no opinion or knew nothing about any of these obscure topics; whereas the less well educated were much more likely to venture an opinion. This is a theoretical puzzle that has persisted to the present day: an "opinion illusion" generated by respondents filling in the cognitive gaps.

Follow-up experiments by my colleagues and me (Bishop, Tuchfarber, and Oldendick 1986), however, failed to find any clear evidence for the hypothesis that giving opinions on obscure or fictitious issues was due simply to a respondent's unwillingness to admit ignorance. If respondents were faking it, it was not obviously explained. Perhaps it was the pressure to answer questions put to respondents by insistent interviewers expecting an answer, as my coworkers and I (Bishop, Tuchfarber, and Oldendick 1986) argued, but that would not explain why so many other respondents in those same experiments would not yield to the identical pressures. A better explanation was needed.

THE IMPUTED MEANING HYPOTHESIS

One such explanation became increasingly plausible: the imputed meaning of ambiguous questions. Various investigators, in fact, had theorized that survey respondents may offer opinions on fictitious or obscure topics because they read meaning into the question in a way that allows them to answer it in terms of a more general attitude toward that psychologically constructed object. My colleagues and I (Bishop et al. 1980, 208), for example, had speculated that respondents who gave an opinion on the fictitious 1975 Public Affairs Act might have "derived a good deal of its meaning from the immediately preceding context of the interview schedule, which consisted of four domestic issues. . . . Inferring that it had to do with the 'government,' albeit vaguely, they would thus rely on their general disposition to trust or mistrust this institution in deciding how to answer." Schuman and Presser (1980, 1223) made a similar argument to explain why so many respondents offered opinions on the obscure Agricultural Trade Act of 1978 and the Monetary Control Bill of 1979, suggesting that respondents without an opinion on an issue "may construct answers by drawing on an underlying disposition not specific to the issue but relevant to it. . . . Respondents make an educated (though wrong) guess as to what the obscure acts represent, then answer reasonably in their own terms about the constructed object." As Smith (1984, 231) summarizes it in his review of the nonattitudes literature: "the imputed-understanding model has respondents taking clues in the question to supply meaning and then answering the question according to a predisposition toward the perceived meaning."

Cognitive social psychologists have taken this hypothesis a step further, linking it to the logic of conversation. Drawing on psychological theories of conversation in everyday life, Schwarz (1995) has argued that merely asking a question about a fictitious or obscure issue in the course of an interview "presupposes that the issue exists—or else asking a question about it would violate each and every norm of conversational conduct." Furthermore, he makes the case that, because respondents have no plausible reason to think the interviewer would ask them a question about something absurd or about a topic that did not exist, they will naturally try to interpret such questions. As questions about fictitious or obscure issues are quite ambiguous, Schwarz (1995, 7–8) hypothesizes that respondents will use the context in which the question is asked "to determine its meaning, much as they would be expected to do in any other conversation" and give "a subjectively meaningful response to *their* definition of the question." Though highly plausible as an explanation, the imputed meaning hypothesis remained essentially untested until a fortuitous experiment was carried out by Richard Morin (1995), director of polling at the *Washington Post*.

THE *WASHINGTON POST* EXPERIMENT[1]

Under Morin's direction the *Post* revisited the classic experiment with the 1975 Public Affairs Act by adding some political nuances to questions in a national weekly poll (February 1995). To half the sample—a random subgroup of about 500 respondents—they asked my colleagues' and my original question: "Some people say the 1975 Public Affairs Act should be repealed. Do you agree or disagree with this idea?" But added to this were two experimental partisan conditions: for one random subsample of about 250 respondents, they reworded the question to read, "President Clinton says the 1975 Public Affairs Act should be repealed. Do you agree or disagree with this idea?" For another random subsample, the question read, "Republicans in Congress say that the 1975 Public Affairs Act should be repealed. Do you agree or disagree with this idea?" Morin's (1995) clever experimental variations created the opportunity to test the proposition that respondents who had no notion at all as to what the Public Affairs Act was would draw upon these partisan clues regarding what Clinton or the Republicans thought about it to answer the question. Morin wanted to check out one other thing: the consequences of the common practice of many survey organizations, including the *Post*, of minimizing the percentage of respondents who have "no opinion" on an issue. Typically, survey interviewers are trained to probe respondents who initially say they "don't know" or have "no opinion" on an issue by asking them which way they "lean" or "which comes closest to your opinion" or by simply repeating the question (cf. Bishop, Tuchfarber, and Oldendick 1986). In Morin's experiment the interviewers first reminded respondents who hesitated to offer an opinion that "there are no right or wrong answers" and then used the following probe: "Which comes closest to the way you feel? Do you agree or disagree that the 1975 Public Affairs Act should be repealed?"

His experiment worked remarkably well. Replicating pretty much what my colleagues and I (Bishop et al. 1980) had found years earlier, Morin discovered that about a third of American adults (32 percent) would offer an opinion on this fictitious topic when the question was asked in its original form. And of those who wouldn't, another 10–11 percent could be induced to give an opinion by simply being pressured with the probe "Which comes closest to the way you feel?" This combination of questioning and probing resulted in more than four out of ten respondents (43 percent) expressing an opinion on a nonexistent issue (table 2.2). Better yet, when given the added partisan cue of "President Clinton" or "Republicans in Congress," the percentage volunteering an opinion rose to more than half for the president's proposal (55 percent) and to nearly half (49 percent) for the Republicans' proposal. This provided clear evidence that many respondents had used these cues to interpret what the question might be about and then answered it in terms of their general partisan disposition toward that psychologically constructed object: either *Clinton's idea* or *the Republicans' idea*.

Table 2.2. Responses to Repealing 1975 Public Affairs Act by Question Wording

	Question wording		
	Ambiguous	*Clinton's idea*	*Republicans' idea*
Agree	24%	25%	22%
Disagree	19	30	27
Don't know	57	45	51
Total	100	100	100
(N =)	(459)	(223)	(220)

Source: National survey for the *Washington Post* conducted by ICR Survey Research of Media, Pennsylvania, February 1995.

Note: Data shown are weighted for household size and population demographics. Not-applicable and refusal responses were excluded from the analysis.

Once activated, partisanship clearly guided how respondents answered the question. When told it was President Clinton's idea, self-identified Democrats tended to favor repealing the Public Affairs Act, whereas Republicans were much more likely to oppose its repeal. But if they heard it was a proposal by the GOP in Congress, Republicans overwhelmingly favored getting rid of it, whereas Democrats opposed the idea by a margin of more than three to one (table 2.3). Psychologically, the gist of the question had become: *If they're for it, I'm against it.* Curiously, self-identified independents answered the questions more like Democrats than Republicans, indicating perhaps that, at the time, their overall partisan leanings generally fell in the same direction. The question cue made a difference for them too.

The *Washington Post* data produced one other striking replication: A respondent's education influenced his or her willingness to venture an opinion. As my coworkers and I (Bishop et al. 1980) had discovered years earlier, less well educated (and black) respondents were significantly more likely to tell interviewers they had an opinion on the Public Affairs Act (table 2.4). Since many of these same respondents identified themselves as Democrats, they were also much more likely to favor repealing the Public Affairs Act when informed that it was President Clinton's idea and to oppose it when it

Table 2.3.   Responses to Public Affairs Act by Party Identification, by Wording

	Democrat	Republican	Independent
Ambiguous wording			
Agree	30%	23%	23%
Disagree	19	19	18
Don't know	51	58	59
Total	100	100	100
(N =)	(150)	(146)	(137)
Clinton's idea			
Agree	24%	17%	35%
Disagree	20	40	35
Don't know	56	43	31
Total	100	100	101
(N =)	(80)	(77)	(49)
Republicans' idea			
Agree	13%	35%	16%
Disagree	45	14	30
Don't know	43	51	54
Total	100	100	100
(N =)	(65)	(77)	(61)

Source: Washington Post/ICR national survey, February 1995.

Table 2.4. Responses to Public Affairs Act by Education, by Wording

	Less than high school	High school graduate	Some college	College graduate
Ambiguous				
Agree	51%	19%	19%	12%
Disagree	14	21	17	22
Don't know	35	59	63	66
Total	100	99	99	100
(N =)	(102)	(160)	(93)	(101)
Clinton's idea				
Agree	46%	29%	18%	9%
Disagree	23	37	28	28
Don't know	31	34	53	63
Total	100	100	100	100
(N =)	(35)	(79)	(60)	(46)
Republicans' idea				
Agree	19%	26%	29%	16%
Disagree	23	28	20	36
Don't know	58	46	51	48
Total	100	100	100	100
(N =)	(43)	(72)	(49)	(56)

Source: *Washington Post*/ICR national survey, February 1995.

was attributed to the Republicans in Congress. And therein lies a clue as to why such respondents are generally more likely to offer opinions on this fictitious topic: because they (the less well educated) may well believe that the Public Affairs Act has something to do with government programs from which they may possibly benefit, the repeal of which would therefore be harmful to their interests. If respondents interpreted the question that way, then the opinions they expressed on the Public Affairs Act became essentially a referendum on the value of government programs in general.

"THE 1995 SOCIAL SECURITY REFORM ACT"

These responses to an ambiguous, fictitious Public Affairs Act were not, however, just an isolated example. Yet another opportunity to test the imputed meaning hypothesis arose as part of an Internet polling experiment conducted during the 2000 presidential election campaign by the Internet Public Opinion Laboratory at the University of Cincinnati (Bishop and Jabbari 2001). Following a series of questions about their attention to the 2000 election campaign, their presidential voting preferences, and what they thought was the most important problem facing the country, respondents to this web-based survey were asked a set of questions on the policy issue of reforming Social Security:

1. "Do you favor or oppose a proposal that would allow people to put a portion of their Social Security payroll taxes into personal retirement accounts that would be invested in private stocks and bonds?"
2. "Thinking about the long-term condition of the Social Security system, if people were allowed to put a portion of their Social Security payroll taxes into accounts that would be invested in the stock market, do you think this would strengthen or weaken the ability to pay benefits to retirees 25 years from now?"
3. "Do you favor or oppose a proposal to repeal the 1995 Social Security Reform Act?"

The first two questions were identical to those asked by the Gallup Organization in its national polls on the Social Security issue in the 2000 presidential election campaign. The third was another red herring, asking about a nonexistent issue: "the 1995 Social Security Reform Act." It was presented online with one of two sets of response categories. On form A, to which half the respondents were randomly assigned, the response categories presented on the computer monitor were: "Favor," "Oppose," and *"Haven't Heard of It."* On form B, to which the other half was assigned, the options were: "Favor," "Oppose," *"Not Sure," "Don't Know,"* and *"No Opinion."* So on both versions of the question, respondents were given a clear and explicit opportunity to say they had not heard of it or did not have an opinion on it one way or the other.

But despite this explicit encouragement to opt out, a remarkably high percentage of respondents offered an opinion on repealing the Social Security Reform Act: about one out of four respondents (25 percent) on form A and a little over one out of five (22 percent) on form B (table 2.5). These figures look all the more remarkable because the respondents to this web survey were much better educated than the average adult (see Bishop and Jabbari 2001), a factor which should have reduced substantially the percentage of respondents volunteering an opinion, given what we know from previous surveys on fictitious or obscure topics.

The relationship of education to offering an opinion on the Social Security Reform Act also varied in an unusual way with the form of the question (table 2.6). On form A the percentage giving an opinion did not vary significantly by education: About three-fourths of the respondents indicated they

Table 2.5.   Responses to Repealing 1995 Social Security Reform Act by Question Form

Form A		Form B	
Favor	13%	Favor	12%
Oppose	12	Oppose	9
Haven't heard it	75	Not sure	26
Total	100	Don't know	39
	(N = 674)	No opinion	14
		Total	100
			(N = 682)

Source: Presidential Election Poll: Campaign 2000. Internet Public Opinion Laboratory, Department of Political Science, University of Cincinnati, October 8–November 7, 2000.

had not heard of it, regardless of their education. But on form B, and contrary to previous research findings (Bishop et al. 1980; Schuman and Presser 1981), highly educated respondents were somewhat more likely than the less well educated to volunteer an opinion on repealing the Social Security Reform Act; they were also more opposed to repealing it, for reasons that are not so obvious. The highly educated were perhaps somewhat more likely to think they knew something about the topic from having answered the previous questions about investing social security funds in the market. They were, in fact, more likely than the less well educated to have expressed an opinion

Table 2.6.   Responses to Social Security Reform Act by Education, by Question Form

Form A	High school or less	Some college	College grad	Postgraduate study
Favor	15%	14%	18%	8%
Oppose	9	11	9	16
Haven't heard of it	76	76	73	76
Total	100	101	100	100
(N =)	(81)	(236)	(110)	(156)

Form B	High school or less	Some college	College grad	Postgraduate study
Favor	11%	12%	18%	11%
Oppose	8	6	5	17
Not sure	30	32	20	21
Don't know	36	37	40	42
No opinion	15	14	18	10
Total	100	101	101	101
(N =)	(98)	(227)	(148)	(209)

Source: Presidential Election Poll: Campaign 2000. Internet Public Opinion Laboratory, Department of Political Science, University of Cincinnati, October 8–November 7, 2000.

on the immediately preceding question about whether investing such funds in the market would strengthen or weaken the ability to pay benefits to retirees twenty-five years from now (Bishop and Jabbari 2001). So while these findings fail to replicate the typical pattern of previous experiments, they support the proposition that respondents, regardless of their education, will impute meaning to ambiguous survey questions from the immediately preceding question context. Psychologically, this situation is not unlike the one in which many respondents may have found themselves when interviewed in the same 2000 election campaign about George W. Bush's proposal to reform the social security system.

OPINIONS ON SOCIAL SECURITY: FACT OR ARTIFACT?

Given the remarkable tendency of even fairly well educated respondents to offer opinions on a nonexistent Social Security Reform Act, how much stock can be put in people's answers to any questions on this topic? How do we know, for example, they are not answering many such questions by simply imputing meaning to policy proposals and concepts about which they have little real knowledge, much less an opinion? As Schuman (2001) observes in his comments on the fine line between fictitious and nonfictitious issues: "What is fictional or non-fictional depends on one's perspective. Some non-fictional items asked on ordinary surveys are probably fictional from the standpoint of many respondents."

As exhibit A, consider the barrage of questions on the Social Security issue asked during the 2000 presidential election campaign, triggered largely by George W. Bush's proposal to reform the system. Shortly after candidate Bush proposed modifying the Social Security system, the Gallup Organization carried out a telling split-sample experiment in one of its national polls (June 2000). Half the sample was asked a question about the proposal that linked it explicitly to Bush; the other half was asked about it without mention of his name:

Form A: "George W. Bush has made a proposal that would allow people to put a portion of their Social Security payroll taxes into personal retirement accounts that would be invested in private stocks and bonds. Do you favor or oppose this proposal?"

Form B: "A proposal has been made that would allow people to put a portion of their Social Security payroll taxes into personal retirement accounts that would be invested in private stocks and bonds. Do you favor or oppose this proposal?"

Gallup repeated the experiment in March of 2001 and discovered once more that the wording of the question made a significant difference in how respondents answered the question (table 2.7). When Bush's name was linked to the proposal, Americans were less supportive than when it was presented as an abstract proposal without any mention of his name (cf. E. Smith 1990).

These results clearly indicate that responses to the question were not about just Social Security reform. Nor should it be surprising to learn that a respondent's partisan identification made a difference in how he or she answered the question. Republicans supported the proposal regardless of whether Bush's name was mentioned, most likely because they already knew it was his idea to begin with. Democrats reacted quite differently. Told that it was Bush's idea, they rejected the proposal by a 49 percent to 41 percent margin. But when it was presented as a generic proposition with no mention of his name, they favored the idea by a whopping margin of 63 percent to 35 percent (Newport 2000). These findings look strikingly similar to the results from the *Washington Post* experiment, which showed sharp partisan differences in reactions to the fictitious Public Affairs Act when it was described as President Clinton's idea versus a proposal by the "Republicans in Congress" (table 2.3). The Gallup experiment also tells us that many respondents may have been answering questions about the Social Security issue based less on what they knew about the specific policy pros and cons and much more on the general meaning they imputed to the question from its context and wording, especially when they didn't know much about it.

Consider one other telling piece of evidence as exhibit B: massive public ignorance. Despite all the publicity given to Bush's proposal during the presidential campaign, many Americans were not very attuned to the issue. Around the same time that a majority of Americans were telling Gallup's interviewers that they favored Bush's proposal to permit people to invest Social Security payroll taxes in the market, 61 percent of them were saying

Table 2.7. Responses to Bush Proposal for Social Security Reform by Question Wording

	June 2000		March 2001	
	With Bush	*Without*	*With Bush*	*Without*
Favor	59%	65%	54%	63%
Oppose	31	30	36	30
No opinion	10	5	10	7

Source: Gallup National Surveys

they did not know which presidential candidate had made the proposal (Princeton Survey Research Associates, June 14–28, 2000). Nearly two-thirds (65 percent) said they either hadn't heard or did not know if Vice President Al Gore favored or opposed the proposal (Shorenstein Center, June 14–19, 2000). Almost half (48 percent) reported they did not know if George W. Bush had even proposed allowing workers to invest such funds in the market; 51 percent didn't know whether or not Bush had proposed reducing Social Security benefits; 56 percent had no idea as to whether he had proposed increasing Social Security payroll taxes; and when asked how closely they had followed news stories about "George W. Bush's proposals about how to make the Social Security program more financially sound," over half (56 percent) said "not too closely," "not at all closely," or "don't know" (Princeton Survey Research Associates, May 26–June 4, 2000).

Follow-up polls told the same story of a poorly informed and inattentive public. Later that month (June 22–23, 2000), a Newsweek poll conducted by Princeton Survey Research Associates found that the vast majority of American adults (70 percent) did not know which of the two presidential candidates had proposed allowing "workers to put up to $2000 a year of tax-deductible savings in retirement accounts outside the Social Security system." A survey sponsored by the Shorenstein Center at Harvard found that close to two-thirds of the adult population still did not know whether presidential candidate Al Gore favored or opposed the proposed reform of the Social Security system (ICR Survey Research, July 26–30, 2000). And by late summer, after all the publicity generated by the presidential nominating conventions, nearly three out of four Americans (73 percent) still said they had heard either "little" or "nothing at all" about the proposed reform (Princeton Survey Research Associates, August 24–September 10, 2000). All this surely meant that the American public had not yet formed an opinion on the issue of reforming Social Security.

But this hardly stopped the pollsters from asking questions about public opinion on Social Security. In fact, the very same *Newsweek* poll (June 22–23, 2000) that had shown much of the public to be relatively uninformed about the issue—not even knowing which of the two presidential candidates had proposed the reform—went on to ask a battery of opinion questions about the topic, including some that first educated respondents about the issue with a presumptive lead-in phrase: "*As you may know*, the presidential candidates have made some proposals to change or supplement Social Security to help Americans save more money for their retirement. One of these proposals would change Social Security to allow workers to invest some of their Social Security payroll taxes in the stock market. In general, do you favor or oppose this proposal?" (emphasis added). Asked of registered voters, the question generated a majority (51 percent) in favor of the proposal; just 36 percent opposed it, and 13 percent answered "don't know." The latter figure indicates more absence of opinion than is typically the case with survey questions, but probably underestimates it significantly because of the implicit expectation in the question's lead-in phrase for respondents to express an opinion, since "they may know" something about it. In this way the wording of the question generated an illusion of public opinion on Social Security where there was, by most polls, considerable ignorance and uncertainty about the proposal at best.

As if that were not enough, other questions asked in the same *Newsweek* poll demonstrated just how malleable public opinion on the issue could be, depending on the way in which the issue was framed. Given an individualistic framing, the majority (55 percent) of the American public thought it was a good idea: "Some people have suggested allowing individuals to invest portions of their Social Security taxes on their own, which might allow them to make more money for their retirement, but would involve greater risk. Do you think allowing individuals to invest a portion of their Social Security taxes on their own is a good idea or a bad idea?" But given a more impersonal framing, a sizable percentage (60 percent) thought it was a bad idea: "Some people have suggested investing some of the Social Security trust fund in the stock market, which might make more money for the fund, but would involve greater risk. Do you think investing some of the Social Security trust fund in the stock market is a good idea or a bad idea?"

Better yet, many of those who said they favored the idea could easily be induced to oppose it by being asked to consider a tradeoff: "You say you generally favor allowing workers to invest some Social Security payroll taxes in the stock market. Would you still favor this proposal if you heard it might require reducing the Social Security benefits that seniors have?" (*Newsweek*, June 22–23, 2000). A substantial majority (57 percent) of the original supporters now said they opposed it. Many other examples of framing effects in questions about this issue could be provided (see the online poll database at the Roper Center for Public Opinion Research), but this should suffice to make the point that the impression of public opinion on Social Security given by such polls during the summer of the 2000 campaign was highly misleading. The public was barely beginning to think about the issue and was a far cry from achieving what Daniel Yankelovich (1991) would call a "public judgment" on the choices and consequences involved in reforming Social Security. American public opinion on this issue was thus, in large part, an illusion generated by the way in which pollsters had posed the questions.

MISSILE DEFENSE: PUBLIC OPINION
AND PUBLIC IGNORANCE

The illusory quality of public opinion on Social Security represents just one of many such illustrations that can be found in numerous national media polls. As exhibit C, consider the elusive character of public opinion that developed around President George W. Bush's proposal for a missile defense system—a déjà vu of Bud Roper's (1983) concerns about the myths of public opinion on the MX missile in the early 1980s. Introduced during the 2000 presidential election campaign, the issue produced sharp partisan debate and a bewildering variation in what the public supposedly thought about it. An early reading of the public's mood by Zogby International (February 2000) suggested there was substantial backing for such a system. Respondents were asked, "Which of the following statements best represents your position on a missile defense system? Statement A: Constructing a national defense system will undermine our nuclear treaty with Russia and produce an unstable international situation. Statement B: Our best hope for long-term defense is developing our own missile defense system and not relying on treaties." Asked this way, the question produced a sizable majority (61 percent) in favor of building a missile defense system instead of relying on treaties with the Russians; less than a third of respondents (29 percent) felt it would undermine our nuclear agreement with Russia and destabilize the international environment; and the rest (11 percent) weren't sure what to think.

Where the public stood on the missile defense issue, however, was not so easily deciphered. Just two months later an ABC News national poll (April 26–30, 2000) indicated that the American public opposed such a system when the issue was framed in terms of its cost-effectiveness and the consequences of building it. This time the question read, "I want to ask you about plans for a land-and-space-based missile defense system in this country. Supporters say it would be worth its estimated 60 billion dollar cost because it would protect the United States from a limited nuclear attack. Opponents say it wouldn't work, would cost too much, and could create a new arms race. How about you: do you support or oppose developing this kind of missile defense system?" By a 53 percent to 44 percent margin, a majority of Americans now opposed the missile defense system, and only a tiny minority (3 percent) said they did not have an opinion on this momentous issue.

Less than a week later the Pew Research Center for the People and the Press (May 2–6, 2000) entered the polling picture with a new national survey on the issue showing that while 90 percent of Americans admitted they had heard "little" or "nothing at all" about the debate over whether the United

States should develop a missile defense system, a decided majority could be coaxed into either favoring it or opposing it depending on how the issue was posed. When the issue was presented as a choice between protecting "the US from missile attack" and the possibility that "it would be too costly and *might* interfere with existing arms treaties with the Russians" (emphasis added), the majority (52 percent to 37 percent) favored developing a ground-and-space-based missile defense system. But when confronted with a choice between developing such a system at the risk of jeopardizing negotiations with the Russians "aimed at reducing the nuclear arsenals in both countries" and holding off on such development to "focus on negotiating further arms reductions with the Russians," the majority (55 percent to 36 percent) opted for holding off and negotiating. Public opinion on missile defense was, in a word, malleable.

A CBS News/*New York Times* poll conducted the following week (May 10–13, 2000) demonstrated just how malleable public opinion on this issue could be. To begin with, the great majority of respondents (64 percent) acknowledged they had heard "not much" or "nothing at all" about the issue of building a missile defense system. Despite this self-admitted ignorance, they favored building such a system by a margin of more than two to one (58 percent to 28 percent), though a sizable percentage volunteered a "don't know." Once they had identified supporters and opponents of the missile defense system with this initial question, the CBS/*New York Times* interviewers then asked a set of follow-up questions containing arguments *against* the respondent's position on the issue. Those who favored the system were asked several such questions. Told "the United States has already spent 60 billion dollars on trying to develop this system," respondents' net support for building it dropped to a 47 percent to 35 percent margin, with 18 percent now unsure about whether it was still a good idea (see analysis by Moore 2001a). Informed that "many scientists conclude it is unlikely that such a system will ever work," the majority of those who initially supported the system now opposed it by a margin of more than two to one (56 percent to 25 percent). And given the further argument that continuing to build such a system would mean "the United States would have to break the arms control treaty we now have with the Russians," they continued to oppose it by a substantial margin (52 percent to 28 percent). The experiment also showed that those who initially opposed building the system could be persuaded in overwhelming numbers to support it (71 percent to 12 percent) by simply being asked, "What if the system had a good chance of working successfully to defend against accidental missile launches?" The what-if quality of the questions in this experiment makes it all sound rather hypothetical, but it tells us how easily respondents can be coaxed into offering an opinion on an issue about which most of them are poorly informed at best.

As Moore (2001a) and many other scholars have argued, this malleability in public opinion most likely reflects how little Americans know about politics and public affairs (see Bennett 1988, 1990; Delli Carpini and Keeter 1991, 1996; Erskine 1962, 1963a, 1963b; Neuman 1986; B. Roper 1983). And, as with the questions on Social Security reform in the 2000 election campaign and "the 1995 Social Security Reform Act," it demonstrates how readily the framing of issues with ambiguously worded survey questions can artificially construct the social reality we call "public opinion." The opinions respondents manufacture on the spot in reaction to such questions may well be real psychologically speaking, insofar as they are based on underlying dispositions toward the constructed object, but they are clearly illusory with respect to the specific substance of the policy issues that the questions were designed to measure in this instance: American public opinion on the merits of a missile defense system and Social Security reform. In each case the net result was a poorly informed public policy debate.

STEM CELL RESEARCH AND
THE PHANTOM PUBLIC

Probably no other recent issue better illustrates the elusive character of public opinion and how it is constructed by the way in which questions are worded than the controversy surrounding federal funding of embryonic stem cell research. As Adam Clymer (2001) observed in a critique of the flurry of polls conducted on the issue when it hit the front burner in Washington, D.C., "American public opinion on the subject doesn't exist—at least not yet. The subject is too new and too complicated." But, as he comments in his ironically titled article, "The Unbearable Lightness of Public Opinion Polls," "Polls seem to say otherwise." An NBC News/*Wall Street Journal* poll he cites found over two-thirds of Americans (69 percent) in favor of stem cell research; an ABC News poll conducted for Beliefnet, a web-based spiritual and religious organization, produced a sizable majority (58 percent) in support of stem cell research and an equally sizable majority (60 percent) that felt federal funding for medical research should include funding for stem cell research. Another poll cited by Clymer, which was commissioned by a special interest organization, the Juvenile Diabetes Research Foundation, likewise discovered that the great majority of Americans, by a margin of more than two to one, supported federal funding of stem cell research. On the other hand, he points to a poll sponsored by the National Conference of Catholic

Bishops showing that the overwhelming majority of Americans (70 percent) were opposed to any federal funding of experiments involving stem cells from human embryos. As if only to confuse matters further, a Fox News/ Opinion Dynamics poll of registered voters showed the American public to be sharply divided on the issue, with 43 percent in favor of stem cell research; 40 percent opposed to it; and a sizable percentage (17 percent) still undecided.

Citing a Gallup poll conducted during the same period, Clymer (2001) argues that most of the volatility in public opinion on this issue can be attributed to a lack of public awareness and variations in the wording of the questions asked by the different polling organizations. Indeed, as the headline for the Gallup News Service (July 20, 2001) announced, "Most Americans in the Dark about Stem Cell Research." According to the poll, only 38 percent of Americans said they were following the debate about federal funding of stem cell research either very or somewhat closely, as compared to 63 percent who were following the story about the missing Washington, D.C., intern, Chandra Levy. Even more telling was the percentage of Americans who admitted they were not very informed on the issue of stem cell research. When asked, "Do you think the federal government should or should not fund this type of research, or don't you know enough to say?" a clear majority (57 percent) said they did not know enough about it to offer an opinion. The rest of the respondents said they favored it by a margin of 30 percent to 13 percent. But in a remarkable demonstration of how to create public opinion where not much existed beforehand, the survey also showed that many Americans would offer an opinion once the issue was explained to them in some detail so that they could feel sufficiently informed to answer the question. Rather elaborate in educating the respondent, the Gallup question read (Roper Center for Public Opinion Research, 2001):

> The kind of stem-cell research the government is considering involves human embryos that have been created in medical clinics by fertilizing a woman's egg outside the womb. An embryo may be implanted into a woman's womb to develop into a baby. If an embryo is not implanted into a woman's womb to develop into a baby, it may be destroyed, either by being discarded or by being used for medical research. Some scientists believe this type of medical research could lead to treatments for such diseases as Alzheimer's, diabetes, heart disease and spinal cord injuries. Given this information, do you think the federal government should or should not fund this type of research?

Informed about the issue in this way, a majority of Americans (54 percent) said they thought the federal government should fund this kind of research; 39 percent said it should not; and the rest (7 percent) remained undecided.

In a somewhat different framing of the issue several questions later, how-ever, the American public appeared to be more concerned about the details of the matter. Told that "one of the issues in this type of research is whether or not the embryos used were developed specifically for stem cell research" and then asked, "Do you think the federal government should or should not allow scientists to fertilize human eggs specifically for the purpose of creating new stem cells?" a majority (54 percent) now said "no." In one sense this merely demonstrates that respondents were paying attention to the nuances of the issue as conveyed by the wording of the question (cf. Newport 2001b on the death penalty), but most of them also had readily acknowledged they had not followed the issue (60 percent said either "not too closely" or "not at all closely"), and a noticeable majority (57 percent) had earlier given the answer "don't know enough to say." So, in the absence of an explicit filter question allowing respondents to say "don't know" or "no opinion," it should not be surprising that so many can be induced to offer an opinion however the question is worded. Given a sufficient number of wording or contextual cues on nearly any topic, respondents will, in the absence of an explicit opportunity to say "don't know," find a way to interpret a question and provide an answer, however vague or ambiguous the question might seem, as evidenced by the well-documented instance of responses to the fic-titious 1975 Public Affairs Act.

The summary of poll results in table 2.8 tells the story of just how dramati-cally public opinion on the issue of stem cell research can vary, depending on how the issue is framed and on how exactly the question is worded—a perplexity that President George W. Bush and his advisers may well have been aware of at the point of his stem cell decision (*Time*, July 23, 2001). Unlike the Gallup poll, which begins by measuring respondents' awareness and attention to the issue, the NBC News/*Wall Street Journal* poll starts by defining the meaning of the stem cell research issue for the respondent and then frames the choice as one between the ethics of using "potentially viable human embryos" (whatever that might mean to respondents) and the value of such research for curing various well-known diseases such as cancer, Alz-heimer's, and Parkinson's. When the question is framed this way, the bulk of the respondents (69 percent) choose the latter. Defining the issue somewhat differently for respondents, the ABC News/Beliefnet poll poses the issue a bit more vaguely as one between those who see it as "an important way to find treatments for many diseases" and others who believe that "it's wrong to use any human embryos for research purposes." Given this elaborate definition and wording, the majority (58 percent) supports the idea of stem cell research. And given little or no further information on the issue in the fol-low-up question, a clear majority (60 percent) also ends up in favor of having

Table 2.8.   Responses to Variously Worded Survey Questions on Stem Cell Research

ABC News/Beliefnet (June 20–24, 2001)

"Sometimes fertility clinics produce extra fertilized eggs, also called embryos, that are implanted in a woman's womb. These extra embryos either are discarded, or couples can donate them for use in medical research called stem-cell research. Some people support stem-cell research, saying it's an important way to find treatments for many diseases. Other people oppose stem-cell research, saying it's wrong to use any human embryos for research purposes. What about you—do you support or oppose stem-cell research?"

Support	58%
Oppose	30
No opinion	12
N	1,022

"The federal government provides funding to support a variety of medical research. Do you think federal funding for medical research should or should not include funding for stem-cell research?"

Should	60%
Should not	31
No opinion	9
N	1,022

NBC News/*Wall Street Journal* (June 23–25, 2001)

"There is a type of medical research that involves using special cells, called stem cells, that are obtained from human embryos. These human embryo stem cells are then used to generate new cells and tissue that could help treat or cure many diseases. I am now going to read you two statements about this type of research. Statement A: Those opposed to this type of research say that it crosses an ethical line by using cells from potentially viable human embryos, when this research can be done on animals or by using other types of cells. Statement B: Those in favor of this research say that it could lead to breakthrough cures for many diseases, such as cancer, Alzheimer's, Parkinson's, and spinal cord injuries, and this research uses only embryos that otherwise would be discarded. Who do you agree with more—those opposed or those in favor?"

Agree more with those opposed	23%
Agree more with those in favor	69
Depends (volunteered)	3
Not sure	5
N	806

Fox News/Opinion Dynamics (July 11–12, 2001)

"Based on what you know, do you support or oppose each of the following? . . . Allowing medical research using tissue from fertilized human eggs commonly called stem cell research."

Support	43%
Oppose	40
Don't know	17
N	900

Gallup Organization (July 10–11, 2001)

"As you may know, the federal government is considering whether to fund certain kinds of medical research known as 'stem cell research.' . . . How closely have you followed the debate about government funding of stem cell research—very closely, somewhat closely, not too closely, or not closely at all?"

Very closely	9%
Somewhat closely	29
Not too closely	28
Not closely at all	32
No opinion	2
N	998

"As you may know, the federal government is considering whether to fund certain kinds of medical research known as 'stem cell research.' . . . Do you think the federal government should or should not fund this type of research, or don't you know enough to say?"

Should	30%
Should not	13
Don't know enough to say	57
No opinion	—*
N	998

"The kind of stem-cell research the government is considering involves human embryos that have been created in medical clinics by fertilizing a woman's egg outside the womb. An embryo may be implanted into a woman's womb to develop into a baby. If an embryo is not implanted into a woman's womb to develop into a baby, it may be destroyed, either by being discarded or by being used for medical research. Some scientists believe this type of medical research could lead to treatments for such diseases as Alzheimer's, diabetes, heart disease and spinal cord injuries. Given this information, do you think the federal government should or should not fund this type of research?"

Should	54%
Should not	39
No opinion	7
N	998

"One of the issues involved in this type of research is whether or not the embryos used were developed specifically for stem cell research. Do you think the federal government should or should not allow scientists to fertilize human eggs specifically for the purpose of creating new stem cells?"

Yes, should allow	38%
No, should not	54
No opinion	8
N	998

National Conference of Catholic Bishops/ICR Survey Research (June 1–5, 2001)

"Stem cells are the basic cells from which all of a person's tissues and organs develop. Congress is considering whether to provide federal funding for experiments using stem cells from human embryos. The live embryos would be destroyed in their first week of development to obtain these cells. Do you support or oppose using your federal tax dollars for such experiments?"

Support	23.9%
Oppose	69.9
Don't know	4.8
Refused	1.3
N	1,013

"Stem cells for research can be obtained by destroying human embryos. They can also be obtained from adults, from placentas left over from live births, and in other ways that do no harm to the donor. Scientists disagree on which source may end up being most successful in treating diseases. How would you prefer your tax dollars to be used this year for stem cell research?" (Options rotated.)

Supporting all methods, including those that require destroying human embryos, to see which will be most successful	17.6%
Supporting research using adult stem cells and other alternatives, to see if there is no need to destroy human embryos for research	66.8
Neither (volunteered)	8.6
Don't know	6.3
Refused	0.7
N	1,013

Juvenile Diabetes Research Foundation (January 12–5, 2001)

"As you may already know, a stem cell is the basic cell in the body from which all other cells arise. Medical researchers have been able to isolate stem cells from excess human embryos developed through in vitro fertilization and fetal tissue that has been donated to research. The medical researchers believe that human stem cells can be developed into replacement cells to cure diseases such as diabetes, Parkinson's, Alzheimer's, cancer, heart disease, arthritis, burns, or spinal cord problems."

Support federal funding	65%
Oppose	26
Don't know	9
N	1,004

Harris Interactive (July 12–16, 2001)

"Based on what you have read or heard, do you think that the federal government should or should not fund stem cell research?"

Should	43%
Should not	27
Depends (volunteered)	3
Not sure	27
N	1,011

Sources: Public Opinion Location Library, Roper Center for Public Opinion Research; Public Agenda Foundation Online (www.publicagenda.org); Juvenile Diabetes Research Foundation (www.jdrf.org).

the federal government include funding for stem cell research in its medical research budget.

In contrast, the Fox News/Opinion Dynamics Poll of registered voters presents the issue with minimal definition and nothing at all in the way of arguments and counterarguments. Posed in this minimalist fashion, the question produces an impression of a deeply divided American public (at least among registered voters), with nearly equal percentages in favor of (43 percent) and opposed to (40 percent) "allowing medical research using tissue from fertilized human eggs commonly called stem cell research" and a sizable percentage of respondents volunteering a "don't know"—an indication that this question, unlike those asked by NBC News/*Wall Street Journal* and ABC News/Beliefnet, does not educate respondents sufficiently to induce them to offer an opinion.

Approaching the issue with a more obvious vested pro-life interest, the National Conference of Catholic Bishops commissioned a poll that persuades respondents to oppose stem cell research by telling them "the live embryos would be destroyed in their first week of development to obtain these cells." Not surprisingly, given this emotional input, nearly 70 percent of the respondents say they oppose "using their federal tax dollars for such experiments." A poll commissioned by the Juvenile Diabetes Research Foundation, an organization with an opposite, but equally obvious, vested interest in stem cell research, includes "diabetes" among the many diseases that human stem cell research could help cure, the combined effect of which results in nearly two-thirds of Americans (65 percent) saying they favor the funding of stem cell research by the National Institutes of Health. Given the pro-research bias in the definition of the issue, it's little wonder that only one out of four (26 percent) respondents oppose it. So with one question form, the public appears to support stem cell research; with the other, it does not—reminding us once more of Walter Lippmann's venerable critique of "the phantom public." Given how little the public probably knew about it at the time, American public opinion on stem cell research was probably not much more than a phantom.

NOTE

1. I would like to thank Richard Morin of the *Washington Post* for granting initial access to the data from this experiment, which are presently archived in the Roper Center for Public Opinion Research at the University of Connecticut.

3

Survey Questions and Reality

> What we observe is not nature in itself, but nature exposed to our method
> of questioning.
>
> —Werner Heisenberg, *Physics and Philosophy*

From the very beginning, public opinion researchers such as Gallup, Roper, and Crossley knew all too well how the results of their polls could be affected by the way in which the questions were worded, the form in which they were presented, and the order and context in which they were asked. As early as 1937, the Gallup Organization designed the first of thousands of "split-ballot" experiments on the way in which questions were asked, primarily to improve on the practice of wording them (Bishop and Smith 1991). But for reasons that are now obscured in the archives of survey research, this vigorous program of experimentation by Gallup and other polling organizations (see Rugg and Cantril 1944) died out not long after the infamous preelection polling failure in the 1948 presidential election, most likely because of the need to focus the resources of the field on the problems of nonprobability sampling revealed by that fiasco.

Though experimentation with the wording of survey questions occurred here and there over the years, not until the 1970s was this line of inquiry revitalized, first by Schuman and Presser (1981) at the University of Michigan's Survey Research Center and shortly thereafter by my associates and me at the University of Cincinnati's Behavioral Sciences Laboratory and Institute for Policy Research. A burst of experimentation since then, including extensive collaboration of academic survey researchers with cognitive and social psychologists (see, e.g., Sudman, Bradburn, and Schwarz 1996; Tanur 1992), has produced complex theoretical models of the question-and-answer process in survey interviews (see, e.g., Tourangeau, Rips, and Rasinski 2000). Suffice it to say that the thrust of this research has been to reinforce, dramatically, the proposition that survey questions not only shape the answers respondents give, but also, more important, construct the social reality we call "public opinion." One of the most powerful factors in this constructive psychological process is the form in which the question is posed to the respondent.

OPEN VERSUS CLOSED WORLDS

Asking survey questions in an open-ended (free-answer) or a closed-ended (forced-choice) form controls the answers respondents give in both obvious and subtle ways. By limiting respondents' choices to two or more fixed categories in a closed-ended question, a pollster forces respondents to interpret the question within the subjective frame of reference he or she has created. But, as Schuman and Presser (1981) have demonstrated in their now classic experiments with these question forms, open-ended, or so-called free-answer, questions can also powerfully constrain how respondents interpret and answer a question by subtly implying a frame of reference. Consider, for example, their experiment with one of the most commonly asked questions in American public opinion research: "What do you think is the *most* important problem facing this country today?" As part of a Detroit Area Study (DAS), they compared people's responses to a nearly identical version of this standard open-ended question, administered to a random half of the sample, with those given to the following closed-ended form, administered to the other half of the sample: "Which of these is the *most* important problem facing this country at present?"

1. Food and energy shortages
2. Crime and violence
3. Inflation
4. Unemployment
5. Decreased trust in government
6. Busing
7. Breakdown of morals and religion
8. Racial problems

On both the open and closed forms of the question, the percentage selecting inflation (13.3 percent and 12.6 percent, respectively) and unemployment (19.1 percent and 19.7 percent, respectively) as the most important problem was virtually the same. But on the closed form, respondents chose crime and violence as the most important problem more than twice as often

CRIME 64

(34.9 percent) as those who had to volunteer it spontaneously on the open form (15.7 percent). In fact, it emerged as the most frequently mentioned problem facing the country on the closed form, whereas it was second most important on the open form, following unemployment and just barely ahead of inflation. By making crime and violence an explicit response category, Schuman and Presser argued, the closed form of the question legitimized it as an option. On the open form, however, they argued that the use of the wording "facing this country" subtly discouraged many respondents from volunteering "crime" as an alternative because it may have been perceived more as a local problem and, therefore, as an inappropriate response to the nationwide frame of reference implied by the wording of the standard open-ended question. The public thus appeared to be much less concerned with crime in this seemingly open construction of the question than when it was posed in a closed-ended form. One version of the question, in other words, made crime and violence seem to be a "real" and significant problem facing the country merely by mentioning it, whereas the other version seemingly obscured its reality and significance. Or did it? As Werner Heisenberg and his philosophical disciples might have put it, how do we know how important crime truly was to the American public at the time, apart from the act of measurement with an open or closed question form?

That the "reality" of a problem facing the country depends so much on the form in which the question is asked became even more conspicuous in a follow-up experiment Schuman and Presser (1981) conducted during the unusually harsh U.S. winter of 1977. In this instance they constructed a new closed-ended version of the question about the most important problem facing the country, using the five most frequently volunteered responses to an open-ended form of the question asked in a previous Detroit Area Study: unemployment, crime, inflation, quality of leaders, and the breakdown of morals and religion. They limited the list to five problems because previous pilot studies had indicated that about five response alternatives was the maximum that respondents could handle effectively in a telephone interview. Among the response alternatives they did not include in the closed form was "food and energy shortages" since it had been volunteered in the DAS by only a very small percentage of respondents (1.7 percent). In February of 1977, the Survey Research Center (SRC) at the University of Michigan administered this closed-ended form of the question, with five response categories, to a random half of a national sample and the standard open-ended version of the question to the other half.

As Schuman and Presser (1981) recount it, while the telephone survey was in the field, a severe bout of winter struck the eastern half of the United States, producing widespread concerns and stories in the press about potential energy shortages. The results of the survey reflected the sudden emergence of the energy crisis, but only among those respondents who were asked the open form of the question, to which more than one out of five (22 percent) volunteered a response coded as "food and energy shortages," second in importance only to unemployment (24 percent) as the most important problem facing the country. Looking at those responses given to the closed form of the question, however, a historian of the future could find barely a trace of the energy crisis during the winter of 1977. Nearly all the respondents given the closed form (99 percent) selected one of the five explicit response categories made available to them, and only 1 respondent out of 592, according to Schuman and Presser, volunteered anything resembling the energy crisis affecting the country, which was coded under "other." With the closed form of the question, then, the energy crisis simply did not exist; only with the open form did it become a reality. Schuman and Presser's fortuitous experiment drove home the point, once more, that respondents will almost invariably limit themselves to the explicit list of choices provided by the pollster and the substantive frame of reference it implies. Rarely, if ever, will they venture beyond his or her framing of "reality."

Just how profoundly the reality of the situation can be defined for respondents comes through in yet another series of experiments on open versus closed questions by Schuman and Scott (1987). As part of a national, monthly telephone survey conducted by the University of Michigan's Survey Research Center (October 1986) they embedded an experiment in which a random half of the respondents received the standard open version of the question about "the most important problem facing this country today." The other half got a specially constructed closed-ended version of the question that included just four *rare* problems, each of which had been volunteered by less than 1 percent of the sample to an open form of the question asked in a previous national poll by the Gallup Organization. In other words, these were extremely insignificant problems as far as most Americans were concerned in the fall of 1986 (the energy shortage of 1977 was a distant memory by then). The closed question offering the four categories of rare problems read, "Which of the following do you think is the most important problem facing this country today—the energy shortage, the quality of public schools, legalized abortion, or pollution? Or if you prefer, you may name a different problem as most important." As proof of the rarity of the problems listed on the closed form, Schuman and Scott (1987) discovered that only a tiny percentage of the respondents receiving the open form of the question spontaneously volunteered any one of them (less than 3 percent). But on the closed form a sizable majority of the respondents (60 percent) selected one of the four rare, artificially created "problems" as the most important facing the country today.

That was not the only reality constructed by the question. Illustrating, once more, the great power of the question form to establish the frame of reference for the respondent, unemployment, the most frequently mentioned problem on the open form (17 percent), was volunteered by only about a third as many respondents (6.2 percent) on the closed form. Even more significant, as Schuman and Scott (1987) point out, a pollster using the closed-ended form of the question would be drawn to the totally misleading conclusion that a rarely mentioned problem (at that time), the quality of public schools, was of the greatest concern to Americans, with nearly one out of three respondents (32 percent) selecting it as the most important problem facing the country, followed by pollution (14 percent) and abortion (8.4 percent). Whereas on the open form the most important problem would appear to be the "reality" of "unemployment" and "economic problems," followed by "international concerns" that preoccupied many Americans, with little or no mention of any of the rare "problems" artificially manufactured on the closed form. Though no competent pollster would ever consider designing a closed-ended question with such rarely mentioned problems as explicit response categories, Schuman and Scott's experiment demonstrates how easily an illusion of the American public's concerns can be generated by the way in which the question and the response categories are constructed. And apart from the long-standing issue of which question form—open or closed— better measures the public's "true" priorities, these well-designed experiments by Schuman and his associates tell us that the framing of survey questions can wittingly or unwittingly construct much of what passes in poll reports and press releases as the reality of public opinion. And this is but one of many ways in which public opinion can be constructed.

DON'T KNOW, NOT SURE, OR NO OPINION?

The framing of survey questions can generate contrasting images of public opinion through another crucial decision pollsters make: whether to give respondents an explicit opportunity to say they have "no opinion" on an issue, that they're perhaps "not sure," or that they just "don't know" anything about it. Because they want to minimize missing data, most polling organizations today typically do not give respondents such an opportunity. In fact, they usually discourage such "don't know" (DK) responses by training interviewers to probe respondents who initially indicate they're "not sure" or "don't know" with follow-up comments like "We're interested in just your general opinion" or by asking them which way they *lean* or whether they feel *closer* to one side or the other. Respondents generally comply with these situational demands of the interview and can be induced, as we have seen, to give opinions even on highly obscure or fictitious issues (see chapter 2). The same situational pressures probably lead many respondents to offer opinions to pollsters on numerous domestic and foreign policy issues, whether they know much about them or not. But the critical question is whether including or excluding such less knowledgeable respondents makes an important difference in the conclusions a pollster draws about the nature and reality of public opinion on a given issue.

The initial verdict from Schuman and Presser's (1981) seminal experiments with the DK response in survey questions suggested that it generally made little or no difference in the results and conclusions. Even though their experiments showed that a sizable percentage of respondents (about 20–25 percent on average) would admit they did not have an opinion on a given issue if asked an explicit filter question such as "Do you have an opinion on that?" the availability of a "no opinion" option generally had no significant effect on the distribution of opinions (pro and con) once the DK responses were excluded from the data analysis (see Schuman and Presser 1981, chap. 4). In one such experiment, for example, they used the standard form of the question (one without an explicit DK alternative) to ask respondents whether they agreed or disagreed with the idea that "the Russian leaders are basically trying to get along with America." In this case, roughly one out of six (15.2 percent) volunteered a "don't know" response. Respondents who received the filtered form (with an explicit "no opinion" option), however, were much more likely to acknowledge they had no opinion (37.6 percent). Nonetheless, once the DK and "no opinion" responses were deleted from the data analysis, there was no statistically significant difference in the percentage of respondents who agreed with the statement about the Russian leaders: 59 percent on the standard form versus 63 percent on the filtered form. A pollster would, in other words, reach essentially the same conclusion regardless of which question form was used: A sizable majority of Americans thought the Russian leaders were fundamentally trying to get along with us.

An independent set of experiments by my colleagues and me (Bishop, Oldendick, and Tuchfarber 1983), however, produced a somewhat different set of results. Like Schuman and Presser, we found that the use of an explicit filter question led many respondents to acknowledge they did not have an opinion, though the percentage varied considerably depending on the topic and how the filter question was worded. On the more familiar and concrete issue of affirmative action for black Americans in jobs and education, for example, asking an explicit filter question, regardless of how it was worded, increased the percentage of "no opinion" responses by only 5–6 percent on average, as compared to the percentage volunteered spontaneously on the standard, unfiltered form. But on more obscure foreign affairs issues, such as whether the United States should resume arms shipments to Turkey, adding a filter question boosted the percentage of "no opinion" responses by 25–50 percent, depending on how it was worded. When asked, for instance, if they had "thought much about the issue" of arms shipments to Turkey, respondents were significantly more likely to say "no" than if they were asked simply "Do you have an opinion on this or not?" In other words, the more strongly worded the filter question, the less likely respondents were to express an opinion. And, as a rule, the more abstract or remote the issue was from the day-to-day concerns of respondents, the greater was the impact of the wording of the filter question.

But unlike Schuman and Presser, my coworkers and I (Bishop, Oldendick, and Tuchfarber 1983) discovered that the use of a filter question made a significant difference in our conclusions about the nature of public opinion on a given issue. One of the key issues we examined was the role of the government versus the private sector in solving the nation's problems. In one randomized experimental condition, respondents were asked an unfiltered version of a standard question from the National Election Studies:

> Now some people think the government in Washington is trying to do too many things that should be left to individuals and private businesses. Others disagree and think that the government should do even more to solve our country's problems. What is your opinion—do you think the government is trying to do too many things that should be left to individuals and private businesses, or do you think the government should do even more to solve our country's problems?

The same exact question was asked of respondents who were given differently worded versions of a filtered question form (see Bishop, Oldendick, and Tuchfarber 1983), which generated "no opinion" responses ranging from 25–35 percent, depending on how strongly the filter question was worded. But more important, public opinion on the role of the government looked rather different with one form of the question than with the other, even when the "no opinion" responses were excluded from the data analysis. Using the unfiltered form of the question, a pollster would conclude that a sizable majority (60 percent) favored having the government take a more activist role in solving the nation's problems. Whereas with the filtered versions of the question, a researcher would reach just the opposite conclusion: a clear majority (54 percent) thought such things should be left to individuals and private businesses.

That wasn't the only example of contrasting realities generated by the form of the question. A similar pattern turned up on a key question in international affairs at the time: whether the respondent favored or opposed the Strategic Arms Limitation Talks (SALT) between the United States and the Soviet Union. Respondents given the standard (filter-free) form were asked:

> Some people say that we should refuse to continue the Strategic Arms Limitation Talks with the Soviet Union until they stop interfering in African affairs. Other people think that limiting the arms race is so important that we should continue the talks despite the involvement of the Soviet Union in African affairs. What is your feeling—do you think we should refuse to continue the Strategic Arms Limitation Talks until the Soviet Union stops interfering in African affairs, or do you think that limiting the arms race is so important that we should continue the talks despite the involvement of the Soviet Union in African affairs?

The same question was asked of those who received different versions of a filtered question form. In this instance the percentage giving a "no opinion" response varied considerably, depending on how strongly the filter question was worded. Asked simply, for example, "Do you have an opinion on this or not?" about one out of four respondents (26 percent) said "no." But when asked, "Have you already heard enough about it to have an opinion?" over half (53 percent) said they had not. Experiments with other versions of the filter question eliminated anywhere from 30–40 percent of the respondents, depending again on how strongly it was worded (see Bishop, Oldendick, and Tuchfarber 1983).

Did this filter question stuff really matter? As with the question on the role of the government versus the private sector, the use of a filter question to screen out the less informed made a significant difference in the distribution of public opinion on the issue. In a fall 1979 Greater Cincinnati survey, for example, the results showed that a pollster would have concluded that a sizable majority of respondents (57 percent) *favored* the SALT II agreement with the Soviet Union if the standard, unfiltered form of the question had been administered; that the public was almost evenly *divided* if the moderately strong filter question—"Have you thought much about this issue?"—had been used (51 percent favored it); or that a clear majority (54 percent) actually *opposed* the agreement if the pollster had used, instead, the most strongly worded filter: "Have you already heard or read enough about it to have an opinion?" So on both the SALT issue and the question about the role of the government versus the private sector in solving our national problems, giving or not giving respondents an explicit chance to say "don't know" or "no opinion" in one way or another produced rather different versions of what was supposedly the reality of public opinion. Yet another way in which the form of the question can construct the reality of public opinion is through the creation of a "middle-of-the-road" position—a seemingly mythical place where a majority of the American public is often said to reside.

THE MIDDLE OF THE ROAD

A key decision in constructing many survey questions is whether to offer respondents a middle alternative on an issue. A question asking respondents, for example, whether they think spending for military defense should be increased or decreased can easily be changed to include the implied middle position, "kept at the present level." The question "Should divorce in this country be easier or more difficult to obtain than it is now?" can likewise be modified to offer respondents the plausible option "stay as it is" (Schuman and Presser 1981, chap. 6). Some pollsters avoid offering respondents such a middle position, probably because they believe that many respondents would choose it as an easy way out of making a decision, as a way to conceal their real opinion, or as a way to appear to have an opinion on the issue when in fact they know little or nothing about it. Other survey practitioners defend the use of middle response alternatives as a logical and meaningful choice in many questions. It is practically unthinkable in American politics, for instance, to ask the question "In politics, as of today, do you think of yourself as a Republican or a Democrat?" and not mention the well-established, middle-like position of independent (the standard Gallup Organization question). Nor would anyone think to ask the question about an individual's political ideology "On most issues, do you think of yourself as a liberal or as a conservative?" and not include "moderate" or "middle of the road" as an explicit alternative.

But on many substantive issues in American politics, the pollster's decision gets more complicated. Take, for example, the issue of abortion. Numerous polls conducted by the Gallup Organization have asked about this controversial issue with a question that offers respondents an explicit and presumably meaningful middle position: "Do you think abortions should be legal under any circumstances, *legal under only certain circumstances*, or illegal in all circumstances?" (emphasis added; see Saad 1999, 2003). In many of the same polls, however, Gallup has asked respondents to classify their position on the abortion issue as if there were no middle ground whatsoever: "With respect to the abortion issue, would you consider yourself to be pro-choice or pro-life?" Given the standard question with a middle-of-the-road option, a clear majority of Americans (55 percent) in a recent national poll chose the moderate position of keeping abortion "legal only under certain circumstances."

About one out of four (27 percent) favored making it legal under any circumstances. And fewer than one out of five (16 percent) thought it should
be illegal in all circumstances, with the rest (2 percent) having "no opinion."
In contrast, given the simple dichotomous version of this controversial issue,
the American public appears to be sharply divided into two almost evenly
split camps: 48 percent pro-choice and 42 percent pro-life (Saad 1999). For-
mulating questions with or without a middle ground on the issue of abortion
thus generates two rather different constructions of the reality of public opinion: on the one hand, a moderate majority; on the other, a deeply divided
nation.

The public's view of the state of the American economy can likewise be
made to appear very different if a middle position is explicitly offered to
respondents, compared to when it is not. In a national poll conducted by the
Gallup Organization (May 10–14, 2001), for example, respondents were
asked, "Right now, do you think that economic conditions in the country as
a whole are getting better or getting worse?" One out of four American adults
(25 percent) said it was "getting better," but the great majority (63 percent)
felt it was getting worse.[1] A small percentage (9 percent) spontaneously volunteered that they thought it was about the "same" and the rest (3 percent)
had "no opinion." At almost exactly the same time (May 10–12, 2001) a CBS
News national poll asked a slightly different question on the same topic, but
with an explicit middle response alternative: "Do you think the economy is
getting better, getting worse, or staying about the same?" In this case only 10
percent of the respondents thought it was "getting better" (versus 25 percent
in the Gallup poll). But as compared to Gallup's reading of the national economic mood, far fewer Americans (44 percent) thought things were "getting
worse" (versus 63 percent in Gallup). In fact, just as many of them (44 percent) believed that the economy was "staying about the same" (versus 9 percent volunteered in Gallup) when that ambiguous definition of economic
reality was offered to them. But which poll represented the "truth" about
American public opinion on the state of the economy? Did Americans think
it was getting better or worse, or staying the same? Reality seemed to depend
on the presence or absence of a status quo alternative. While suggestive, this
comparison of the Gallup and CBS News polls represents at best a quasi-
experimental test of what may be called the middle position effect.

More controlled experiments with the middle response alternative, however, have demonstrated that the effect is a reliable and typically sizable one.
Even on everyday subjects, on which most people would be expected to have
relatively well-formed opinions impervious to such manipulations, such as
the topic of divorce, experiments with a middle option have shown how easily public opinion on the matter can be recast. In a now classic investigation

of the middle position effect, Schuman and Presser (1981, chap. 6) asked respondents one of two versions of a question on the divorce issue. Half the sample, at random, received a form of the question that omitted a middle alternative (the "omitted form"): "Should divorce in this country be easier or more difficult to obtain than it is now?" The other half got a version with an explicit middle option (the "offered form"): "Should divorce in this country be easier to obtain, more difficult to obtain, or stay as it is now?" Surprisingly, given the everyday familiarity of the topic, the form of the question made a significant difference in the results and the corresponding impression of public opinion. A sizable plurality (about 45 percent) of those getting the omitted form of the question favored the conservative option of making it more difficult to get a divorce than it is now, whereas fewer than three out of ten (29 percent) thought it should be easier. More than one out of five (22 percent), however, spontaneously volunteered that divorce should "stay as it is," suggesting that a middle position on the divorce issue occurred readily to many respondents. Indeed, when given such a status quo option explicitly, on the offered form of the question, a significant plurality (40 percent) chose it; the percentage in favor of making divorce more difficult dropped from 45 percent to 33 percent, while advocates of making it easier fell from 29 percent to 23 percent. The reality of public opinion on the divorce issue thus seemed to depend heavily on how the question was framed, with or without a middle plank, so to speak.

Or did it? As Schuman and Presser (1981, chap. 6) discovered in these and other experiments, offering a middle alternative will typically alter the distribution of public opinion because it draws respondents with less intense feelings away from the polar positions on an issue. As they also found, however, if the middle responses given on both forms of the question are excluded from the data analysis, a researcher will generally draw the same conclusions about the distribution of public opinion on an issue (e.g., about the ratio of those in favor of making divorce more difficult to those in favor of making it easier). While this is often true, statistically speaking (but see Bishop 1987 for some significant exceptions to their findings), the day-to-day practice in the world of public opinion research makes it highly unlikely that pollsters will exclude middle responses from the data analyses and presentations in their press releases. If anything, pollsters often hype results showing that the public supports the status quo on some matter by saying things are OK as they are. A good example comes from the early months of President George W. Bush's administration, when there was widespread speculation in the mass media and Democratic political circles about the undue influence of Vice President Dick Cheney on public policy matters. But a Gallup poll released at the time (Jones 2001a) trumpeted the fact that a substantial majority (61 percent) of Americans thought Dick Cheney had the "right amount of power" in the Bush administration. The public, in other words, appeared to support the political status quo, largely, I would argue, because this middle position was offered explicitly to respondents at the end of a question on a topic they probably knew little or nothing about, making it the easy way for most of them to go. Such is the illusion of public opinion generated by a middle position.

THE WORDING OF THE QUESTION

Countless examples in both the popular and scholarly literatures have told us that how a question is worded—its emotional tone, whether it leads or does not lead the respondent, whether it is balanced or imbalanced, whether it presents one or both sides of an issue—can make a critical difference in the answers respondents give (see Schuman and Presser 1981 for some classic demonstrations). Probably one of the best examples comes from a well-known experiment conducted as part of the General Social Survey (GSS) by the National Opinion Research Center at the University of Chicago (Rasinski 1989). In a series of questions about the nation's spending priorities, respondents were told, "We are faced with many problems in this country, none of which can be solved easily or inexpensively. I'm going to name some of these problems, and for each one I'd like you to tell me whether you think we're spending too much money on it, too little money, or about the right amount." One random subgroup was asked about whether we were "spending too much, too little, or about the right amount" on "assistance to the poor," whereas another random subgroup was asked instead about spending on "welfare." As might be expected, the results differed dramatically, depending on which words were used. In one of several such experiments, less than a fourth of the respondents (23 percent) said we were spending "too little" on "welfare," whereas a sizable majority (63 percent) thought "too little" was being spent on "assistance to the poor." The choice of words obviously changed how respondents interpreted the meaning of the question, from one about the possibly deserving poor to one about the probably undeserving recipients of welfare, producing two rather different pictures of public opinion on a vital social policy issue.

In some cases the change in meaning due to variations in wording appears to be much subtler. As Schuman and Presser (1981) have shown in their replications of a classic experiment on whether the United States should "allow" or "forbid" public speeches against democracy, the tone of the question can make a profound difference in the results. Repeating an experiment carried out originally in the 1940s, Schuman and Presser found that, while Americans had become much more supportive of free speech in the 1970s, regardless of how the question was worded, they were still much more likely to support restricting free speech when the question read, "Do you think the United States should *allow* public speeches against democracy?" (emphasis added). When asked in this way, about 45 percent (on average) of the respondents in their national surveys would say "no" (not allow it). But when asked, "Do you think the United States should *forbid* public speeches against democracy?" (emphasis added), only about 25 percent on average would say "yes" (forbid it). To forbid something and not to allow it are logically equivalent response alternatives, but psychologically they are not. One form of the question seems to have more to do with allowing something that might harm our democratic society, whereas the other form appears to focus the respondent's attention more on the First Amendment implications of controlling free speech (see Bishop 1992). Many respondents evidently pick up on this subtle difference in the tone of wording and answer the questions accordingly, thereby creating rather different impressions of American public opinion on freedom of expression.

Offering respondents a strong counterargument on an issue can alter the meaning of a question just as much, if not more (Schuman and Presser 1981, chap. 7). To take a conspicuous, contemporary example, consider public opinion polls on the death penalty. For the past twenty-five years or so, responses to the standard question asked by the Gallup Organization ("Are you in favor of the death penalty for a person convicted of murder?") would suggest that the overwhelming majority of Americans support the death penalty without reservation. And even though such public support has declined somewhat in recent years, press releases from the Gallup News Service continue to reinforce this impression of a harsh and vengeful public with such headlines as "Two-thirds of Americans Support the Death Penalty for Convicted Murderers (Jones 2001b). Much less well known until fairly recently, however, are other Gallup questions on the death penalty that show Americans to be significantly less supportive of the death penalty option when given a meaningful alternative of life in prison without the possibility of parole. In fact, not long after these poll results were released, the Gallup Organization conducted a split-sample experiment (see Jones 2003) in which approximately half the respondents were asked the standard question about the death penalty: "Are you in favor of the death penalty for a person convicted of murder?" The other half were asked a more balanced version: "If you could choose between the following two approaches, which do you think is the better penalty for murder—the death penalty, or life imprisonment with absolutely no possibility of parole?" To the standard question, two-thirds of Americans (67 percent) again said they were for the death penalty, with only 28 percent opposed to it and 5 percent having no opinion. But in response to the more evenly balanced framing of the issue, they were much less likely to favor the death penalty option (49 percent chose it) and just about as likely to favor the alternative of life imprisonment with no possibility of parole (47 percent) as they were to favor the death penalty. These experimental results on a topic on which most Americans would seem to have well-formed opinions illustrate once more how two contrasting images of the reality of public opinion on an enduring social issue can be created simply by framing the issue differently in the wording of the question.

To drive the point home, table 3.1 gives another striking demonstration of how the reality of public opinion gets constructed through variations in question wording. In this case, the questions are on a social policy issue about which many Americans remain relatively uninformed and thus highly malleable: school vouchers. Depending upon the choice of wording, one could generate a liberal, a conservative, or a moderate majority or plurality on one side of the issue or the other (cf. Newport and Carroll 2001). How then does one tell policy makers, the press, and the public which, if any, of these results represent what Americans really want on the issue of school vouchers? Psychologically speaking, most survey methodologists would probably say that all these results are "real" given a specific wording of the question. Epistemologically speaking, however, it all gets rather fuzzy even for educated consumers of public opinion polls.

QUESTION ORDER AND CONTEXT

Important as it might be, the wording of questions may be the least of pollsters' worries, as it is much more on the surface than another consideration that survey researchers have become ever more aware of: How the order and context in which a question is asked can make a dramatic difference in what public opinion on an issue appears to be. One of the best-known examples in the literature has come from experiments with the order in which questions were asked about the controversial issue of abortion. First demonstrated by Schuman and his colleagues at Michigan (Schuman, Presser, and Ludwig 1981; Schuman and Presser 1981) and later replicated by my associates and me at Cincinnati (Bishop, Oldendick, and Tuchfarber 1985), the "abortion context effect" emerged when respondents were asked two questions about the issue in either the following sequence or in the reverse sequence: (1) "Do you think it should be possible for a pregnant woman to obtain a legal abortion *if she is married and does not want any more children?*"

Table 3.1.   Variations in Public Support for School Vouchers by Question Wording

Experimental Comparisons
Gallup (January 5–7, 2001)

Form A: "Please tell me whether you would vote for or against the following proposition. Would you vote for or against giving parents the option of using government-funded school vouchers to pay for tuition at the public, private or religious school of their choice?"

For	62%
Against	36
DK/no opinion	2

Form B: "Please tell me whether you would vote for or against the following proposition. Would you vote for or against a system giving parents government-funded school vouchers to pay for tuition at a private school?"

For	48%
Against	47
DK/no opinion	5

Quasi-Experimental Comparisons
CBS News/*New York Times* (September 27–October 1, 2000)

"Please tell me if you agree or disagree with the following statement. Parents should get tax-funded vouchers they can use to help pay for tuition for their children to attend private or religious schools instead of public schools."

Agree	45%
Disagree	50
DK/no opinion	5

***Washington Post*/Kaiser/Harvard 2000 Election Values Survey (September 7–17, 2000)**

"Do you favor or oppose providing parents with tax money in the form of school vouchers to help pay for their children to attend private or religious schools?"

Favor	49%
Oppose	47
DK/no opinion	4

Pew Research Center/Princeton Survey Research Associates (August 24–September 10, 2000)

"I'd like your opinion of some programs and proposals being discussed in this country today. Please tell me if you strongly favor, favor, oppose, or strongly oppose each one. . . . Federal funding for vouchers to help low- and middle-income parents send their children to private and parochial school."

Favor/strongly favor	53%
Oppose/strongly oppose	44
DK/no opinion	3

NBC News/*Wall Street Journal* (August 10–11, 2000)

"Let me read you two positions on school vouchers. Between these positions, which do you tend to side with more? Position A: Government should give parents more choices by providing taxpayer-funded vouchers to help pay for private or religious schools. Position B: Government funding should be limited to children who attend public schools."

Position A (supports vouchers)	56%
Position B (opposes vouchers)	38
DK/no opinion	6

University of Maryland Survey Research Center (June 23–July 9, 2000)

"Do you favor or oppose establishing a school voucher program that would allow parents to use tax funds to send their children to a private school?"

Favor	50%
Oppose	45
DK/no opinion	5

Washington Post/Kaiser/Harvard 2000 Election Values Survey (May 11–22, 2000)

"I'd like you to think about students who attend what some people call 'failing schools.' These are low-ranking, poor-quality public schools where students' academic performance is low and has not improved in the past three years. I'm going to read descriptions of two federal programs that have been proposed to deal with the problem of failing schools. For each, please tell me whether you favor or oppose it. The program would provide parents of a child in a failing public school with a $1,500 federal voucher that they could use to send their child to another school. Parents could use the money to help pay the cost of a private school, or to send their child to another public school outside their district. Would you favor or oppose this program?"

Favor	48%
Oppose	49
DK/no opinion	3

University of Connecticut/Heldrich Center at Rutgers (May 2000)

"I am going to read you a list of education policies and practices that some suggest will improve public education. For each, please tell me if you favor such a policy or oppose such a policy: Provide vouchers to help parents send their children to private school."

Favor	39%
Oppose	57
DK/no opinion	4

University of Connecticut (April 3–26, 2000)

"Please tell me whether you agree or disagree with each of the following statements: Parents should have the option of sending their children to religious schools instead of public schools using 'vouchers' or 'credits' provided by the federal government that would pay for some or all of the costs."

Agree	64%
Disagree	34
DK/no opinion	2

Newsweek/Princeton Survey Research Associates (March 9–10, 2000)

"I'm going to describe the positions of two candidates for president (in 2000) on some different issues. I'll call them Candidate A and Candidate B. After I describe their positions on each issue, tell me which candidate you would be more likely to vote for based only on this issue. On the issue of education, Candidate A calls for reforming education by giving parents vouchers to help send their children to the school of their choice, including a private or church-run school. Candidate B says vouchers are the wrong kind of education reform and would be damaging to our public-school system. Based only on this issue, would you be more likely to vote for Candidate A or Candidate B?"

Candidate A	54%
Candidate B	40
DK/no opinion	6

Source: Adapted from Newport and Carroll (2001); Public Opinion Location Library, Roper Center for Public Opinion Research; and the Polling Report (www.pollingreport.com).

Good cr

and (2) "Do you think it should be possible for a pregnant woman to obtain a legal abortion *if there is a strong chance of serious defect in the baby*?" (emphasis added). Typically, when the question about the woman who is married and does not want any more children is asked first, respondents will more likely say "yes" to an abortion. But when it is asked after the question about the birth defect situation, they tend to oppose it, probably because it does not appear to be as good a reason for having an abortion by comparison. For example, in one of their original experiments with this topic, Schuman, Presser, and Ludwig (1981) discovered that a sizable majority of American adults (61 percent) would favor an abortion for a married woman who did not want any more children if the question was asked first. But they were much more divided on the issue if it was asked after the question about abortion in the case of a birth defect; in fact, a majority (52 percent) was opposed to it when the questions were posed in that sequence. So in one instance, public opinion appears to strongly support a woman's right to have an abortion if she does not want any more children; in the other, it does not, largely because of the order and context in which the questions were asked.

Nor is this just one isolated academic example of how variations in question order can dramatically affect polling results. Public opinion in a 1997 Gallup poll on threats from weapons of mass destruction also looked quite different depending on the order in which the following two questions were presented (Moore 1999, 25):

1. "How likely is it, in your view, that a terrorist group will attack the United States using *chemical or biological weaponry* sometime in the next ten years (very likely, somewhat likely, somewhat unlikely, very unlikely)?"
2. "How likely is it, in your view, that a terrorist group will attack the United States using *nuclear weaponry* sometime in the next ten years (very likely, somewhat likely, somewhat unlikely, very unlikely)?"

As Moore (1999) discovered, a clear majority (53 percent) of respondents thought it was either "very likely" or "somewhat likely" that a terrorist organization would attack the United States using nuclear weapons when it was asked as the first question in the sequence, but when it was asked after the question on chemical or biological weaponry, the percentage thinking this way dropped dramatically to 41 percent. Similarly, a much larger percentage (71 percent) of respondents thought a biological or chemical attack was likely when asked about it first rather than second (62 percent). In each case, the threat presented second does not appear as plausible or "real" in juxtaposition with the threat presented first. As in the experiment with the abortion issue, the order and context generates a different impression of the reality of public opinion by altering the meaning and interpretation of the following question. As in everyday life, the meaning of language and what seems real is almost always context dependent.

THE INFLUENCE OF RESPONSE ORDER

As if this were not enough, pollsters must contend as well with a growing experimental literature telling them that the nature of public opinion on an issue can be significantly influenced by the order in which the response alternatives for a question are presented to the interviewee (Bishop and Smith 2001; Holbrook et al. 2003; Moore and Newport 1996). In some instances the order in which the alternatives are presented (particularly in telephone surveys) produces a "recency effect"—a tendency to choose the last-mentioned response alternative. In other instances (self-administered mail and Internet surveys), the order of the response alternatives will often generate a "primacy effect," or a tendency to choose the alternatives presented at the beginning of the list.

One of the best examples of such an effect turned up in a series of experiments on response order conducted by the Gallup Organization (Moore and Newport 1996), in this case involving a question on the then-current issue of tax reform. The question presented two alternatives—one of which favored the current tax system, the other of which favored a new flat tax system:

> Thinking about the federal tax system—which of the following would you prefer? The current system in which people with large incomes pay higher tax rates than people with smaller incomes—and taxpayers can take deductions for charitable contributions, interest paid on home mortgages, and other items, or a different system in which all people would pay a flat tax rate of 17 percent regardless of income and no deductions would be allowed. Families with four or more people and incomes of less than $36,000 per year would pay no income tax.

Approximately half the respondents were read the question with the current tax alternative presented first and the flat tax alternative presented second (form A); the other half were presented with these response alternatives in the reverse sequence (form B). Not surprisingly perhaps, it made a noticeable difference in the results and the conclusions a pollster would draw about what the American people "really thought" about the federal tax system. When the flat tax alternative was presented *last* (as in form A), a clear majority of Americans (56 percent) appeared to favor this radical change. But when it was presented as the *first* option in the question (as in form B), only 43 percent supported it; in fact, a majority (52 percent) now seemed to favor the status quo (the current tax system), which had been presented as the second option—an excellent example of a recency effect in telephone surveys. In this instance the recency effect generated a quite different reality.

An equally telling example of a primacy effect showed up in an exit poll experiment reported by Mitofsky and Edelman (1995). As part of a large set of exit polls conducted for the major news networks by the Voter Research and Surveys in the 1992 presidential election, respondents were asked: "Which one or two issues mattered most in deciding how you voted today?" In one version of the self-administered questionnaire, respondents were given *nine* possible alternatives presented in the following order; in the other version, they received the reverse sequence:

Health care
Federal budget deficit
Abortion
Education
Economy/jobs
Environment
Taxes
Foreign policy
Family values

Respondents were noticeably more likely to select an issue when it appeared at or close to the beginning of the list than when it was presented at the end of the list. For example, family values was chosen twice as often (20 percent) when it appeared at the beginning of the list than at the end (10 percent). Health care was picked by nearly one out of four respondents (24 percent) as the issue that mattered most in deciding how they voted for president, if it was placed at the start of the list, but was selected by only 15 percent of the respondents when it came at the tail end of the list. So depending on which version of the questionnaire was used, a journalist or news anchor could have reported a different story about what issues really mattered most to the voters in the 1992 American presidential election. Such was the dependence of the reality of public opinion in the 1992 election on how the response alternatives were sequenced in the question.

THE DANGER OF POLLS AS REFERENDUMS

In his presidential address some years ago to the American Association for Public Opinion Research, Howard Schuman (1986) warned the polling profession of the dangers of what he called "the referendum point of view," by which he meant the overemphasis in poll reports on the simple marginal percentages telling us how many people are on one side of the issue or the other, what percentage of them favor or oppose the proposal, approve or disapprove of it, and the like. Consider, for example, the following headlines from various poll releases by the Gallup News Service in 2001, headlines that often reflect the majority-rule bias built into our democratic political culture:

"Majority of Americans Say Roe v. Wade Decision Should Stand." (January 22, 2001)

"Americans Consider Global Warming Real, but Not Alarming." (April 9, 2001)

"Vast Majority of Americans Think McVeigh Should Be Executed." (May 2, 2001)

"Majority Considers Sex before Marriage Okay." (May 24, 2001)

"Americans Agree with Supreme Court Ruling on the Use of School Facilities for Religious Group Meetings." (June 12, 2001)

"Slim Majority of Americans Still Approve of Bush's Performance." (July 3, 2001)

"Microsoft Still Enjoys Public Favor." (July 5, 2001)

As we now know from a long line of experimentation and the many examples presented in this chapter, the results of such polls could have turned out quite differently had the questions been asked in another form, been presented in one context rather than another, or been worded more or less abstractly, and with or without a particular affective tone. As Schuman (1986) reminds us, "Respondents feel enormously constrained to stay within the framework of a question." Change the framework, and you change responses to the question and, with them, what public opinion on that issue appears to be. Most professional pollsters know this, and yet many of them continue in their poll reports, press releases, and presentations of poll results

Good paper quote

to the powers that be to emphasize the absolute percentages in favor of this or that position, as if the poll were a referendum on public opinion. The danger of polls as referendums is that they can seriously mislead us into believing that the percentages presented in poll reports literally represent a picture of public opinion—a naive belief that Schuman rightfully labels "survey fundamentalism." Instead, they may represent mostly how the reality of public opinion gets constructed through the way in which the questions are framed, worded, and presented to respondents. To take a page from Heisenberg once more, if we've learned nothing else in public opinion research these past thirty years or so, we've learned that what we observe in our polls is not reality in itself, but reality exposed to our method of questioning.

NOTE

1. The poll findings cited in this chapter on Americans' opinions on the economy were compiled from the Roper Center for Public Opinion Research's online Public Opinion Location Library (POLL) and the Polling Report (www.pollingreport.com).

4

The Changing American Voter: Fact and Artifact

Artifacts are in the mind of the beholder.

—Howard Schuman

Because they construct the reality of public opinion at any given point in time, survey questions can produce equally illusory impressions of change over time. Indeed, the question of how much the American voter has changed over time has become one of the most enduring controversies in political science. Much of it has centered on the question of whether Americans think about candidates, issues, and political parties in liberal-conservative terms or whether they are, as Kinder (1985) has cleverly put it, ideologically innocent. Evidence from national surveys in the 1950s made it unmistakably clear that the vast majority of Americans were devoid of ideological thinking (see, e.g., Campbell et al. 1960, cited in Kinder 1985). But more than anything else, it was the research of Philip Converse (1964), published in his article "The Nature of Belief Systems in Mass Publics," that put the nail in the coffin. Using data from 1956 to 1960 from the National Election Studies (NES), conducted by the Michigan Survey Research Center (SRC), Converse first demonstrated that only a very tiny percentage (2–3 percent) of the American public thought in abstract ideological terms (left-right or liberal-conservative) when asked what they liked or disliked about the Democratic and Republican parties. A small percentage (9 percent) were what he called "near-ideologues," who made a looser and somewhat less sophisticated use of such concepts in describing what they liked or disliked about each of the two political parties. But most respondents (88 percent), as he showed, lacked any semblance of ideology in how they thought about the Democrats and the Republicans and reacted instead in terms of their own group's self-interests, in response to the nature of the times (e.g., war, recession), or in a way that indicated they did not think about policy issues at all in evaluating the political parties. Such was the inability of the mass public to think in ideological terms.

Even more compelling were the data on what Converse called ideological "constraint," by which he meant the degree of psychological consistency in an individual's beliefs or opinions on various domestic and foreign policy issues. Knowing, for example, that an individual favored a government guarantee of employment for everyone who wanted a job would lead us to expect that he or she would also be likely to favor having the government help people to get subsidized medical care, and vice versa if the individual were opposed to such governmental involvement. In other words, we would expect the majority of citizens in American society to display a degree of liberal-conservative consistency in their beliefs and opinions across a range of issues that corresponded at least roughly to the ideological thinking that we take for granted among journalistic, political, and policy-making elites. As Converse realized, that too was a cardinal assumption underlying traditional democratic theory's "rational voter."

But his incisive analysis of survey data from a national sample of the general public and an elite sample of Democratic and Republican candidates for the U.S. House of Representatives in the 1958 election said it just wasn't so. Comparing responses to questions on a variety of domestic and foreign policy issues—employment, aid to education, federal housing, fair employment practices to prevent racial discrimination, foreign economic aid, foreign military aid, and U.S. involvement in other parts of the world—Converse discovered that the opinions expressed by the Democratic and Republican candidates for Congress seemed much more ideologically consistent and predictable than those given by ordinary citizens. The correlations between responses to domestic issues and between those given to domestic and foreign policy issues were, in fact, more than twice as high, on average, in the elite sample of congressional candidates than in the sample of ordinary citizens (see P. Converse 1964, 228–29). So abysmally low were the correlations for the general public that Converse concluded that their opinions were essentially "unconstrained" by any abstract conceptual yardstick, such as liberal-conservative ideology, and that such an ideological assumption was warranted only among the more elite segments of American society.

As if these data were not already damaging enough, based on his analysis of repeated interviews with respondents in the SRC 1956–1960 election panel study (P. Converse 1970), Converse discovered that not only were the opinions of ordinary citizens ideologically inconsistent at any one point in time, but they were also highly unstable from one interview to the next. So inconsistent and unstable were these opinions that Converse could only conclude that the great majority of respondents were more or less inventing their opinions on the spot, expressing what he called "nonattitudes" on most domestic and foreign policy issues. People were offering opinions, he contended, mostly to avoid admitting their ignorance of the issues and to satisfy the demand of the interviewing situation that they have an opinion. Thus did Converse's withering, empirically based critique of the nature of belief systems in the American mass public rock the foundations of democratic theory and set the research agenda for the next several decades of public opinion research in political science (see Zaller 1992). The dominant image that emerged from this seminal research was that, when it came to thinking abstractly about politics and public policy issues, the American electorate was essentially clueless.

THE REVISIONIST CONTROVERSY

The image of an ideologically clueless electorate dominated the discipline for over a decade with few, if any, serious challenges (cf. Luttbeg 1968). Not until the mid-1970s, when Norman Nie and his associates (Nie with Andersen 1974; Nie, Verba, and Petrocik 1976, 1979) reanalyzed the data from the National Election Studies with new evidence from surveys conducted between 1964 and 1976, was Converse's critique called into question. The revisionists led by Nie and his colleagues now claimed that, beginning with the 1964 presidential election, the American public had become much more ideological in its thinking about the candidates, the parties, and the issues, largely in response to the clear ideological differences between conservative Republican candidate Barry Goldwater and big-government Democrat Lyndon Baines Johnson. The political environment, Nie and others argued, had radically changed, especially in comparison to the more ideologically quiescent Eisenhower era of the 1950s examined by Converse. The mass public, they hypothesized, had responded in kind—an ideological reaction that continued throughout the turbulent atmosphere of civil rights demonstrations, race riots, antiwar protests, and the social and cultural changes of the 1960s and early 1970s. The American voter had changed.

The key piece of evidence supporting the revisionists' claim of an ideologically charged electorate came from a replication of Converse's earlier analysis of ideological "constraint." From 1956 to 1960, they agreed, the data looked identical to what Converse had previously discovered: little or no consistency between the public's opinions on various domestic and foreign policy issues. But all of a sudden in 1964 the answers that respondents gave to questions about the same issues became much more strongly correlated with one another. Respondents, for example, who took a liberal stance on the role and size of the government on social welfare matters tended to express a liberal outlook not only on related issues, such as racial integration, but also on Cold War relations with Communist countries. So too did conservative respondents appear to answer questions on the same issues in a more ideologically consistent manner (see Nie with Andersen 1974; Nie, Verba, and Petrocik 1976, 1979, chap. 8). Indeed, the American mass public now appeared to be just as ideologically constrained in its liberal-conservative views of the issues as the elite congressional respondents Converse had studied in the 1958 national election. Not only that, but this newly emergent pattern of liberal-conservative ideological thinking in the mass public appeared to persist throughout the turbulent political atmosphere of the times and into the 1968 and 1972 national elections. The temper of the times had, in effect, dramatically altered the ideological quality of the electorate, creating what Nie and his colleagues called the "changing American voter."

Or so it seemed. Just as the thesis of a changing American voter was beginning to take hold as the new conventional wisdom in the discipline, two independent teams of researchers—my colleagues and I at the University of Cincinnati (Bishop et al. 1978, 1979; Bishop, Tuchfarber, and Oldendick 1978) and another team at the University of Minnesota (Sullivan, Piereson, and Marcus 1978)—both demonstrated that it was all an illusion. What had changed, we each argued with convincing experimental evidence, was the way in which the questions about the policy issues were worded, beginning with the 1964 SRC National Election Study. Prior to that time (1956–1960), the survey questions on domestic and foreign policy issues that had formed the basis of Converse's (1964) critique of mass belief systems had all been asked in a standard agree-disagree format, preceded by a simple filter question: "Do you have an opinion on this or not?" But beginning in the SRC 1964 national survey, respondents were asked about the same issues in a rather different form; they were now given a choice between an argument and a counterargument on each side of the issue, preceded by a noticeably stronger filter question: "Have you been interested enough in this to favor one side over the other?" Table 4.1 shows the striking difference in the two question forms on the jobs issue (for a detailed account of these and other changes in question forms in the controversy, see Bishop et al. 1978, 1979). Though Nie and his associates vigorously disagreed that the changes in ideological constraint they had discovered, beginning with the 1964 election, were merely an artifact of changes in the form and wording of the SRC's questions, their own in-house, methodological experiment clearly indicated otherwise—a scientific story that has never been fully told until now. Nor has Converse's (1964) original comparison of the questions asked of the elite

Table 4.1.   Wording of Questions and Response Categories on Jobs Issue in the National Election Studies: SRC 1956–1960 vs. 1964–1968 Question Forms

SRC 1956–1960 form: "The government in Washington ought to see to it that everybody who wants to work can find a job. Now would you have an opinion on this or not? [IF YES] Do you think the government *should* do this?" (HAND *R* CARD)

    1. Agree strongly; government definitely should
    2. Agree but not very strongly
    3. Not sure; it depends
    4. Disagree but not very strongly
    5. Disagree strongly; government definitely should not
    8. Don't know (volunteered)
    0. No opinion

SRC 1964–1968 form: "In general, some people feel that the government should see to it that every person has a job and a good standard of living. Others think the government should just let each person get ahead on his own. Have you been interested enough in this to favor one side over the other? [IF YES] Do you think the government should see to it that every person has a good job and a good standard of living, or should let each person get ahead on his own?"

    1. Should see to it that every person has a good job and a good standard of living
    2. Should let each person get ahead on his own
    3. Other; depends (volunteered)
    8. Don't know (volunteered)
    0. Not interested enough

Source: Adapted from SRC election survey questionnaires, 1956–1968, NES.

congressional sample and of the mass public sample ever been fully illuminated. A lot has been overlooked.

Illusions of Comparable Questions

Conspicuously missing from both editions of *The Changing American Voter* (Nie, Verba, and Petrocik 1976, 1979) is any analysis of an in-house methodological experiment conducted by the National Opinion Research Center (NORC) in December 1973 (amalgam survey 4179). Designed explicitly by Nie and his associates to assess whether the changes in question wording and format introduced by the SRC in 1964 (and again in 1972) had any impact on the striking increase in the ideological consistency of the political attitudes of the American public, the experiment gets but a brief mention in a footnote (n. 10) to the first published report of their findings in the *Journal of Politics* (Nie with Andersen 1974) and no attention at all in their subsequent publication of *The Changing American Voter*. The findings from the original experiment did show up, however, in an unpublished master's thesis and in an unpublished conference paper by one of Norman Nie's graduate students (Rabjohn 1976, 1977). The data were also released by NORC to my colleagues and me (Bishop et al. 1978, 1979; Bishop, Tuchfarber, and Oldendick 1978) during the height of the controversy in the literature and have since been archived at the Inter-university Consortium for Political and Social Research (ICPSR; study no. 7556). Contrary to the counterclaims and impressions created by Nie and his colleagues at the time, the data from their own experiment (NORC, December 1973) demonstrated that the wording of the questions asked about the various domestic and foreign policy issues by the SRC in the 1950s, 1960s, and 1970s was far from comparable. Indeed, this methodological artifact became the most plausible explanation for their "changing American voter."

Table 4.2 gives an example from the NORC 1973 experiment of just how unlike those questions were. Consider, for instance, the question about whether the government in Washington should guarantee employment (and living standards). To begin with, the distribution of public opinion on this issue varied substantially depending on which form of the question was asked. When respondents in the NORC 1973 experiment were asked the original pre-1964 SRC version of the question, the vast majority (86 percent) of them agreed with the statement, "The government in Washington should see to it that everybody who wants to work can find a job." Only 11 percent disagreed, and the rest (3 percent) said they were "not sure." But when given

Table 4.2. Opinions on Jobs Issue by Question Form in December 1973 NORC Experiment

SRC 1956–1960 form: "The government in Washington ought to see to it that everybody who wants to work can find a job. Do you have an opinion on this or not? Do you think the government *should* do this?"

Agree/agree strongly	86%
Not sure/depends	3
Disagree/disagree strongly	11

SRC 1964–1968 form: "In general, some people feel that the government should see to it that every person has a job and a good standard of living. Others think the government should just let each person get ahead on his own. Have you been interested enough in this to favor one side over the other? Do you think the government should see to it that every person has a good job and a good standard of living, or should let each person get ahead on his own?"

Government should see to it	59%
Other/depends (volunteered)	5
Let each person get ahead on own	36

Source: Adapted from Rabjohn 1977.

both an argument and a counterargument on the issue (the SRC 1964–1968 form), a noticeably smaller majority (59 percent) accepted the liberal proposition that "the government should see to it that every person has a job and a good standard of living," whereas a sizable minority (36 percent) bought the conservative counterargument that "the government should just let each person get ahead on his own," and the rest (5 percent) were unsure of where they stood (see Rabjohn 1977 for a detailed summary of the frequency distributions on the issues used in the December 1973 NORC experiment). So when given the earlier version of the question (pre-1964), the public appeared to be much more liberal on the government-guaranteed jobs issue than when given the later version.

Another striking difference in the comparability of the two question forms shows up on the issue of federal aid for schools. Asked the pre-1964 SRC form of the question, the great majority (77 percent) agreed with the idea that "if cities and towns across the country need help to build more schools, the government ought to give them the money they need." Just one out of five (19 percent) disagreed with this liberal notion and the rest (5 percent) weren't sure. Given a persuasive counterargument on the issue in the SRC 1964 version of the question, however, less than half (45 percent) endorsed the liberal idea that "the government in Washington should help towns and cities provide education for grade and high school children." In contrast, a majority of respondents (52 percent) accepted the conservative counterargument that "this should be handled by the states and local communities," and the remainder (2 percent) were undecided. Public opinion on the school aid issue thus appeared to be rather liberal with one form of the question and conservative with the other.

But each of these contrasts pales by comparison with the questions asked about what Nie and his associates call "the size of government." The pre-1964 SRC form of the question replicated in their NORC 1973 experiment asked respondents whether they agreed or disagreed (on a five-point scale) with the following statement: "The government should leave things like electric power and housing for private businessmen to handle." Because this question was supposedly not repeated in any form whatsoever after the SRC 1960 election study, Nie and his colleagues substituted a much more general and vague question about the scope of the federal government in their 1973 NORC experiment, as well as in their original analysis of the changing American voter. It read as follows: "Some people are afraid the government in Washington is getting too powerful for the good of the country and the individual person. Others feel that the government in Washington is not getting too strong for the good of the country. Have you been interested in this enough to favor one side over the other?" This "size of government" question, first introduced in the SRC 1964 election study, can hardly be regarded as comparable to the earlier SRC version of the question. Yet the impression that they were comparable was perpetuated by, among other things, the superficial similarity of the percentages giving liberal and conservative responses to the two questions (see Rabjohn 1977). Curiously, Nie and his colleagues also appeared to overlook a question in the 1964 postelection interview that was much more comparable in content, though not in form, to the pre-1964 version of the question on the role of the government in housing and electric power: "Some people think it's all right for the government to own some power plants while others think the production of electricity should be left to private business. Have you been interested enough in this to favor one side over the other? [IF YES] Which position is more like yours, having the government own power plants or leaving this to private business?" This question's conspicuous absence from any of their publications and analyses of the changing American voter remains a mystery to say the least.

No political scientist or pollster today, however, or anyone familiar with the now extensive literature on question wording and context effects, would regard any of the pre- and post-1964 SRC questions used by Nie and his colleagues as comparable. If anything, these questions would be considered textbook examples of how changes in the wording of questions can dramatically affect the results and conclusions of public opinion surveys, creating an illusion in this instance of a "changing American voter," when all that really changed was the way in which the questions were asked. As Kinder (1985, 666) summarizes the outcome in his review of the revisionist controversy, "It is now clear that most of the apparent change in opinion structure is artificial, produced not by political metamorphosis but by mundane alterations in question wording."

Questions about Converse's Questions

But all this, I would contend, was not the only illusion in a classic controversy about the ideological character of the American voter. Strangely neglected throughout it all, Converse's original comparison of ideological consistency in the mass public with that of a congressional elite was based on what most survey researchers today would regard as decidedly noncomparable questions. At the time, Converse (1964) insisted that "the questions posed to the two samples were quite comparable, apart from adjustments necessary in view of the backgrounds of the two populations involved." What did he mean by "adjustments"? As he explains in a much neglected footnote in the history of this controversy (1964, n. 21), "As a general rule, questions broad enough for the mass public to understand tend to be too simple for highly sophisticated people to feel comfortable answering without elaborate qualifications." He then lists in summary form the pairs of questions asked of the mass and elite samples. At first glance the questions appear to be superficially similar in content. But a closer look at the original questionnaires and documentation for the SRC 1958 election studies shows that the questions asked of the two samples were remarkably unlike in multiple ways (cf. the ICPSR codebooks for the 1958 National Election Study and the 1958 American Representation Study: Candidates).

To begin with, the questions asked of the elite sample of congressional candidates were all partly open-ended, and respondents were allowed, if not encouraged, to give qualified answers, including volunteered middle positions such as "depends on situation."[1] Furthermore, the questions posed to Converse's elite sample typically included a substantive argument as well as a counterargument on the issue that foreshadowed the controversial changes in question form later analyzed by Nie and his colleagues in the revisionist flap. In sharp contrast, those questions asked of the mass public in the 1958 survey were all closed-ended, in a standard agree-disagree format typically used in the National Election Studies. The agree-disagree form was presumably what Converse meant by questions "too simple for highly sophisticated people to feel comfortable answering without elaborate qualifications." However defensible it may have seemed at the time, we now know from a number of experiments on open versus closed questions, and on forms including an argument and counterargument, carried out by Schuman and his associates (Schuman and Presser 1981; Schuman and Scott 1987), that a survey's results and conclusions can vary considerably depending on which question form is used—not to mention the further influence of acquiescence with the agree-disagree format used with Converse's mass public sample.

Take, for instance, the question asked of the elite congressional sample on the issue of government-guaranteed employment. Not only was the question asked in a partly open-ended form (see the SRC 1958 codebooks), but it also presented a strong counterargument against the involvement of the federal government: "Do you think the federal government ought to sponsor programs such as large public works in order to maintain full employment, or do you think that problems of economic readjustment ought to be left more to private industry or state and local government?" Notice too that the argument in favor of federal involvement includes sponsoring "programs such as large public works." None of these elements and arguments appeared anywhere in the question on the jobs issue asked of the general public (cf. table 4.1). Instead, respondents from the general public were asked simply whether they agreed or disagreed (on a five-point scale) with the rather vague, one-sided proposition, "The government *ought* to see to it that everyone *who wants to work* can find a job" (emphasis added).

The questions on federal aid to education followed the same pattern. The elite congressional sample was asked a partly open-ended question about the issue with a balanced argument and counterargument: "Do you think the government should provide grants to the states for the construction and operation of public schools, or do you think the support of public education should be left *entirely* to state and local governments?" Whereas the question put to members of the general public asked just whether they agreed or disagreed with the one-sided, worthy-sounding proposition, "If cities and towns around the country need help to build more schools, the government in Washington ought to *give them the money they need*" (emphasis added).

Just as noncomparable was one of the most notable items in Converse's entire critique, one that he used as the centerpiece of his evidence on the instability of mass belief systems (P. Converse 1970): the question on electric power and housing. For the mass public, it appeared in the typical unbalanced, agree-disagree format: "The government should leave things like electric power and housing for private businessmen to handle." But when posed to the elite congressional candidates, it looked like a much more balanced, quasi-open-ended question and curiously omitted any reference at all to "electric power": "Do you approve the use of federal funds for public housing, or do you generally feel that housing can be taken care of better by private effort?"

Converse's SRC questions on dealing with racial discrimination seem superficially similar in content at first blush, but look much more incomparable on closer examination. While the elite sample was asked a partly open-ended question about a specific policy proposal—"Do you think the federal government should establish a fair employment practices commission to prevent discrimination in employment?"—the general public was given a somewhat leading, agree-disagree statement that talked about racial discrimination in jobs as well as housing: "If Negroes are not getting fair treatment in jobs and housing, the government should see to it that they do."

Similarly, on the question of foreign economic aid, the general public received a one-sided proposition to agree or disagree with: "The United States should give economic help to the poorer countries of the world even if those countries can't pay for it." In contrast, the elite sample was presented with a balanced set of options on a more specific policy issue, in a partly open-ended format, including a middle response alternative: "First, on the foreign economic aid program, would you generally favor expanding the program, reducing it, or maintaining it about the way it is?" In form and focus the two questions could not be more unlike.

The questions on foreign military aid look just as noncomparable. For the mass sample the issue was posed as a single-sided, anti-Communist proposition to agree or disagree with: "The United States should keep soldiers overseas where they can help other countries that are against Communism." But for the elite sample the issue was framed as a broader, partly open-ended choice among three policy options: "How about the foreign military aid program? Should this be expanded, reduced, or maintained about as it is?"

Nor, finally, were the questions on U.S. involvement in foreign affairs any more comparable than any of the other pairs in Converse's analysis. When posed to the general public, the question was offered as a one-sided, isolationist statement to be agreed or disagreed with: "This country would be better off if we just stayed home and did not concern ourselves with problems in other parts of the world." Whereas for Converse's elite sample, the question became a much broader, partly open-ended query about our future involvement in world affairs: "Speaking very generally, do you think that in the years ahead the United States should maintain or reduce its commitments around the world?"

With the benefit of several decades of methodological hindsight, it now seems rather remarkable that the questions asked of Converse's elite and mass samples could ever have been regarded as comparable. The questions differed sharply in form and focus and, in a number of instances, in content as well—not to mention the measurement errors that may have occurred in coding the responses to the partly open-ended questions asked of Converse's elite sample of congressional candidates (see, again, the ICPSR codebook for the 1958 American Representation Study: Candidates). In the absence of a controlled experiment, we can never know for sure just how different Converse's original results, which showed dramatic differences in ideological constraint between the elite and the mass public, would have turned out had he used the same exact questions for each group. But knowing what we now know about the significant effects of question wording in the revisionist controversy about the changing American voter, plus the massive evidence that has since been accumulated on question form effects in public opinion surveys, it seems plausible that using the same questions for each group would have made a substantial difference in Converse's results and conclusions. Some might well want to perish the thought that Converse's findings on mass-elite differences in ideological constraint could have been mostly an artifact of question wording and format, an illusion that has misled generations of researchers. Could it all have been for naught? Perish the thought!

FACT AND ARTIFACT IN THE
NATIONAL ELECTION STUDIES

The "changing American voter" controversy has become probably one of the most memorable object lessons in how the results of political attitude and public opinion surveys can be generated by pure methodological artifact. But, contrary to what many political scientists might have concluded, this episode constitutes more than just an isolated example of confounded measurement; it may, in fact, represent the proverbial tip of an iceberg of noncomparability that has surfaced over time in the National Election Studies (Abramson 1990; also see National Election Studies 1995–2000). Other methodological artifacts in the NES have become much more visible with the passage of time, as scholars such as Abramson, Silver, and Anderson (1987); Bartels (2002); Bishop, Oldendick, and Tuchfarber (1982, 1984); Eubank and Gow (1983); and Sears and Lau (1983; also see Lewis-Beck 1985) have uncovered the unintended consequences of changes in question order and context in this well-established time series. What is fact and what is artifact in the NES has thus become a significant methodological concern.

A Drop in Civic Duty?

For many Americans, voting in elections is a matter of civic duty. As Campbell et al. (1960, cited in Abramson, Silver, and Anderson 1987) concluded in their classic analysis of the American voter, "the strength of a person's sense of citizen duty has a very great influence on the likelihood of his voting" (105). The SRC has typically measured this central construct by using a four-item scale of agreement or disagreement that includes such statements as, "It isn't so important to vote when you know your party doesn't have any chance to win." Looking at the long-term trend in responses to such items, Abramson and his associates (Abramson, Silver, and Anderson 1987) found that the American electorate's overall feelings of citizen duty had remained remarkably positive and stable from election to election between 1952 and 1980. On three of the four items, the great majority of Americans (80 percent or more) strongly supported the norm of civic duty. Abramson and his colleagues have argued that, because of this conspicuous lack of variation across elections, the NES investigators assumed the Citizen Duty Scale could not possibly explain the well-documented decline in the American voter's participation between 1960 and 1980. For this and other reasons (available space in the interview schedule), the NES Board of Overseers decided to drop three of the four citizen duty questions from the 1984 national election survey, keeping just the one that had produced a more even balance of agree and disagree responses in previous election surveys: "If a person doesn't care how an election comes out then that person shouldn't vote in it." In the 1980 election survey, when it was asked as part of the four-item civic duty scale, 59 percent of the respondents disagreed with this statement, indicating that the majority of Americans clearly felt they had a duty to vote regardless of what they thought about the likely outcome of the election. In the 1984 election survey, however, when it was presented by itself, the percentage disagreeing with this statement dropped precipitously to just 43 percent, suggesting that sometime during the early 1980s the sense of civic duty in the American electorate had eroded for some unknown reason. Perhaps, in the spirit of ad hoc explanations of spikes in the trend line—exemplified by the changing American voter controversy—it was somehow due to the sense of national "malaise" that had been developing during President Carter's administration, a sort of delayed aftereffect stemming from a prolonged period of stagflation and the 444-day hostage episode in Iran.

Tempting as such after-the-fact explanations might have been, Abramson and his colleagues (Abramson, Silver, and Anderson 1987) thought the apparent decline in citizen duty was implausible for a variety of reasons. To begin with, as they note, this decline of feelings of civic duty should have decreased voter turnout, but voter participation actually increased a bit between the 1980 and 1984 elections. Furthermore, as they point out, other indicators of support for the political system during the same period, such as feelings of political efficacy, political trust, and interest in the outcome of the elections, all ticked up rather than down. Though changes in such indicators had not been related to overall trends in civic duty in previous election periods (1960–1980), the pattern of increased support for the political system between 1980 and 1984 suggested that something else was responsible for the apparent decline in feelings of citizen duty, something much more mundane than a fundamental change in public attitudes: a methodological artifact.

A plausible suspect was also near at hand: changes in question order and context. In the 1984 election survey the question about whether a person should vote if he or she doesn't care about the outcome of the election had been asked all by itself. But in the 1956–1980 national election surveys it had always followed two other questions about civic duty, both of which typically generated a high degree of disagreement: (1) "It isn't so important to vote when you know your party doesn't have a chance to win," and (2) "So many other people vote in the national elections that it doesn't matter much to me whether I vote or not." That they disagreed with these two statements (usually 80 percent or more did so) would imply to most respondents that they must also disagree with the following item: "If a person doesn't care how an election comes out he shouldn't vote in it." But when this proposition was presented to respondents in the 1984 election survey, where it was the first question in a series of items asked in an agree-disagree format, the question context no longer implied disagreement with statements opposed to the civic norm of voting (see the 1984 survey questionnaire items in Abramson, Silver, and Anderson 1987). The percentage disagreeing with the proposition, as the question order and context hypothesis would predict, fell, from 59 percent in 1980 to 43 percent in 1984. A methodological artifact thus seemed plausible.

That wasn't the only piece of evidence in Abramson and his colleagues' favor. Making an even more persuasive case for their artifact hypothesis, they unearthed a mound of indirect evidence from a little known, unpublished experiment with the order and context of the civic duty items in the 1952 National Election Study. In this early SRC experimental venture, the standard four questions about civic duty appeared in various locations as part of a larger randomized experiment with five other questions on a respondent's feelings of political efficacy. Two of these randomized question sequences mirrored the order in which the civic duty questions were asked from 1956 to 1980; the other sequence matched the order used in the 1984 survey (see Abramson, Silver, and Anderson 1987, 904). The results showed, as expected, that respondents were significantly more likely to disagree with the idea that if "a person doesn't care about how an election comes out he shouldn't vote in it" when it came after the other citizen duty items than when it preceded them. In a nutshell, the apparent decline in feelings of citizen duty (1980–1984) in the National Election Studies was just that: an apparent decline, an illusion generated by a methodological artifact.

A Decline in Public Faith in Elections?

If voting in elections is a matter of civic duty, then the American public's faith in elections becomes a critical indicator of the responsiveness of our democratic government. For nearly three decades the SRC has monitored public confidence in the American electoral process by asking respondents the following question: "How much do you feel that having elections makes the government pay attention to what the people think—*a good deal, some,* or *not much?*" Measured by responses to this single item, the American electorate's faith in elections has fallen off substantially over time (1964–1996), with the steepest decline occurring between the 1980 and 1984 presidential elections (Bartels 2002). Historians, journalists, and various political pundits might be readily tempted to attribute such an overall decline to a number of factors, especially the growth of negative campaign ads, not to mention the mass media's increasingly cynical coverage of politicians and elections ever since the Vietnam War and Watergate. Such an interpretation would seem to fit the cultural wisdom about the character of American politics in the post-Vietnam era—prior to September 11, 2001.

But, once more, the decline turned out to be more apparent than real. As with the seeming decline in feelings of citizen duty discovered by Abramson and his colleagues (Abramson, Silver, and Anderson 1987), Bartels (2002) has convincingly demonstrated that most of the decrease in the American electorate's faith in elections since the early 1970s is the result of a change in the order and context in which the question was asked. Prior to the 1984 national election survey, the question about the public's belief that "having elections makes the government pay attention to what the people think" had always been asked right after the following two, closely related questions on public confidence in the responsiveness of the political system: (1) "Over the years, how much attention do you feel the government pays to what people think when it decides what to do—a good deal, some, or not much?" and (2) "How much do you feel that political parties help to make the government pay attention to what the people think—a good deal, some, or not much?" But, beginning with the 1984 election study—the very same survey in which Abramson and his associates (Abramson, Silver, and Anderson 1987) uncovered the artifact in the civic-duty time series—the question on faith in elections was relocated in the questionnaire and asked immediately after the following block of questions on beliefs about trusting the "government in Washington," government waste, special interests, and crooked politicians (Bartels 2002):

1. "How much of the time do you think you can trust the government in Washington to do what is right—*just about always, most of the time,* or *only some of the time?*"
2. "Do you think that people in government waste *a lot* of the money we pay in taxes, waste *some* of it, or *don't waste very much of it?*"
3. "Would you say the government is pretty much run by a *few big interests* looking out for themselves or that it is run *for the benefit of all* the people?"
4. "Do you think that *quite a few* of the people running the government are crooked, *not very many* are, or do you think *hardly any* of them are crooked?"

As Bartels points out, the American public answered these four questions in a generally negative manner throughout this period. So it is not surprising that when the question on the public's faith in elections was asked in this negative context at the time of the 1984 election survey, responses to it declined most dramatically. In that context it was most likely interpreted as just one more question on the corrupt government, politicians, and special interests in Washington. Providing even more evidence for the question context hypothesis, Bartel's analysis clearly shows that the strength of the relationship between responses to the question on faith in elections and those given to three of these four questions—trust in government, special interests, and corrupt politicians—was significantly stronger from 1984 to 1996, following the change in question order. Furthermore, his multivariate analysis of the NES time series suggests that there has been "no significant trend in public faith in elections since 1964." As he summarizes it, "the change in question order . . . wipes out most of the apparent decline in faith in elections after 1972, controlling for aggregate changes in more general attitudes toward the political system . . . wipes out most of the apparent decline before 1972" (Bartels 2002). This apparent change in the character of the American electorate was, in the words of that old Chicago song, "just another illusion."

A Falloff in Attention to Politics?

Most political scientists today probably take for granted the idea that democracy functions best when the average citizen pays attention to politics and becomes better informed about public affairs. How much attention Americans pay to what is going on in government and public affairs has indeed become a useful indicator of the political health of our democratic system. So too has the public's interest in elections and political campaigns emerged as a vital indicator of the degree of apathy in the American electorate. Given the significance of the American public's interest in electoral politics, the SRC has monitored it since the early 1950s with the following question, typically asked near the beginning of the interview: "Some people don't pay much attention to the political campaigns. How about you—would you say that you have been/were very much interested, somewhat interested, or not much interested in following the political campaigns (so far) this year?" Beginning with the 1952 national election survey, responses to this question have fluctuated from election to election, with interest in the campaign typically being somewhat higher in presidential election years than in off-year congressional elections. But curiously, as the NES time series shows (figure 4.1), the indicator of interest in election campaigns dropped precipitously from 1976 to 1978, a falloff that was much larger than the usual decline from presidential to nonpresidential years. The percentage of respondents saying, for example, that they were "very interested" in following the political campaigns fell from 37 percent in 1976 to 22 percent in 1978, while the percentage indicating they were "not much interested" rose from 21 percent in 1976 to 34 percent

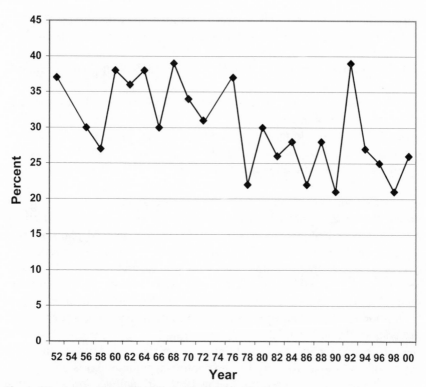

Figure 4.1   Interest in Political Campaign: 1952–2000

Response: Very much interested
Source: National Election Studies.

in 1978. Any number of after-the-fact explanations could have been generated to account for this apparent rise in political apathy, including the "malaise" hypothesis that was so prevalent in the political atmosphere of President Jimmy Carter's administration.

But, once more, a methodological artifact loomed as a far more plausible hypothesis. As part of a larger project on survey question effects, my associates and I (Bishop, Oldendick, and Tuchfarber 1982) discovered that the order and context in which the question on campaign interest had been asked had changed significantly from one election to another. Similar to the practice in all the preceding election surveys, the question about interest in the 1976 political campaign was asked near the beginning of the interview, but not until shortly after another set of opening questions about the respondent's attention to the race between the presidential candidates:

1. "Who do you think will be elected president in November?"
2. "Do you think it will be a close race or will [answer to 1] win by quite a bit?"
3. "How about here in [R's state]? Which candidate for president do you think will carry this state?"
4. "Do you think it will be a close race in [R's state] or will [answer to 1] win by quite a bit?"
5. "Generally speaking, would you say that you personally care a good deal which party wins this presidential election this fall, or that you don't care very much which party wins?"

In the 1978 postelection survey, however, the question about interest in the political campaign appeared in a completely neutral question context because it was the very first item in the interview. Thus it seemed plausible that respondents who were asked about their interest in the campaign right *after* a set of closely related questions about the presidential race (the 1976 context) would be more likely to infer that they were interested in the campaign than those who were asked about it right off the bat with no contextual cues from prior questions (the 1978 context). Indeed, merely being made to think more about the presidential race in answering the questions could be sufficient to get many respondents to think they were interested in the campaign.

One other piece of evidence for the context hypothesis shows up in figure 4.1. With the curious exception of the 1992 national election survey, the American electorate's reported interest in political campaigns has remained noticeably lower beginning with the 1978 election. But ever since then, the question about interest in the campaign has appeared as the first item in the interview, suggesting that this altered context is largely responsible for the striking discontinuity in the trend that occurred between 1976 and 1978.

Nor was this the only measurement artifact lurking in the 1978 election survey. The electorate's general interest in public affairs plummeted just as precipitously as its interest in following the political campaigns that year. The percentage of respondents who said they followed what was going on in government and public affairs "most of the time" fell from 38 percent in 1976 to just 23 percent in 1978 and has remained around that level ever since (figure 4.2). What could possibly have happened in just two years to produce so dramatic a change in Americans' attentiveness to public affairs? Again, in the absence of any plausible substantive explanation, my colleagues and I (Bishop, Oldendick, and Tuchfarber 1982, 1984) suspected a measurement artifact: a change in question context. In this instance, however, the change in context was subtle, though no less powerful than the one responsible for the decline in campaign interest. As in many previous election studies, the

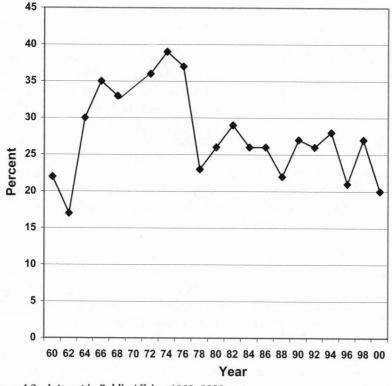

Figure 4.2   Interest in Public Affairs: 1960–2000

Response: Most of the time
Source: National Election Studies.

standard NES question on attention to public affairs was asked in the 1976 postelection interview *after* a number of other questions on such topics as the respondent's involvement in the presidential campaign; conversations he or she may have had with others about the outcome of the election; perceptions of various governmental institutions (e.g., Congress) and the power of the government in different domains (e.g., regulation of business); attitudes toward various groups in society (e.g., women, blacks); trust in institutions such as Congress and the Supreme Court; and confidence in various levels of government. In other words, this was a question context that was likely to imply to the respondent that he or she paid attention to what was "going on in government and public affairs."

In contrast, many of the questions used in the 1978 survey implied just the opposite. Unlike the 1976 survey, the 1978 survey also asked respondents a large number of difficult questions somewhat earlier in the interview about their knowledge of the congressional and senatorial candidates running in their region, including, among many other things: (1) whether they knew if their incumbent U.S. representative had done anything special for the people in their congressional district and (2) whether they knew how their representative had voted on any particular legislation (see Bishop, Oldendick, and Tuchfarber 1982, 185–86). Since most respondents were unlikely to know such things (over 80 percent could not answer either of these two questions correctly), their lack of knowledge in this context clearly implied that they must have not been paying much attention to what was "going on in government and public affairs." As with the apparent change in attention to political campaigns between 1976 and 1978, a change in the order and context of the questions thus seemed to be the most plausible explanation of the otherwise inexplicable drop in the public's general interest in government and public affairs.

Two well-designed, randomized experiments confirmed the artifact hypothesis (see Bishop, Oldendick, and Tuchfarber 1982 for the details; also see Bishop, Oldendick, and Tuchfarber 1984). In one such experiment, respondents were more likely to think they were interested in following the political campaigns that year if they were asked about it immediately after, rather than before, other questions about the presidential election. In the other experiment, respondents were less likely, as predicted, to think they followed what was going on in government and public affairs if they were asked about it immediately after, instead of before, a difficult set of knowledge questions about their congressional representative identical to those used in the 1978 National Election Study. Changes in question order and context, then, had evidently explained the original puzzling drop in the trend line.

So, once more, an apparent change, in this case the American public's interest in electoral politics and public affairs, turned out to be just as illusory as Nie and others' changing American voter, the drop in civic duty identified by Abramson and his colleagues, and the decline in the public's faith in elections described by Bartels. All that had changed was the order and context of the questions. And all this, I suspect, is but the proverbial tip of the iceberg in the evolution of the ever-changing question order and context within the survey questionnaires designed for the National Election Studies (for an earlier account, see Abramson 1990 on the decline of comparability over time in the NES). Methodological artifacts in the NES may, in fact, account for far more of the apparent variance in the political attitudes and opinions of the American voter over time than has heretofore been suspected. How much is true change and how much is artifact remains to be seen.

Nor, as we will see in the following chapters, is the theme of artifact and illusion confined to just a few isolated examples in the National Election Studies. Indeed, I am far from the first to suggest that apparent changes in American public opinion can be rather misleading, if not illusory (chapters 5 and 6). In a classic and still controversial study, Sullivan, Piereson, and Marcus (1979) demonstrated that a seemingly dramatic increase in Americans' tolerance of groups such as Communists, Socialists, and atheists over a twenty- to twenty-five-year period was mostly an illusion, an artifact of a change in the evaluative meaning of the questions used to measure these political attitudes. And by no means am I the first to contend that the results of public opinion polls presented in the mass media may represent an illusion (chapter 7). Elliot King and Michael Schudson (1995) make a compelling case for how polls on presidential approval can be seriously misconstrued in their illuminating article titled "The Press and the Illusion of Public Opinion: The Strange Case of Ronald Reagan's 'Popularity.'" Artifacts, as Howard Schuman (1982) rightly reminds us, may well be in "the mind of the beholder," representing research opportunities to better understand the meaning, nuances, and ambiguities of survey questions. True, but outside the survey research beltway, such methodological artifacts often become factoids about the reality of public opinion in the mass media and in the minds of the mass public.

NOTE

Examination of the footnotes to the NES Codebook for the *1958 American Representation Study: Candidates* (ICPSR Study 7226, Note 2) indicates that responses to these seemingly closed questions were actually recorded verbatim as if they were partially open-ended questions and then coded subsequently into five-point Guttman scales.

5

September 11's Ephemeral Opinions

> Public opinion is easily changed; it rises as quickly as it falls because it
> changes its subjects.
>
> —Ferdinand Tonnies, *Kritik der Offentlichen Meinung*

Understanding how public opinion changes, its moods, cycles, and dynamics, has become one of the biggest problems in public opinion research today. Responding to that theoretical challenge, numerous scholars have tried to explain how public opinion changes in response to real-world events, mass media coverage of social and political issues, and cultural shifts in values (see, e.g., Abramson and Inglehart 1995; Davis 1992; Page and Shapiro 1992; T. Smith 1990; Stimson 1999). Though these authors have invariably offered highly plausible accounts of changes in public opinion, none has explicitly considered a rival, and potentially much more parsimonious, explanation: simply that the meaning and interpretation of the survey questions used to monitor public opinion over time has changed. As nearly every public opinion analyst is aware, a cardinal assumption in asking any survey question is that it should mean the same thing to all respondents: the "same stimulus principle." Likewise, when a question is repeated over time, it should mean essentially the same thing the second time as it did the first time: the "constant stimulus principle." If these vital assumptions cannot be met, then valid comparisons across time and respondents become extremely difficult, if not impossible.

As William Foddy has identified the issue in his superb sociological treatise on the theory and practice of questionnaire design in survey research, "if respondents typically search for contextual clues to help them interpret a question, different respondents may attend to different clues so that they end up with quite different interpretations. When this happens, it makes little sense to compare respondents' answers with one another, since the different

91

answers are, in essence, answers to different questions" (1993, 21). Foddy finds fault as well with a key assumption underlying the use of closed-ended survey questions: that answers to survey questions can be meaningfully compared because respondents answer the questions in the same way. From his symbolic-interactionist perspective, he argues that "if different respondents give different meanings to key concepts and adopt different perspectives, they will, in fact, be answering different questions . . . the fact that every respondent has been exposed to the same words is no guarantee that they will have understood the question in the same way" (Foddy 1993, 140).

Most pollsters clearly recognize this problem in another guise when, for example, there has been a noticeable change in the wording or context of a question in a well-established time series, such that it becomes difficult to separate real change from variations in wording or context (see, e.g., chapter 4 on a classic case in the National Election Studies: Bishop et al. 1978, 1979; Sullivan, Piereson, and Marcus 1978; Nie, Verba, and Petrocik 1976, 1979). The problem of wording variations also arises quite frequently in comparing the conflicting results of polls on the exact same topic across different survey organizations. The difference in wording almost invariably amounts to a difference in the meaning of the question, making such comparisons fraught with invalidity. As a consequence, public opinion analysts rightly regard differences in the meaning of survey questions resulting from changes in wording and context as particularly troublesome in interpreting poll results.

Strangely, however, public opinion analysts and political scientists have been much less attentive, if not oblivious, to how the meaning of survey questions can vary across respondents and over time even when the wording and context of the question remain constant (for a notable exception, see Fee 1981; Nie, Verba, and Petrocik 1976, 1979). Such variations in meaning create a survey measurement artifact that is essentially equivalent to those that result from changes in question wording and context. This problem represents one of the most serious threats to the validity of poll results in general, and makes the interpretation of changes in public opinion particularly challenging. In culture, as in nature, the underlying dynamics of a problem often become much more transparent under extreme conditions or unusual circumstances. The events of September 11, 2001—the terrorist attacks on the World Trade Center in New York and the Pentagon in Washington, D.C.—represent exactly such an episode in American public life, one that produced an apparent sea change in American public opinion.

In the wake of the terrorist attacks of September 11, multiple indicators of public opinion and the mood of America changed dramatically. President Bush's approval ratings surged to an all-time high. Ratings of Congress also soared to record heights. The influence of religion in American life looked stronger than ever. Trust in government spiked up to levels not seen since the mid-to late-1960s. Satisfaction with "the way things are going in the United States at this time"—a standard indicator of the general mood of the nation—shot up sharply. And perhaps to no one's great surprise, terrorism became "the most important problem facing this country today" (see, e.g., Moore 2001b). But what were the abrupt shifts in all these well-established indicators really measuring? Did they represent what survey researchers would call "true changes" in American public opinion, or were they telling us something else? Here I will make the case that these apparently dramatic changes were largely, if not entirely, ephemeral—an artifact of transitory changes in the meaning and interpretation of some standard questions in American public opinion polls.

A SURGE IN PRESIDENTIAL APPROVAL

Consider the most conspicuous example of change: presidential approval. Just before the events of September 11, George W. Bush's approval ratings in the Gallup time series had slipped to a razor-thin majority of 51 percent (see figure 5.1). Right after the terrorist attacks, his approval ratings skyrocketed to record levels, reaching a high of 90 percent in late September (21–22) and then holding in the low to mid-80s for months thereafter, followed by a steady decline to nearly pre–September 11 levels by late February of 2003 (58 percent in a CNN/*USA Today*/Gallup poll conducted February 17–19, 2003). Characteristically, political analysts and pundits viewed the surge in approval ratings after September 11 as just one more example of the classic rally-round-the-flag effect. The country and its partisan Democrats, Republicans, and independents alike had all suddenly united behind the president in a time of crisis. But had public opinion of "the way George W. Bush is handling his job as president" really changed? I would argue that all that had really changed was how respondents were interpreting the meaning of this standard question, a result of what political psychologists would call a "priming effect" generated by mass media coverage of the events of 9/11 and their aftermath. While this simple "change of meaning" hypothesis may strike some readers as a highly plausible but utterly obvious observation, to my knowledge, it has never been systematically considered as a rival explanation for fluctuations in presidential approval ratings. And while there appears to be no direct evidence revealing how respondents actually interpret standard questions about presidential approval, we do have a considerable chunk of indirect evidence from open-ended follow-up questions about "why" Americans approve or disapprove of the way the president is handling his job.

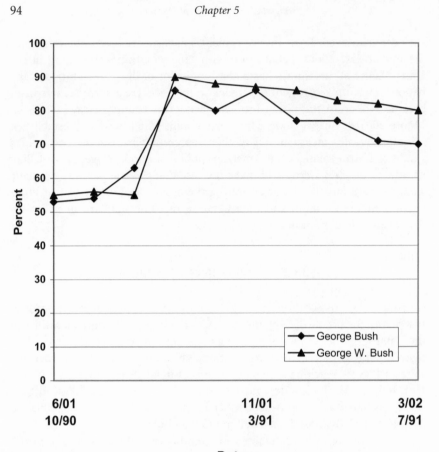

Date

Figure 5.1   Like Father, Like Son: Presidential Approval Ratings

Question: Do you approve or disapprove of the way . . . is handling his job as president?
Source: Roper Center for Public Opinion Research, University of Connecticut. Surveys by the Gallup Organization and by Gallup/CNN/*USA Today.*

To its great credit, the Ohio Poll at the University of Cincinnati has routinely included in its quarterly survey just such a follow-up probe on presidential approval for the past twenty years or so. Modeled in large part after the standard Gallup measure, the initial question asks respondents: "Generally speaking, do you approve or disapprove of the way [name] is handling his job as president?" Next, respondents are probed on how strongly they approve or disapprove of the president's performance or, if in doubt as to whether they approve or disapprove, which way they "lean." They are then asked, "And could you tell me why it is you approve/disapprove of the way [name] is handling his job as president?" In November 2001, President

Bush's approval ratings in the Ohio Poll reached a record high of 87 percent, very much as they did in the rest of the country (Rademacher 2001). And, not surprisingly, when asked why they approved or disapproved of the way he was handling his presidential duties, well over half the respondents mentioned something about his dealings with the war on terrorism and foreign policy in general or his leadership and communication during the terrorism crisis (table 5.1). The responses to this "why" question do not, of course, literally represent statements of causality. Instead, they appear to be plausible justifications or rationalizations for the respondent's approval or disapproval of the president, best thought of as simply cognitive by-products of how the initial approval question was being interpreted at the time it was asked. In this particular instance, the content of the responses to the open-ended "why" probe strongly suggests that for many respondents the initial approval question was being heard, psychologically, as, "Do you approve or disap-

Table 5.1. Reasons for Bush's Job Approval Rating: November 2001 Ohio Poll

Reasons for Approval:	Percent
Approve of U.S. "war on terrorism"/terrorism policy/foreign policy (total)	43
Approve of "war on terrorism"/terrorism policy	37
Approve of attacks on Afghanistan	4
Approve of foreign/military policy (in general)	2
Strong leader/leadership/strong leadership during terrorism-related crises (total)	11
Strong leader/leadership (in general)	5
Performs well in crisis situations (in general)	5
Strong leadership of country during terrorism-related crises	1
Doing a good job (in general)	8
Addressing most important issues (in general)	3
Morals/religious/values	2
Takes positions on issues and follows through on them	2
Good communication/keeping nation informed about terrorism/response	2
Agree with issue/policy positions (in general)	2
Other reasons for approval	15
Don't know why approve	2

Reasons for Disapproval:	
Disapprove of U.S. "war on terrorism"/terrorism policy/foreign policy (total)	4
Disapprove of "war on terrorism"/terrorism policy	3
Disapprove of attacks on Afghanistan	1
Disapprove of foreign/military policy (in general)	(less than 1)
Other reasons for disapproval	6
Don't know why disapprove	(less than 1)
	(N = 787)

prove of the way George W. Bush is handling his job as president—*that is, in dealing with this terrorism war situation we're in right now?*"

Compare this psychological context with the one that existed when the approval questions were asked a few months earlier in a July 2001 Ohio Poll. At that time a solid majority of Ohioans (60 percent) approved of the way George W. Bush was handling his job as president, 29 percent disapproved, and the rest (10 percent) said either "neither" or "don't know" (Rademacher and Shaw 2001). The responses to the "why" probe were scattered all over the lot. As would be expected, there was no mention whatsoever of terrorism, and just a small cluster of responses related to President Bush's tax policies, which had been the subject of previous media coverage (table 5.2). The same scattered pattern had shown up just a few weeks earlier in a national Gallup poll that reported the verbatim answers given by 877 respondents to a very similar "why" question. As in the July Ohio Poll, these responses, especially in uncategorized, verbatim form, were spread all over creation (Gallup News Service 2001a). Indeed, this is fairly typical during normal times, when there is not any specific focus on the news about the president and what he's doing. Under such normal circumstances, the standard approval question must seem like a rather vague query to most respondents. What could the interviewer possibly mean by "the way he is *handling his job* as president?" For that matter, what is meant by "*approve*" or "*disapprove?*" In other words, in more normal periods, when there's not a lot of news about the president, this rather vague question becomes subject to multiple interpretations. For some respondents, it gets interpreted as a question about his economic or foreign policies; for others, it becomes a question about his personal character, morals, or religious values; for still others, it's just a question about whether they like him as a Republican; and ad infinitum.

By contrast, when a crisis emerges, as in the period following September 11, and the president becomes the focus of attention, the meaning of the question becomes much less ambiguous for most respondents. It comes to mean, largely, how is the president handling his duties in the *present situation?* The meaning of this normally ambiguous question, in other words, becomes homogenized, and the verbatim responses to the open-ended "why" probe cluster into fewer categories—for example, about terrorism, as was the case in the November 2001 Ohio Poll. Responses given to the presidential approval question in polls taken after September 11 thus became incomparable with those given prior to that because respondents were answering essentially different questions. And if the meaning of the question cannot be held constant, all such comparisons become invalid. One is not comparing an apple with an apple.

A relatively sound comparison can, however, be made between the post-

Table 5.2.   Reasons for Bush's Job Approval Rating: July 2001 Ohio Poll

Reasons for Approval:	Percent
Tax cut policies/approve cutting taxes	12
Doing a good job (in general)	7
Morals/religious/values	4
Have not heard anything bad about him	4
Honest/trustworthy/keeps promises	4
Better than previous presidents	2
Foreign/military policy	2
Approve, but too early to tell	2
Takes positions on issues and follows through on them	2
Agree with issue/policy positions (in general)	1
"Character"	1
Economic policies/improving economy/unemployment low	1
Education policy positions/proposals	1
Cabinet appointments	1
Restoring respect to the presidency	1
Trying to help everyone/listens to everyone	1
Strong leader/leadership	1
Addressing most important issues (in general)	1
Country is in good shape	1
"I just like him"	1
Position on abortion	1
Better than previous/current Democratic leaders	1
Trying to do good job/Democrats stopping him	1
Other reasons for approval	6
Don't know why approve	7

Reasons for Disapproval	
Tax cut policies/disapprove cutting taxes	3
"He's a Republican"/respondent is a Democrat	3
Not qualified to be president, relies on others to make decisions	3
Energy policy	2
Did not win the election fairly	2
Environmental policy	2
Dishonest/don't trust him	2
Foreign/military policy	2
"For the rich"	2
"I just don't like him"	1
Disagree with issue/policy positions (in general)	1
Economic policies/not improving economy/unemployment higher	1
Social Security policy	1
Education policy	1
"For corporations/big business"	1
Policies not helping constituent groups (e.g., elderly, working class, minorities)	1
Health care/health insurance policies	1
Other reasons for disapproval	5
Don't know why disapprove	1
	(*N* = 722)

9/11 approval ratings and those of an earlier period: the time when George W. Bush's father was president during the Persian Gulf War (cf. Parker 1995). In both cases, not only were the questions on presidential approval asked under roughly similar circumstances, but they also dealt with two politically and psychologically similar individuals with the same name. In these two instances, it seems highly likely that respondents interpreted the question on presidential approval in much the same way. Not surprisingly, with the social contextual meaning of the question held relatively constant, we find that the approval ratings for George W. Bush resemble his father's ratings during the height of the Gulf War rather closely (figure 5.1). The average for the elder Bush during the first quarter of 1991 was 82.7 percent, whereas for George W. Bush it was 86 percent during the period of October 20, 2001–January 19, 2002 (Jones 2002). The difference of 3.3 percent in the two averages falls within the bounds of the recommended allowance for the sampling error of a difference between two percentages. So with the meaning of the question essentially the same for respondents across the two periods, the approval ratings for the two presidents, father and son, are for all practical purposes identical, leading us to conclude that under the same social-psychological circumstances, no real change in presidential approval occurs. Nor does simply naming it a rally-round-the-flag effect explain anything. For it is only when the meaning of the question is altered by events that such an illusion of change appears. And this represents but one conspicuous example of how interpreting shifts in public opinion as true change can be seriously misleading, if not entirely invalid.

AN UPSURGE OF TRUST IN GOVERNMENT

Another dramatic example of illusory changes came from polls telling us that, in the wake of September 11, Americans had become much more trusting of the federal government (see figure 5.2). "Now, Government Is the Solution, Not the Problem," said the headline in the *New York Times* just a couple of weeks after the attacks on the World Trade Center and the Pentagon (Toner 2001). "Suddenly, Americans Trust Uncle Sam" was the buzz in the *Times* in early November, in response to polls showing a sharp rise in the percentage of Americans who said they now trusted the government in Washington to do what was right (Stille 2001). Chiming in again a few weeks later, the *Times* declared, "Big Government Is Back in Style" (Apple 2001).

What happened? Had the American public undergone a genuine change of heart about the leviathan in Washington that had been the object of increasing distrust for over thirty-five years? Were all the new books purport-

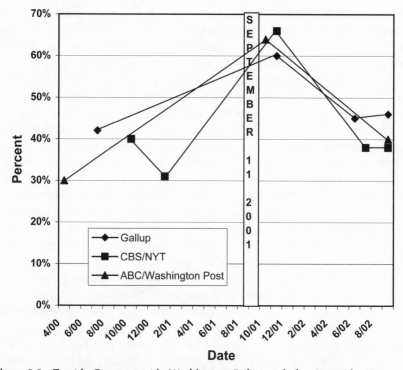

Figure 5.2 Trust in Government in Washington: Before and after September 11
Response: Most of the time/just about always

ing to explain a thirty-year trend of declining trust in government—like *Why Americans Don't Trust Government* and *The Trouble with Government*— suddenly obsolete? Some scholars (interviewed by Stille 2001) sensed the possibility of a fundamental realignment in how Americans viewed government. Robert Putnam, author of *Bowling Alone* and coeditor of the new volume *Disaffected Democracies*, which attempts to explain the decline of trust in government across developed nations, suggests that part of the upsurge in trust after September 11 might be due to a "rallying around the flag in a time of crisis . . . but that part of it reflects something deeper. . . . The events made us all realize the government does important work" (cited in Stille 2001, A13). Like other scholars interviewed by Stille, who hunt for a more general theory of why trust in government and other institutions rises and falls over time, Putnam looks naturally for political, economic, or cultural explanations for the sudden upsurge in trust after September 11. Many political and social scientists, for example, think automatically of the civil rights and anti-Vietnam protests of the 1960s as the origin of the long-term decline in trust in government (see, e.g., Nye, Zelikov, and King 1997), a trend that was supposedly reinforced by the scandals of Watergate, the Iran-Contra affair, and the Clinton-Lewinsky saga. Digging through the piles of polling data after 9/11, many scholars and analysts came to believe, as in the proverbial tale, there must be an explanatory pony in here somewhere.

As with the surge in presidential approval, however, a much simpler and parsimonious explanation of the upward spike in trust lay at hand, namely, a change in how respondents interpreted the standard question on trust in government before and after September 11 (see Langer 2002a for a strikingly similar observation). Consider the wording of the one question that has been repeatedly cited as exhibit A in virtually all of the poll reports and scholarly analyses to date. First asked by the University of Michigan in its long-running series of national election studies, it reads, "How much of the time do you think you can trust the government in Washington to do what is right—just about always, most of the time, or only some of the time?" When asked this question in a CBS/*New York Times* poll in January 2001, only 31 percent of Americans said they trusted the government in Washington to do what was right "most of the time" or "just about always."[1] But in a *Washington Post/* ABC News poll asking the same question just two weeks after September 11, trust in the federal government soared to a level not seen since 1965: 64 percent of Americans now told interviewers that they trusted the government in D.C. to do what was right "most of the time" or "just about always." Though this trust indicator declined to 55 percent in a CBS/*New York Times* poll in late October of 2001 and fell to 47 percent in a follow-up poll by the same organizations in early December, it still looked quite robust by recent historical standards, having reached a low of 21 percent in an October 1994 survey by the University of Michigan.

But how should changes in response to this well-established indicator of trust in government be interpreted? To begin with, it seems highly unlikely that respondents interpreted the meaning of this vague question in the same way after September 11 as they had before that tragic date. What, for example, could "trust the government in Washington to do what is right" possibly mean to them? Most likely, "trust in government" now meant trusting the present administration in Washington, symbolized by George W. Bush and his cabinet, to do the right thing in dealing with the terrorists, the anthrax threats, and other aspects of the then-current crisis. Just as they did for presidential approval, the events of September 11 and their aftermath altered and homogenized the meaning of the standard question about trust in government for the great majority of respondents. The upward spike in the poll figures (figure 5.2) did not represent any fundamental change in the American public's trust or distrust of the government in Washington but merely an illusion of change generated by how respondents interpreted the question.

Compelling evidence for the change-in-meaning hypothesis comes from a timely experiment designed by Gary Langer, director of polling for ABC News. Recognizing that the larger societal context had changed because of the events of September 11, Langer (2002b) suspected that the standard question about trust in government, which was most likely interpreted in normal times as a question about how the government was handling issues such as the economy, Social Security, health care, education, and the like, now meant trusting the government in Washington to deal with terrorism. To test this proposition, ABC News conducted a split-sample experiment with the wording of the trust in government question as part of a national poll in January 2002. Half the respondents, at random, received form A of the question, and the other half received form B:

Form A: "When it comes to handling *national security and the war on terrorism*, how much of the time do you trust the government in Washington to do what is right? Would you say just about always, most of the time, or only some of the time?" (emphasis added)

Form B: "When it comes to handling *social issues like the economy, health care, Social Security, and education*, how much of the time do you trust the government in Washington to do what is right? Would you say just about always, most of the time, or only some of the time?" (emphasis added)

The results of the experiment were rather telling. Whereas two out of three respondents (68 percent) said they could trust the government to handle national security and the war on terrorism "just about always" or "most of the time," only 38 percent could trust it to the same degree to handle the social and economic issues facing the country—a percentage similar to those observed prior to September 11, 2001, with the standard question on trust in government. As Langer (2002b, 9) concludes, "That suggests that what mainly changed after September 11 was the subject—not so much the level of trust, but the focus of that trust. Before the attacks, people were chiefly expressing their low trust in government's ability to handle social issues. After September 11, they were referring primarily to their high trust in its ability to fight terrorism." In other words, what changed was how respondents were interpreting the meaning of the question before and after 9/11. Psychologically, they were answering essentially different questions.

Partisan Reactions

Another telling piece of evidence from Langer's (2002b) research turns up in his analysis of how trust in government shifted over time among various political subgroups. Shortly after September 11, trust in government rose 19 percent among self-identified Democrats, moving up from 42 percent in a March–April 2000 poll by ABC News and the *Washington Post* to 61 percent in a poll conducted September 25–27, 2001. But it increased much more among Republicans and independents, for whom trust in government was initially a lot lower. For independents, it went from 27 percent in March–April 2000 to 62 percent in the September 25–27, 2001, poll—an increase of 35 percent. But for Republican identifiers it changed even more dramatically, shooting up from 25 percent in March–April 2000 to 73 percent, a jump of 48 percent, which was two and a half times as large as the increase among self-identified Democrats.

Most telling of all, however, was the reaction of self-identified "conservative Republicans." In March–April 2001, just 22 percent of them said they trusted the government in Washington to do what was right "just about always" or "most of the time." But shortly after 9/11, in the September 25–27, 2001, poll by ABC News and the *Washington Post*, trust in the government in Washington soared to 75 percent among these chronic critics of bloated government. This represented a boost of 53 percent, which was nearly five times the size of the increase among self-identified Democrats (11 percent) during the same time period. Clearly, for such ideological critics of big government, trusting the government in Washington no longer meant what it once had. As Langer (2002b, 10) reflects, "How plausible is it that conservative Republicans suddenly and massively abandoned their long-standing skepticism of government activism?" Not likely at all. It is much more likely, he suggests, that their newfound trust in the "government in Washington" was an expression of two things: (1) it was now led by George W. Bush, a conservative Republican, and (2) it could be trusted to do what was right with regard to terrorism. For ideologically conservative Republicans, then, the standard question on trusting the federal government in Washington no longer meant what it once had, and that was what generated the apparent change. Nor was this just another isolated example of illusory changes in public opinion after the events of September 11.

A RISE IN THE INFLUENCE OF RELIGION

The role of religion in American life also appeared to loom much larger following the events of September 11 than it ever had before. Two months after the terrorist attacks (November 13–19, 2001), a national survey sponsored by the Pew Forum on Religion and Public Life discovered that the vast majority of respondents (78 percent) believed the influence of religion in American life was increasing (Pew Research Center 2001). Just eight months earlier, however, an identical survey by the Pew research group had found that only 37 percent of respondents believed the influence of religion was on the rise. In fact, not since 1957, when the Gallup organization asked the question for the first time, had Americans so fervently believed in the growing role of religion in our society, and even then, the percentage believing in it (69 percent) was noticeably less than it was in the aftermath of September 11 (see figure 5.3).

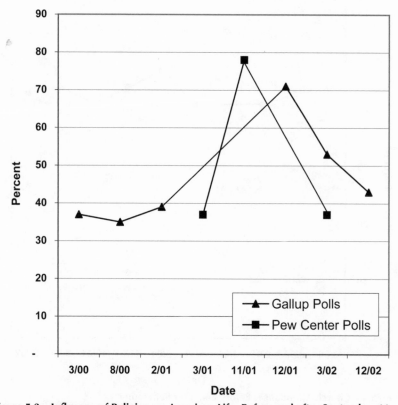

Figure 5.3   Influence of Religion on American Life: Before and after September 11

Response: Increasing
Question: "At the present time, do you think religion as a whole is increasing its influence on American life or losing its influence?"
Source: Roper Center for Public Opinion Research, University of Connecticut.

But despite what the public seemed to believe about the rising influence of religion in American life, there was little or no evidence that Americans themselves had actually become more religious in their beliefs and behavior after 9/11 (see Gallup News Service 2001b; Newport 2002b). Attendance at churches, synagogues, and other places of worship, for example, showed a slight uptick in the week or so immediately after September 11, but remained otherwise unaffected in the weeks and months thereafter (see figure 5.4). Nor was there any indication that religion was playing a more significant role in the personal lives of Americans. The percentage saying religion was "very important" in their own lives increased a tad in a Gallup poll conducted

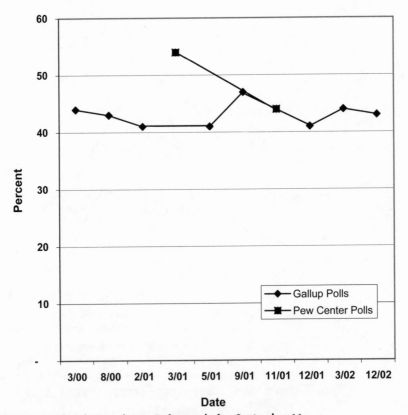

Figure 5.4 Church Attendance: Before and after September 11

Response: Yes
Gallup question: "Did you, yourself, happen to attend church or synagogue in the last seven days, or not?"
Pew Center question: "Did you, yourself, happen to attend church, synagogue, or any other place of worship in the last seven days?"
Source: Roper Center for Public Opinion Research, University of Connecticut.

shortly after 9/11, but then faded away in small fluctuations in the months that followed (figure 5.5). Perhaps most telling of all, the belief about the growing influence of religion in the United States proved to be just as transient. In yet another national survey by the Pew research group (Pew Research Center 2002a), the percentage of Americans believing in the rising influence of religion dropped dramatically to 37 percent—exactly where it had been one year before in a March 2001 poll (figure 5.3).

What could possibly explain such extraordinary variations in the American public's perceptions? Once more, a change in the meaning and interpretation of the question is the most plausible explanation. Prior to the events of 9/11, the question probably meant to most respondents something like

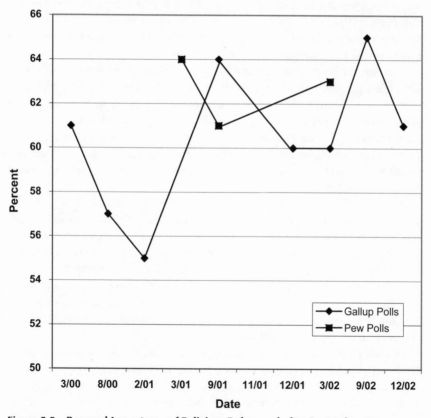

Figure 5.5   Personal Importance of Religion: Before and after September 11

Response: Very important
Question: "How important would you say religion is in your own life—very important, fairly important, or not very important?"
Source: Roper Center for Public Opinion Research, University of Connecticut.

whether they thought the *moral influence* of religion in American life was increasing or decreasing. But in the weeks and months right after the events of September 11, when Americans everywhere—on the steps of the Capitol, at public gatherings, and even during the seventh-inning stretch—were singing "God Bless America," the question most likely became for many respondents a question about whether the influence of America's ritualistic and publicly patriotic "civil religion" was increasing (see Bellah 1967, cited in McLean 2003). Thus, for a brief period, it became a question concerning our belief about the unique religious character of the American nation and whether it had some special protection from God in the crisis atmosphere created by the events of September 11. With so much singing and talking about God blessing America, and countless pledges of allegiance and public prayer events publicized in the mass media, it would seem plausible to most respondents that such public proclamations of all this religiously infused patriotism was sufficient evidence that the influence of religion in American society was surely increasing.

Some suggestive evidence for the "surge of civil religion" hypothesis comes from a simple content analysis of the nation's newspapers before and after September 11. With perhaps some lag factor, the "God Bless America" effect (figure 5.6), as it might be called, parallels rather closely the rise and fall of the perceived influence of religion in American life shown in figure 5.3. Right after September 11, mentions of "God Bless America" surged dramatically and then tapered off steadily as the months went by. The civil religion mood was fading away.

Once the crisis period had passed, by late February and March of 2002, the standard Gallup question most likely reverted to its original meaning for the bulk of respondents, becoming again a question largely about whether they believed that the influence of religion on Americans' moral values was increasing or decreasing. Meaning essentially the same thing that it had meant in March of 2001, the results in March 2002 were identical, with a little more than a third of Americans (37 percent) each time saying they thought "religion as a whole is increasing its influence on American life." The September 11 effect had faded away.

Another persuasive piece of evidence comes from analyzing changes in the psychosemantic links between the personal importance of religion to Americans, their attendance at church or synagogue, and the perceived influence of religion on American life before and after September 11. As shown in table 5.3, the psychological association between the importance of religion in one's own life and whether one believes the influence of religion in American life is increasing or decreasing was fairly small in magnitude as of March 2001 (gamma = .12). So too was the link between church or synagogue atten-

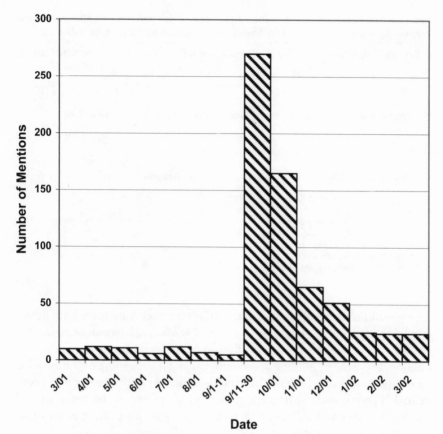

Figure 5.6   The "God Bless America" Effect: Mentions in U.S. Newspapers

Source: Lexis-Nexis Academic Universe, General News.

dance and beliefs about the influence of religion in the United States rather weak prior to 9/11, though statistically significant (gamma = .17). But by November 2001, the psychological meaning of the rising influence of religion in American life became noticeably more connected with both the respondent's attendance at church or synagogue (gamma = .37) and with the importance of religion in his or her own life (gamma = .36). Four months later, however, as the events of September 11 began to fade, the psychosemantic association between these religious indicators started to decline as well (gamma = .22 and .29, respectively), suggesting that the meaning of the question about the influence of religion in the United States was changing once again. In sharp contrast, attendance at churches, synagogues, or other places of worship and the importance of religion in one's own life remained

Table 5.3.   Relations among Personal Importance of Religion, Church Attendance, and Perceived Influence of Religion on American Life: Before and after September 11

I. Personal Importance of Religion and Perceived Influence of Religion on American Life

	Mar. 2001	Nov. 2001	Mar. 2002
Gamma =	.12**	.36***	.29***

II. Church Attendance and Perceived Influence of Religion on American Life

	Mar. 2001	Nov. 2001	Mar. 2002
Gamma =	.17***	.37***	.22***

III. Church Attendance and Personal Importance of Religion

	Mar. 2001	Nov. 2001	Mar. 2002
Gamma =	.75****	.74****	.72****

Source: Pew Research Center for the People and the Press (people-press.org).
**Statistically significant at the .01 level.
***Statistically significant at the .001 level.
****Statistically significant at the .0001 level.

strongly and consistently linked in the minds of most Americans both before and after September 11 (gamma = .75, .74, and .72). So, once more, the events of 9/11 had generated an illusion of a significant change in public opinion, this time by altering and homogenizing the meaning of the question about the influence of religion in American life. As with the surge in presidential approval and the upsurge of trust in government, the steep rise and fall in the perceived influence of religion in American life appears to be almost entirely ephemeral.

FADING EPHEMERA OF SEPTEMBER 11

A rereading of American public opinion one year later by the Gallup Organization indicated that, with few exceptions, the effects of September 11 had proved to be rather short-lived. As Gallup analyst Lydia Saad observes in her anniversary report of September 11, 2002, Americans' trust in their government "has reverted to pre-attack levels," and their confidence in the federal government to handle both domestic and international problems "has subsided to pre-attack levels" as well. The percentage of Americans who favored a more activist role for the federal government in solving the nation's problems had likewise faded with the passage of the one-year anniversary. Prior to September 11, as Saad notes, a solid majority of Americans (55 percent) thought that the government was "trying to do too many things that should be left to individuals and businesses"; only 36 percent said "government should do more to solve our country's problems," and the rest (9 percent) had "no opinion." Shortly after the terrorist attacks of 9/11, however, a Gallup survey (October 5–6, 2001) found that public opinion had flipped: the percentage thinking the government was doing too much to deal with our problems dropped dramatically from 55 percent to 41 percent, whereas the percentage of Americans who felt the government should do more to solve our national problems increased significantly from 36 percent to 50 percent, most likely because they now interpreted the question to mean the role of the federal government in dealing with the country's immediate problem of terrorism. But one year later, as the events of September 11 faded from the nation's collective short-term memory, a new Gallup survey (September 5–8, 2002) demonstrated that the American public had once more reversed its view of the role of government and "by a 50 percent to 43 percent margin, the plurality again believed that the government is doing too much" (Saad 2002). The question, in other words, had probably regained much of the conventional meaning it had prior to September 11: big government versus private sector solutions to the nation's social and economic problems.

Polls conducted by the *Los Angeles Times* and by Princeton Survey Research Associates (cited by Saad 2002) showed the same ephemeral pattern on the question of whether Americans were willing to sacrifice some of their civil liberties to deal with terrorism. Shortly after the Oklahoma City bombing in April of 1995, a *Los Angeles Times* poll indicated that nearly half (49 percent) of Americans thought "it will be necessary for the average person to give up some civil liberties" to "curb terrorism." But as the events of the Oklahoma bombing faded from the public's collective memory, the percentage thinking such restrictions on civil liberties were "necessary" dropped to around 30 percent in follow-up surveys conducted approximately one year later (March 28–31, 1996) and two years later (April 3–6, 1997). All that had really changed was the meaning of the question.

"MOST IMPORTANT PROBLEM FACING THE COUNTRY"

Ditto, it would appear, for the question about the "most important problem facing the country." One of the most significant indicators in American public opinion polling today, this standard indicator used by Gallup and numerous other polling organizations has measured the nation's priorities for decades. In one form or another since 1939, Gallup has been asking Americans a question much like this: "What do you think is the most important problem facing this country today?" Paying close attention to this well-established Gallup measure, political scientists, journalists, politicians, pundits, and policy analysts have long regarded responses to it as a vital indicator of the real concerns of the American public. Many other scholars have treated it as a social indicator par excellence of long-term trends in the American public's issue consciousness, reflecting the agenda-setting function of the mass media. Along with presidential approval and consumer confidence, it has become one of the most frequently monitored barometers of the changing mood, cycles, and dynamics of public opinion in American life. But does this question measure what it appears to measure? And, if not, to ask Schuman's (1998) validity question, do we understand what it is measuring, even if what it is measuring is partly or entirely different from what it is intended to measure?

First of all, except perhaps for a few naive observers, responses to the "most important problem" question do not resemble anything like a reasoned judgment about the nation's priorities. Instead, the evidence from the communications and cognitive psychological literatures would suggest that the question elicits largely top-of-the-head reactions from respondents (e.g., "the economy") that reflect topics made salient to them by the mass media's coverage of events (see Zaller 1992). A more parsimonious explanation of the same data is that mass media coverage of events simply alters the meaning and interpretation of the most important problem (MIP) question.

Once again, the events of 9/11 give us a glimpse at how the causal process works. Shortly before September 11, responses to this standard question in the national Gallup poll varied considerably. Though a noticeable percentage (34 percent) of respondents mentioned the economy and related economic matters (e.g., unemployment, taxes) in the immediately preceding month (Gallup, August 16–19, 2001), the rest of the responses were scattered all over the lot (e.g., 9 percent mentioned education; 6 percent, crime and violence; 4 percent, environment and pollution; 3 percent, poverty, hunger, and homelessness; 2 percent, immigration and illegal aliens; 1 percent, abortion; etc.). The responses varied widely, I would argue, because the question was inherently ambiguous and therefore subject to multiple interpretations. After September 11, however, the question became much less ambiguous for many respondents. Not surprisingly, the Gallup polls taken in the weeks and months after those tragic events found that terrorism was now the most important problem facing the country (46 percent), along with the fear of war or "feelings of fear" (10 percent) and concerns about national security (8 percent) and related issues (Gallup, October 11–14, November 28, 2001). As with the questions about presidential approval and trust in government, the events of September 11 had homogenized the meaning of the MIP question. For the great majority of respondents, it now meant simply the obvious problem of terrorism and its aftermath of national insecurity. Looking at similar data, Langer (2002b, 9) also observes how closely the sharp rise and fall in trusting the government in Washington parallels changes in responses to Gallup's question on the most important problem facing the country: "Mentions of terrorism, war and national security as the MIP soared from nowhere to 64 percent in the days after September 11, just as 'trust' soared. By January mentions of terrorism as the most important problem had subsided to 35 percent, just as 'trust' had subsided."

Theoretically speaking, these data on the impact of September 11 suggest that a rather mundane change in the meaning and interpretation of the MIP question provides the most plausible, parsimonious explanation for what many scholars call the agenda-setting effect of the mass media. Measurement-wise, most respondents struggle not with figuring out what problems are really facing the country but rather with how to interpret this vague and ambiguous question. The events of September 11 just simplified that cognitive task. These results also suggest that responses to the MIP question, so heavily relied upon by political analysts and policy makers to discern the American public's priorities, cannot be compared over time because, psychologically speaking, respondents are often answering different questions whose meanings have shifted with events. The findings for the MIP question, the presidential approval question, the questions on trust in government, and the influence of religion in American life—even questions in the Gallup poll on consumer confidence, which also shot up briefly after the events of September 11 and then faded away like a mirage (see Jacobe 2003)—all underscore the ephemeral quality of public opinion and its great dependence on the transitory meaning of survey questions.

IT'S NOT ALL JUST AN ILLUSION

But before throwing out the baby with the bathwater, we should remind ourselves of the many instances in which variations in responses to survey questions do represent true changes. Take, for instance, the well-known fluctuations in presidential candidate preferences in the trial heats and tracking polls during the 2000 election campaign between Bush and Gore, the 1996 campaign between Clinton and Dole, or any other campaign. When candidate preferences shift over time, we typically regard these shifts as representing some combination of true change and random instability due to sampling and measurement error, rather than some form of systematic error such as the meaning of the question changing from time 1, to time 2, to time

3. Bush and Gore or Clinton and Dole remain essentially constant in meaning across respondents and over the campaign period. We are comparing an apple with an apple. To take another illustration, if a national poll told us that the percentage of Americans reporting that their houses or apartments have been broken into in the last twelve months has more than doubled, we would most likely regard those figures as an indication of true change plus random error and perhaps some systematic error in recall, but we would not be worrying about whether the meaning of the question had changed. We are comparing an orange with an orange. Finally, as an example of short-term change, consider once again the events of September 11. In October of 2001, respondents in a CBS/New York Times poll were asked, "How likely do you think it is that there will be another terrorist attack in the next few months—very likely, somewhat likely, not very likely, or not at all likely?" Over half (53 percent) thought it was "very likely." When the same question was repeated in a CBS/New York Times poll a few months later (early January of 2002), however, the percentage thinking another such terrorist attack was "very likely" dropped dramatically to just 18 percent. This striking shift in the public's perception most likely represents a real change because it does not seem plausible that the core meaning of the phrase "another terrorist attack" could have changed much, if at all, in such a short period of time. For most respondents the question probably continued to mean an attack like the one that occurred on September 11, though for some it might also have come to mean things like anthrax attacks and other forms of terrorism. But, by and large, we are still comparing apples with apples, at least in the short run.

Not so when we deal with the many vague questions that have become our stock in trade in public opinion research today. Trying to measure the overall mood of the nation, the Gallup Organization often asks Americans, "In general, are you satisfied or dissatisfied with the way things are going in the United States at this time?" Many polling organizations also like to ask the following favorite: "Do you think things in this country are generally going in the right direction or do you feel things have gotten pretty seriously off on the wrong track?" While respondents readily answer such questions and the trend lines recording their reactions rise and fall with events, the meaning of these types of questions probably fluctuates just as rapidly as the events themselves, making any comparisons over time essentially meaningless. We are not comparing apples with apples. At best, we can only guess at what our questions mean to respondents. And just because the responses to such questions correlate with this or that demographic variable (age, race, sex) doesn't tell us anything about what that common variance might mean.

WHAT NEEDS TO BE DONE

Many years ago at the annual conference of the American Association for Public Opinion Research (AAPOR), President Paul Lazarsfeld (1950–1951) urged AAPOR members to think about "the obligations of the 1950 pollster to the 1984 historian." Among other things, he warned us that the 1984 historian might well "reproach us for not having given enough thought to what he will want to know about 1950." Lazarsfeld believed that historians would especially want to understand the meaning of current events lest they become unable, in the Orwellian sense, to compare the present with the past. Were he alive today, I think he would be reminding pollsters once more of their obligations to historians who will want to understand, in great depth, the meaning of American public opinion following the events of September 11: what the surge in presidential approval actually *meant*, what the boost of trust in government *meant*, what the rise in the perceived influence of religion *meant*, and what the change in a pile of other indicators *meant*. Much of the meaning of those historical social facts can only be guessed at now. As a deeply skeptical observer might ask, How much of what we think we know about American public opinion following the events of September 11, 2001, is historical fact, and how much of it is pure artifact? It's certainly not the factual equivalent of documenting the historical authenticity of the collapse of the World Trade Center on that date.

In the future, we can heed Lazarsfeld's sage advice by taking advantage of a technique recommended, likewise many years ago, by Howard Schuman (1966; see also T. Smith 1989, chap. 9) to assess the validity and meaning of closed questions: the random probe technique. It will require some methodological experimentation and investment of resources on our part, but it will benefit both pollsters and historians in the future if we get in the habit of randomly probing random subsamples of respondents, on a regular basis, about *what they mean* when they say they approve or disapprove of how George W. Bush, for example, is handling his job as president; *what they mean* when they say they trust the government in Washington to do what is right "always" or just "some of the time"; *what they mean* when they say they think the influence of religion in American life is "increasing"; *what they mean* when they say they are satisfied with "the way things are going in the United States at this time"; and *what they mean* when they say "things in this country are generally going in the right direction" or that "things have gotten pretty seriously off on the wrong track." That now is our obligation to future pollsters and historians.

But our obligation does not end there. The ephemeral opinions and illusions of change generated by the events of September 11 would not be so worrisome if they represented an isolated instance of misunderstanding public opinion. On the contrary, I will contend in the following chapters that this episode represents a microcosm of a much larger problem of artifact and ambiguities in understanding political attitudes and public opinion, especially when monitored over time. False impressions of American public opinion may indeed be far more common than anyone has suspected. One such impression that has taken hold in political science, public opinion circles, and the popular culture is that Americans had, at least prior to September 11, lost faith in their "government in Washington." In the following chapter we take a critical look at this widespread conventional wisdom in American politics, along with other ambiguities of measurement, such as asking Americans to classify themselves as "liberal," "moderate," or "conservative" and as a "Democrat," a "Republican," or an "independent." As we will see, the ambiguity of such terms in survey questions and the measurement artifacts they generate can create much of what I call the illusion of public opinion.

NOTES

The epigraph is based on Tonnies's observations of what he thought of as the ephemeral public opinion of the day (*Offentlichen Meinung des Tages*), as translated by Hanno Hardt and Slavko Pichal in *Ferdinand Tonnies on Public Opinion: Selections and Analyses* (Lanham, Md.: Rowman & Littlefield, 2000), 184.

1. The poll findings cited in this chapter on American public opinion on trust in government, presidential approval, the influence of religion, and the most important problem facing this country were compiled from the Roper Center for Public Opinion Research's online Public Opinion Location Library (POLL) and the Polling Report (www.pollingreport.com).

6

Ambiguities of Measurement

The words of things entangle and confuse.

—Wallace Stevens

The dramatic impact of the events of September 11 on the meaning of questions about presidential approval, trust in government, the "most important problem facing the country," and the influence of religion in American life underscores the critical importance of understanding how respondents interpret the questions we ask them (see, e.g., Belson 1981; Brady 1985; Cantril and Fried 1944; Fee 1981; Tannenhaus and Foley 1982). But does it represent just an isolated instance, or, more likely, is it but the proverbial tip of the iceberg? As I will argue, there are numerous such examples of question ambiguities and apparent changes in well-established indicators of political attitudes and public opinion, and these changes are due almost entirely to subtle and, in some cases, substantial shifts in the meaning of survey questions over time. First, we will look at a serendipitous example that emerged as a by-product of my earlier work on the controversy about "the changing American voter" (cf. chapter 4). Next, we reexamine a commonly used question about the political ideology of the American public, finding it loaded with ambiguity and exhibiting changes over time that are largely an artifact of measurement—one that points, in turn, to an even bigger fish: political party identification. Finally, taking a clue from the impact of September 11 (chapter 5), we revisit the National Election Studies (NES) time series on trusting the "government in Washington" and discover how trends on this measure may have been misinterpreted for many years. Ambiguous political concepts, as Tannenhaus and Foley (1982) reminded us years ago, threaten the validity of measurement in survey interviews and questionnaires in ways that remain unresolved today.

"HELPING COUNTRIES AGAINST COMMUNISM"

A serendipitous illustration of the measurement problem facing the field cropped up as part of a larger research controversy about the changing American voter (Bishop et al. 1978, 1979; Nie, Verba, and Petrocik 1976, 1979; Sullivan, Piereson, and Marcus 1978; also see chapter 4). Rather accidentally, I discovered a puzzling replication by Nie and his associates (National Opinion Research Center [NORC], December 1973) of a question on the Cold War issue of American military involvement overseas. Originally designed by the University of Michigan's Survey Research Center (SRC), the question asked respondents whether they agreed or disagreed with the following statement: "The United States should keep soldiers overseas where they can help countries that are against communism. Do you have an opinion on this or not?" If respondents said they had an opinion on it, they then indicated the extent to which they agreed or disagreed with the statement on a five-point scale. Not surprisingly, at the time of the SRC 1956 National Election Study, the great majority of respondents (73 percent) agreed either "strongly" or "somewhat" with this Cold War stance. Two years later, the 1958 national election survey revealed that the percentage of Americans agreeing with this proposition had increased to 79 percent, and by the time of the 1960 presidential election contest between Cold War warriors Kennedy and Nixon, the figure had swelled to virtually a national consensus: *81 percent.*

But when NORC repeated the question verbatim in December of 1973, it found that the American public had become sharply divided on the policy of "keeping soldiers overseas where they can help countries that are against communism." Had Americans radically changed their views of the Cold War against Communism? Or, more likely, did the question, though worded identically, no longer mean what it had meant during the late 1950s and early 1960s? Back then, it most likely would have been interpreted as a question about keeping troops in Europe and the NATO countries to deal with the military threat of the Soviet bloc and perhaps in South Korea and the Pacific to thwart Communist China. By December of 1973, however, the question probably meant just one thing to most U.S. respondents: Vietnam. And because of that fundamental change in meaning, the responses to this question were no longer comparable to those measured in the Cold War era. International military events and cultural trends in American society had changed what it meant to "help other countries against communism." Psychologically speaking, it was as though the wording of the question itself had been changed. One was no longer comparing an apple with an apple. And this represents just one of the more obvious ambiguities in measuring changes in American public opinion. Somewhat subtler is the ambiguous concept of political ideology.

"LIBERAL, MODERATE, OR CONSERVATIVE?"

Pollsters, politicians, and political scientists have long found it difficult to talk about American politics without thinking about it ideologically. The urge to classify the public into "liberals," "conservatives," and "moderates" has become practically instinctive in the press as well as in academe. Journalists almost invariably interpret the outcomes of presidential and congressional elections (e.g., Reagan's election in 1980 and his reelection in 1984, the Republican capture of the House of Representatives in 1994, Clinton's victory in 1996) as signaling a liberal or conservative shift in the makeup of the electorate. Regardless of their methodological reservations, scholars such as Knight and Erickson (1997), Nie, Verba, and Petrocik (1976, 1979), Robinson and Fleishman (1988), Smith (1990), and Stimson (1999) find it just as irresistible to characterize swings in public opinion as indicating a change in the ideological mood of the country. No less enamored of this way of thinking, pollsters have continually reinforced the image of an ideological American public by asking respondents in their surveys to identify themselves as "liberal," "moderate," or "conservative." And despite the inherent ambiguity of these terms, respondents have been obliging them by readily answering such questions for over sixty years.

Like a lot of other pioneering survey measurements, it probably all began with the Gallup Organization, in what was then known as the American Institute for Public Opinion (AIPO). Inspired no doubt by the turbulent economic and political climate of the 1930s, AIPO asked respondents in an April 1937 national poll to answer the following question: "In politics, do you regard yourself as a radical, a liberal, or a conservative?" Since that auspicious beginning, the ideological identification question has evolved and multiplied into various forms not only at Gallup but at a host of other survey organizations as well. As Robinson and Fleishman (1988) have previously demonstrated, substantial "house effects" exist in how the question has been framed, including how many answer categories are offered to respondents (two to as many as seven or eight), whether respondents are offered an explicit middle or neutral category, and whether an explicit filter question is used to screen out respondents who are unfamiliar with such terms as "liberal" or "conservative." Because of these question variations, it has become rather difficult to draw any definitive conclusions about whether the American public is becoming more "conservative" ideologically, as many contemporary observers have frequently contended.

Trends in Ideological Self-Identification

Take the most recent era of trend data gathered in the National Election Studies and in the NORC General Social Survey (table 6.1). Considering only the

Table 6.1. Trends in Liberal-Conservative Self-Identification: NES and NORC GSS, 1972–2000

Year	Liberal		Moderate		Conservative	
	NES	GSS	NES	GSS	NES	GSS
1972	25	—	38	—	37	—
1974	29	31	36	40	36	30
1975	—	30	—	40	—	31
1976	24	28	38	40	38	32
1977	—	30	—	39	—	32
1978	27	29	36	38	36	33
1980	26	27	31	41	43	34
1982	23	29	34	40	42	31
1983	—	24	—	41	—	35
1984	26	24	33	40	41	36
1986	24	24	37	41	39	35
1988	24	27	31	36	45	35
1990	24	28	36	36	39	37
1992	27	—	31	—	42	—
1994	18	27	34	36	47	37
1996	24	25	32	38	44	36
1998	24	28	37	37	39	34
2000	27	27	32	40	41	34

Source: National Election Studies, NORC General Social Survey, Inter-university Consortium for Political and Social Research (ICPSR), University of Michigan.

NES results, we would conclude, much as Knight and Erickson (1997) have argued, that there has been an unmistakable conservative trend in the American electorate, beginning around the 1980 national election, peaking initially at the time of the 1988 presidential election, and then surging to an all-time high during the year of the Republican Party's Contract with America in 1994, when nearly half of the American public (47 percent of those who answered the question) identified itself as "conservative"; about a third as "moderate"; and less than a fifth as "liberal." The drop in the percentage of those who called themselves "liberal" was indeed quite dramatic, falling from 27 percent in the 1992 NES survey to just 18 percent in 1994. Strangely, however, this conservative trend is barely evident, if at all, in the data collected by the NORC General Social Survey (GSS) during approximately the same time period. Though there was a small increase in the percentage of respondents who identified themselves as "conservative" in the GSS during the 1970s (from 30 percent in 1974 to 34 percent in 1980), it was only about half as large as that recorded in the NES (from 36 percent in 1974 to 43 percent in 1980). Furthermore, in the NORC GSS, there was no evidence of any increase whatsoever in the percent of Americans calling themselves "conservative" between 1986 and 1988, whereas in the NES the percentage identifying as "conservative" jumped noticeably from 39 percent in 1986 to 45 percent in 1988. Nor was there any trace at all in the GSS of the "conservative surge" observed by Knight and Erickson (1997) in the NES during the early '90s. The percentage of Americans who identified themselves as "conservative" in the 1994 GSS (37 percent) was, in fact, identical to the figure reported in the 1990 GSS, as for all practical purposes were the percentages identifying as "moderate" and "liberal." What explains the inconsistency between these two well-established time series?

Once more, the form in which the questions were asked probably accounts for most of the difference. In the NORC GSS interviews the standard ideology question reads as follows: "We hear a lot of talk these days about liberals and conservatives. I'm going to show you a seven-point scale on which the political views that people might hold are arranged from extremely liberal— point 1—to extremely conservative—point 7. Where would you place yourself on this scale?" The NES question appears to be quite similar, but includes at the end an explicit filter question: "We hear a lot of talk these days about liberals and conservatives. I'm going to show you a seven-point scale on which the political views that people might hold are arranged from extremely liberal to extremely conservative. Where would you place yourself on this scale, *or haven't you thought much about this?*" (emphasis added).

Not unexpectedly, this strongly worded filter question, which is part of a long-standing tradition at the Michigan Survey Research Center for screening out respondents with "nonattitudes," typically gets a sizable percentage of respondents to say they have not thought much about such an abstract seven-point scale on how liberal or conservative they might be. The percentage opting out of classifying themselves because of this NES filter question has averaged around 27 percent over the years, whereas the percentage who volunteer a "don't know" (DK) in response to the unfiltered GSS version of the question has generally hovered around just 4–5 percent. Further analysis of these data suggests that the bulk of the respondents removed by the filter question in the NES would most likely have chosen the response category "moderate, middle of the road" had they been given the GSS version of the question. In the critical comparison year of 1994, for example, the percentage of respondents removed by the NES filter was approximately a fourth (24 percent), and the percentage choosing the middle category was a little over a fourth (26 percent). In contrast, only 3.4 percent of the respondents to the GSS in 1994 volunteered a DK response, but more than a third (35 percent) chose the middle category. Respondents removed by the NES filter also tended to be significantly more Democratic in their party identification (data not shown here). So the "conservative upsurge" observed in the NES by Knight and Erickson (1997) looks, in large part, like a measurement artifact of a difference in the form of the question used to measure a respondent's ideological self-identification. And that's just the beginning of the problems with these measures.

Ambiguities of Ideological Self-Labels

Far more problematic is the meaning of such labels as "liberal," "moderate," and "conservative." Do they mean essentially the same thing to all respondents in any given survey? And, what is even more critical for examining trends over time, does it mean the same thing to call oneself a "liberal" or "conservative" in the year 2002, for example, as it did in 1992, 1982, or 1972? Most observers would agree that these terms are unusually ambiguous and therefore subject to multiple interpretations by survey respondents, and that such interpretations are highly susceptible to shifts in meaning across questionnaire contexts and over time. Only rarely, however, have survey organizations made any attempt to probe the meaning of these widely used ideological self-labels. One notable exception occurred in the 1978 National Election Study (cf. replications in later NES surveys), in which respondents were directly asked, in an open-ended set of questions, to tell interviewers what the terms "liberal" and "conservative" meant to them: "People have different things in mind when they say that someone's political views are liberal or conservative. We'd like to know more about this. Let's start with liberal. What sorts of things do *you* have in mind when you say that someone's political views are liberal? And, what do you have in mind when you say that someone's political views are conservative?"

As Conover and Feldman (1981) discovered, the meaning of such terms can vary considerably across respondents, even when answers to these open-ended questions are coded into fairly broad categories, such as references to "change" and "recent social issues." Though they found there was some shared meaning of these terms between those who identified themselves as liberal and those who called themselves conservative (e.g., references to "fiscal policies"), the two groups differed significantly in the frequency with which they used various definitional categories. Self-identified liberals, for example, were more than twice as likely (52.3 percent) as self-identified conservatives (23.5 percent) to make some reference to "change" (e.g., acceptance or resistance to change and new ideas) in specifying what they meant when they said someone's political views were "liberal." Whereas self-identified conservatives were noticeably more likely than self-proclaimed liberals to mention something about "fiscal policies" (33.5 percent versus 9.3 percent), "socialism/capitalism" (14.7 percent versus 7.5 percent), and "New Deal issues" (22.1 percent versus 10.9 percent) to indicate what they meant by the same term (see table 4 in Conover and Feldman 1981). Conversely, conservatives were far more likely than liberals to refer to "fiscal policies," such as government spending (41.8 percent versus 12.2 percent), when explaining what they had in mind when they said someone's political views were "conservative." And this says nothing about the even greater ambiguity of such terms for those who identified themselves as "moderate/middle of the road" (27 percent of the sample in 1978). Nor does it tell us anything about how the meaning of these highly ambiguous labels may have changed in American politics over the past quarter of a century. Comparisons of self-identified "liberals," "moderates," and "conservatives" across survey respondents and over time thus become impossible, if not a fundamentally meaningless exercise. Once more, one is not comparing an apple with an apple.

"DEMOCRAT, REPUBLICAN, OR INDEPENDENT?"

If public opinion researchers and political scientists have found it difficult to talk about American politics without thinking about it ideologically, they have found it nearly impossible to analyze it without the concept of political party identification. The party identification question was developed in the early days of opinion polling by the Gallup Organization and refined theoretically by the Michigan Survey Research Center in the early 1950s (see, e.g., Campbell et al. 1960, chap. 6), and since then, party identification has become the single most important factor in explaining how Americans cast their votes (Miller and Shanks 1996). Since the late 1940s, the Gallup Organization has measured this personal self-identification by asking respondents, "In politics, as of today, do you think of yourself as a Republican, a Democrat, or an Independent?" Whereas at the University of Michigan Survey Research Center, the question has read as follows since 1952: "Generally speaking, do you usually think of yourself as a Republican, a Democrat, an Independent, or what?" Though considerable controversy has surrounded these two rival measures of partisanship (Bishop, Tuchfarber, and Smith 1994; Abramson and Ostrom 1991, 1994; MacKuen, Erickson, and Stimson 1989; MacKuen et al. 1992), most academic and commercial polling organizations today continue to ask some variation of one of these two forms (box 6.1). Along with age, race, sex, education, religion, and the like, it has become essentially a standard demographic question in virtually every American public opinion poll.

But, as with the terms "liberal," "moderate," and "conservative," the

---

BOX 6.1
Questions on Political Party Identification by Academic and Commercial Polling Organizations in the United States

"Generally speaking, do you usually think of yourself as a Democrat, a Republican, an Independent, or what?" (ABC News/*Washington Post*)

"Generally speaking, do you usually consider yourself a Republican, a Democrat, an Independent or what?" (CBS News/*New York Times*)

"Do you consider yourself a Democrat, a Republican, an Independent or none of these?" (Ipsos-Reid/*Cook Political Report*)

"Regardless of your party registration or how you have voted in the past, do you usually think of yourself as a Democrat, or a Republican, or an Independent, or as something else?" (*Los Angeles Times*)

"Generally speaking, do you think of yourself as a Democrat, a Republican, an independent, or something else?" (NBC News/*Wall Street Journal*)

"In politics today, do you consider yourself a Republican, Democrat or Independent?" (Pew Research Center for the People and the Press/ Princeton Survey Research Associates)

Source: Public Opinion Location Library, Roper Center for Public Opinion Research.

---

same measurement issues arise: Do the terms "Democrat," "Republican," and "independent" mean the same thing to all respondents? Does it mean the same thing today to call oneself a "Democrat," "Republican," or "independent" as it did in 1992, 1982, 1972, 1962, or 1952? Are these terms just somewhat less ambiguous in meaning than "liberal" "moderate," and "conservative," but subject nonetheless to different interpretations by different respondents and just about as susceptible to variations in meaning over time? And if the meaning of these terms does vary significantly over time, what does that tell us about apparent trends in party identification, such as the well-established decline of partisanship and the significant growth of political "independents" that began in the mid-1960s, surged in the 1970s, and peaked in the 1980s (see Miller and Shanks 1996)? Do such trends mean what we think they mean—a genuine loosening of the American public's psychological ties to the two major political parties—or something partly or entirely different from what has heretofore been the common wisdom?

A vital clue to possible changes in the meaning of political party identification comes, coincidentally, from its well-documented association with political ideology. Since the early 1970s, the correlation between these two measures has increased noticeably, not only in the NES time series, but also in the NORC GSS (table 6.2). Calling oneself a "Democrat," for example, has become increasingly connected with calling oneself a "liberal," and "Republican" with "conservative." Knight and Erickson (1997) have mustered evidence suggesting that this pattern of increasing correlation over time occurs almost entirely among respondents they classify as "ideologically sophisti-

Table 6.2. Correlations between Party Identification and Ideological Identification in the NES and the NORC GSS, 1972–2000

Year	NES	GSS
1972	.32	—
1974	.35	.16
1975	—	.25
1976	.39	.20
1977	—	.21
1978	.35	.19
1980	.39	.18
1982	.42	.23
1983	—	.31
1984	.41	.24
1985	—	.28
1986	.37	.29
1987	—	.29
1988	.41	.28
1989	—	.28
1990	.34	.28
1991	—	.26
1992	.44	—
1993	—	.36
1994	.51	.31
1996	.57	.35
1998	.47	.36
2000	.51	.33

Source: National Election Studies, NORC General Social Survey, ICPSR, University of Michigan.
Note: Coefficients shown are Pearson product-moment correlations.

cated"—over half the sample (55 percent) in their 1994 analysis. But it may not be so much a matter of growing ideological sophistication in the American public that accounts for the increasing correlation between these measures as it is a simple increase in the sheer frequency with which the terms "Democrat" and "liberal," and "Republican" and "conservative," have been associated with each other in the mass media. And the greater an individual's exposure to the mass media coverage of politics, the more likely he or she is to associate such terms with one another. Better-educated respondents, for example, should be more likely to attend to political coverage in the mass media and should therefore be more likely to associate such terms with one another than their less well educated counterparts, as the results in table 6.3 readily confirm. Notice too that the correlations between party identification and ideological identification are consistently higher in the NES than in the GSS, suggesting that the strength of the relationship itself is, in part, an artifact of which question form is used. In brief, these central political concepts appear to be plagued with ambiguity across respondents and over time, making comparisons problematic to say the least.

TRUSTING THE "GOVERNMENT IN WASHINGTON"

As the polls have told us for years, or at least until fairly recently, the American public's trust in the government in Washington has declined significantly over a forty- to fifty-year period, albeit with puzzling upward surges here and there (figure 6.1). Supposedly Americans had lost much of their faith in government by the time of the 1994 national congressional election. As political scientist Gary Orren (1997, 80) sums it up in his review "Fall from Grace," "By 1994, public sentiment had completely reversed itself in comparison with the halcyon 1950s: from three out of four Americans trusting the government to three out of four mistrusting the government, a turnaround rarely seen in public opinion." That's not all. As he tells it, "This trend of

Table 6.3.   Correlations between Party Identification and Ideological Identification by Level of Education in the NES and the NORC GSS: Year 2000

Education level	NES	GSS
High school or less	.35	.20
Some college	.44	.35
College graduate	.66	.52

Source: National Election Studies, NORC General Social Survey, ICPSR, University of Michigan.
Note: Coefficients shown are Pearson product-moment correlations.

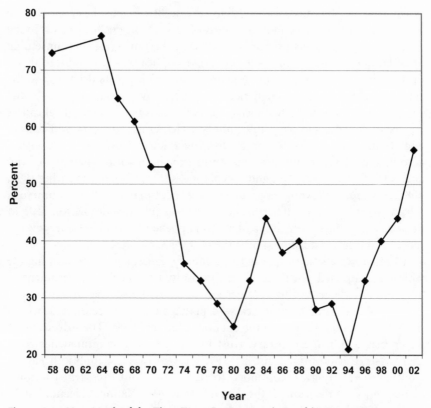

Figure 6.1   How Much of the Time Trust Government in Washington: 1958–2002

Response: Most of the time/just about always
Source: National Election Studies

mounting disillusionment is mirrored in a host of survey questions that track opinions on other aspects of political trust, confidence in government, and government responsiveness" (Orren 1997, 81). He also believes the drop in confidence is deep-seated and not just a transitory thing: "Today's cynicism is fueled by a deeper set of accumulated grievances with political authority, institutions, and processes in general—grievances that cut across party and ideology. Not just a temporary slump, the ensuing cynicism has lasted for three decades, during which time mild discontent has for many citizens turned into outrage and loathing" (Orren 1997, 79). Strangely, however, as pollster and political scientist David Moore (2002a) has observed, none of this cynicism seems to have resulted in any serious consequences or loss of legitimacy for our democratic system of government, raising the question of what the decline in confidence really means (also see Eisinger 1999).

Figuring out the causal forces driving the decline in trust has proved to be just as problematic. For sundry scholarly observers, the decline of trust in the federal government has presumably reflected the impact of such unsettling episodes in our national life as the civil rights upheaval and racial turbulence of the 1960s, the anti–Vietnam War protests, the Watergate debacle, and the Iran-Contra affair; increasingly negative media coverage; dwindling "social capital"; and a host of other social, cultural, economic, and political causes (see Nye, Zelikov, and King 1997; also see Hetherington 1998; see Erickson and Tedin 2001, 155–59, for a basic overview). None of these causal accounts, however, quite measures up in explaining all the patterns of rise and fall in figure 6.1. As Nye and his colleagues (Nye, Zelikov, and King 1997, 268) conclude following their exhaustive examination of the numerous scholarly explanations offered to date, "At this point we know too little to draw a single conclusion about what has happened to confidence in government (and other institutions) over the past three decades."

All these explanations appear to be equally inadequate in accounting for what has happened just since 1994. Curiously, trust in the "government in Washington" seems not to have been affected by the scandal and impeachment episodes of the Clinton years—a perhaps telling piece of evidence, as in the dog that didn't bark in the Sherlock Holmes story "The Adventure of Silver Blaze." On the contrary, trust in the federal government has risen sharply since it bottomed out in 1994, the year of the Republican Party's Contract with America, continued to rise throughout President Clinton's second term of office, and, if the data from the 2002 National Election Study are accurate, has climbed even higher since George W. Bush took office—reaching a level not seen since the early years of the Nixon administration in 1970. What could Bill Clinton's and George W. Bush's administrations possibly have in common to give rise to such a striking upward shift in public confidence? Is it possible that this well-established indicator is measuring something partly or entirely different from what we think it is measuring? How much of the fluctuation in trust is fact, how much of it artifact?

The artifact hypothesis has indeed become a plausible rival explanation for what's going on. As political scientist and Gallup pollster David Moore (2002a) has argued with data from Gallup surveys, Americans' apparent distrust of the government in Washington should be regarded as mostly a myth, an artifact of question wording, rather than as an indicator of any real, substantive disaffection with the institutions of our democracy. We have been dependent for far too long, as he puts it, on "just one question": the standard measure first introduced in the University of Michigan Survey Research Center's 1958 National Election Study and replicated ever since, with seemingly minor exceptions, by various commercial and academic survey organizations. But variations in question wording (and context) are not the only possible source of artifact in the NES time series on trust in government. Far more troubling is the problem of what the standard NES trust question means to respondents at any given point in time and, more important, what it has meant over time.

The Comparability Issue

The core of the question as it has been asked in just about every SRC election survey reads: "How much of the time do you think you can trust the government in Washington to do what is right—just about always, most of the time, or only some of the time?" In the preface to this and other questions in the series on trust in government, the SRC has also urged respondents to think about the government in general when giving their answers (box 6.2): "Now I'd like to talk about some of the different ideas people have about the government in Washington and see how you feel about them. These opinions don't refer to Democrats and Republicans in particular but just to the government in general." This preface and instruction to respondents, which has generally *not* been included in other academic and commercial organizations' replication of the question, becomes crucial because if most respondents are thinking of particular Democratic and Republican officeholders, or just the party controlling the White House and/or Congress, when answering the question, then it may not mean the same thing to all respondents. And if the meaning of the question varies, then valid comparisons become impossible because such variation violates a cardinal assumption of scientific survey

---

BOX 6.2
The Standard NES Question on Trust in Government

"Now I'd like to talk about some of the different ideas people have about the government in Washington and see how you feel about them. These opinions don't refer to Democrats and Republicans in particular but just to the government in general—for example: How much of the time do you think you can trust the government in Washington to do what is right—just about always, most of the time, or only some of the time?"

Source: SRC 1958 National Election Study, ICPSR, University of Michigan.

measurement: that the question should mean the same thing to all respondents at any one point in time (the same stimulus principle), and that when it is repeated over time, it should mean essentially the same thing the second time as it did the first time (the constant stimulus principle; see Groves 1989 on a "fundamental tenet of scientific measurement," chap. 10).

Just such a problem of comparability now plagues the long-established SRC/NES series on trust in government, particularly the most frequently used indicator of trusting "the government in Washington to do what is right." Because of the vague and ambiguous wording of this question, I will argue, changes in the American public's faith in government have become confounded with partisanship and with approval and evaluations of specific presidents in specific historical periods, among other things, and are thus inseparable from artifacts of survey measurement. As a practical consequence, trend data on trusting the government in Washington need to be routinely disaggregated by presidential approval and partisanship, as well as by the standard demographics, so that the meaning of the question can be at least partially disambiguated. But let it be clear at the outset: I am not saying that all the observed changes in trust in government over the past forty years or so are merely artifacts of survey measurement, but rather that the standard NES question is measuring something quite different than has been widely assumed and that we have some vital clues as to what else it is getting at (cf. Abramson and Finifter 1981). It is not about just the institution of government in general.

Clues from the Reagan Era

Indeed, a vital clue to the problem now facing us has been sitting in full view for some time. Consider the work of Jack Citrin and Donald Green (1986) on the resurgence of trust in government during the Reagan years. In sharp contrast with other scholars in the field, they argue that their research confirms Citrin's long-standing contention "that when Americans express trust or mistrust in 'government' their answers largely reflect their *feelings about the incumbent national administration*" (emphasis added). Using data from the 1980, 1982, and 1984 NES surveys, they found "strong and consistent connections at the individual level between party identification, liking the incumbent president, approving his job performance and voting for him, on the one hand, and trust in government, on the other." They also present considerable evidence that it was the incumbent president's persona, or his perceived character and leadership qualities, along with approval of his job performance, that accounted for much of the upsurge in trust in government during the Reagan era. In other words, a significant portion of the semantic meaning of the standard question on trust in government may be specifically linked to the incumbent president. Furthermore, as we learned in the previous chapter, the meaning of trusting the government in Washington can become intimately linked to how the president has dealt with specific events in a particular historical period. Thus, the meaning and interpretation of the NES trust question has probably varied significantly over time, depending on the salience of events such as the Vietnam War, Watergate, and September 11, to name only the most obvious.

Clues from September 11

Another clue sitting out in full view turned up in the polls conducted shortly after the events of September 11, 2001. To the great surprise of many observers, Americans had suddenly become much less cynical about the federal government: They expressed levels of confidence not seen since the late 1960s (see, again, figure 5.2, chap. 5). What had happened? Had the American public undergone a fundamental change of mind about the government in Washington that had been the object of so much distrust for so many years? Hardly. Were all the scholarly analyses purporting to explain a thirty- to forty-year trend of declining trust in government totally obsolete? Unlikely. As with the surge in presidential approval after 9/11, however, a much simpler and more parsimonious explanation of the upward spike in trust was "hidden in plain sight": namely, a change in how respondents were interpreting the standard question on trust in government before and after September 11 (see chapter 5). When asked the standard question in a CBS/*New York Times* poll in January 2001, only about a third (31 percent) of Americans said they trusted the government in Washington to do what was right "most of the time" or "just about always." But shortly after 9/11, trust in the federal government had soared to 55 percent in another CBS/*New York Times* poll (October 2001). An even more spectacular surge in trust turned up in an ABC News/*Washington Post* poll conducted just two weeks after the events of September 11, in which 64 percent of Americans told interviewers that they trusted the government in D.C. to do what was right "most of the time" or "just about always," a level unseen since the early years (1966) of President Lyndon Johnson's administration (see, again, figure 6.1). Adding to the independent replications, the exact same pattern appeared in polls done by the Gallup Organization: Trust in the government in Washington had leaped from 42 percent in July 2000 to 60 percent in October 2001. Confidence in the leviathan on the Potomac seemed to be back in style.

But how should such changes in response to this well-established NES indicator be interpreted? To begin with, it seems highly unlikely that respondents interpreted the meaning of this ambiguous question in the same way after September 11 as they had before. What, for example, could "trust the government in Washington to do what is right" possibly mean to them? Most likely, as argued earlier, it now meant trusting the *present administration in Washington*, symbolized by *George W. Bush* in particular, to do the right thing in dealing with the terrorists, the anthrax threats, and other aspects of the crisis situation. In other words, just as they did for presidential approval, the events of 9/11 altered and homogenized the meaning of the standard question about trust in government for most respondents. The apparent upsurge in trust did not necessarily indicate any fundamental change in the American public's trust or distrust of the government in Washington. Furthermore, as the memories of September 11 faded from public consciousness, the spike of trust in government steadily decayed (see, again, figure 5.2). Was it all just an ephemera?

Digesting the results of a Gallup poll conducted approximately a year after September 11, 2001, Gallup pollster David Moore (2002b) takes issue with the speculation by many observers that the sharp rise in trust after September 11 signaled perhaps a new era in Americans' view of the federal government: "Some observers speculated that this more positive sentiment toward government could represent a significant and long-term reversal in the public's generally skeptical view—perhaps returning the country to the high levels of trust measured before Vietnam and Watergate. Today, however, that speculation seems misplaced. The levels of trust . . . have fallen to just three percentage points above the pre-9/11 levels" (2).

A poll report by the Pew Research Center, "One Year Later" (2002b), reached the same conclusion: "Over the past year, many of the dramatic reactions of the public to the events of Sept. 11 have slowly faded. The spike in trust in government is mostly gone . . . and even President Bush's approval ratings have come down from the stratosphere." Americans, in other words, were no longer interpreting the standard question about trust in government the way they had in the immediate aftermath of 9/11. Psychologically, they were now answering a *different question*, one that was probably much closer in meaning to those asked just prior to the events of September 11. And as the "rally round the flag" effect faded, so too did President Bush's approval ratings, suggesting that the two indicators—presidential approval and trust in government—were perhaps measuring some of the same thing.

But these parallel patterns in the polling data, before and after September 11, may be telling us something far more important. Together with the convincing demonstration in the NES by Citrin and Green (1986) showing a strong connection at the individual level between approving the president's job performance and trusting the government in Washington "to do what is right," these patterns suggest that the standard question on trust in government has probably *not* meant the same thing to respondents over the past forty years or so. In fact, I would argue that the meaning of this standard indicator is heavily confounded with, among other things, partisanship and approval of specific presidents during specific periods in time. Though there may be some elusive core meaning to the question that has persisted over time, analysis of the NES data will show that respondents during various electoral periods have been answering essentially different questions about trusting "the government in Washington." How much of the apparent decline, and variations, in trusting the federal government is fact and how much is artifact is uncertain. If nothing else, it should be clear from the data presented here that the standard NES question on trust in government is measuring something partly or entirely different from what has been intended (cf. Schuman 1998 on the meaning of *validity* in the context of survey measurement). The data also suggest there may be insurmountable problems of invalidity with this and similar subjective social indicators in the NES and public opinion surveys more generally.

Presidential Approval and Trust in Government: 1972–2002

As exhibit A, consider the link between trust and the president. As the trend lines in figures 6.2 and 6.3 tell us, trusting the government in Washington to "do what is right" depends, in significant part, on whether the respondent approves or disapproves of the incumbent president, which, as we know from a sizable literature, depends heavily on a respondent's partisanship. To take the most obvious example, look at the data for 1972. Among those who approved of President Nixon's job performance, a substantial majority (62 percent) said that they trusted the government in Washington to do what was right either "always" or "most of the time." But among those who disapproved of his performance, only about a third (32 percent) felt the same way (figure 6.2). Though the relationship varies in magnitude from election period to election period, we find essentially the same pattern throughout all the other presidencies: Those who approve of the president's job performance tend to trust the government in Washington significantly more than those who disapprove of the way he is handling his job. And, not surprisingly, the more strongly the respondent approves or disapproves of the president, the sharper the contrast becomes (figure 6.3).

The figures from the 2002 National Election Study make the case even more compelling. Among those who reported that they "strongly" approved of the way George W. Bush was handling his job as president, nearly two-

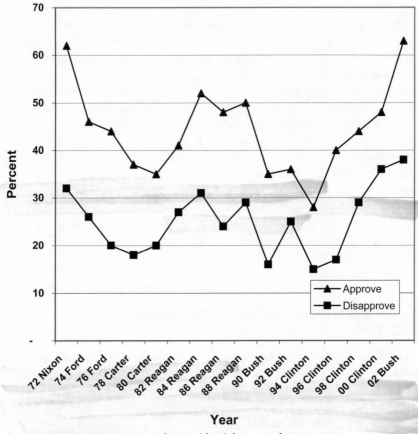

Figure 6.2   Trust in Government by Presidential Approval: 1972–2002

Source: National Election Studies.

thirds (65 percent) said they trusted the government in Washington to do
what was right "just about always" or "most of the time." Whereas among
those who "strongly" disapproved of how he'd been handling his job, only
about a third (34 percent) felt the same way about the "government in Washington." Trusting the government in Washington had thus become, in significant part, a question of whether you trusted the administration and
policies of George W. Bush—a pattern that breaks down sharply along partisan lines, as we know from numerous polls.

Consider as one other curious piece of evidence the failure of trust in government to decline during the second Clinton administration, especially in
1998, when the Lewinsky scandal and the prospect of impeachment were

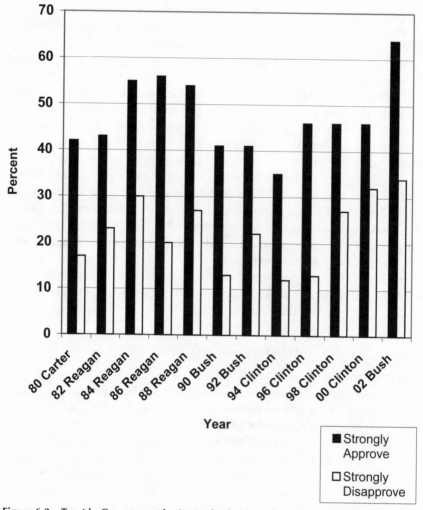

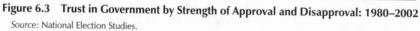

Figure 6.3 Trust in Government by Strength of Approval and Disapproval: 1980–2002
Source: National Election Studies.

reaching a peak. Surely this was a time when a great many Americans should have had significantly more doubts about the legitimacy and trustworthiness of their leader and the ability of the government in Washington "to do what is right," but, curiously, they did not. As with the dog that didn't bark in the Sherlock Holmes story "The Adventure of Silver Blaze," trust in government did not decline. Instead, it rose sharply between 1996 and 1998 (see figure 6.2), along with the job approval ratings for the intensely familiar and popular president, Bill Clinton—ratings that, as we all remember, were divided deeply along partisan lines. Trusting the government in Washington to do what was right had become, in significant measure, a matter of whether you trusted Bill Clinton's administration to do what was right under the circumstances of the time (see chapter 7).

To sum up, a substantial percentage of the respondents in each of these NES surveys appear to be interpreting the standard trust question not as intended, as one about "the government in general," but rather in large part as one about whether they trust the incumbent president and his administration "to do what is right" in the present circumstances: whether they trusted Nixon during the specific circumstances of his time (e.g., Vietnam, Watergate), Ford during his, Carter during his, Reagan during his, George H. W. Bush during his, Clinton during his, and George W. Bush during his tenure. The contextual and semantic meaning of the question, in other words, is significantly *incumbent* and *situation* specific and therefore not comparable over time. Respondents are not being exposed to the same psychological stimulus: "the government in Washington" has meant essentially different things to different respondents at different points in time. We're not, in other words, comparing an apple with an apple.

Partisanship and Trust in Government: 1958–2002

The bar graph in figure 6.4 tells the same story in another way. We find, not surprisingly, that the strength of a respondent's partisanship can make a significant and substantial difference in whether he or she trusts the government in Washington to do what is right. In fact, one of the most telling blips in figure 6.4 occurred between 1964 and 1966, which marks the beginning of a sharp decline in the NES trust indicator, one that began well before the height of the Vietnam protest period that many scholars regard as a precipitating cause (see, e.g., Nye, Zelikov, and King 1997, 264–76). Notice that, during this period, trust in government declined most sharply among those who identified themselves as "strong Republicans," dropping from 66 percent in 1964 to 47 percent in 1966. Whereas among "strong Democrats," trust in the government (of LBJ) remained essentially unchanged and extremely high: 80 percent in 1964 and 77 percent in 1966. The reaction of Goldwater partisans to Johnson's victory and his Great Society programs seems to be the most plausible explanation for this precipitating drop in trusting the government in Washington—a hypothesis that has been sorely neglected in all the scholarly analyses to date.

That's only part of the partisanship story. As the protests against the Vietnam War surged between the time of the 1968 election and the climactic

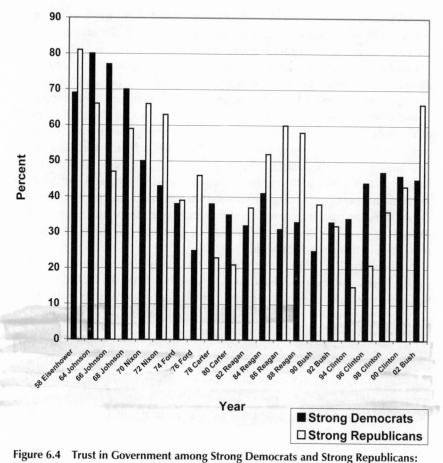

Figure 6.4   Trust in Government among Strong Democrats and Strong Republicans: 1958–2002

Source: National Election Studies.

Nixon-McGovern contest of 1972, trust in the government in Washington "to do what is right" dropped steadily among strong Democrats, but actually increased and remained quite high among strong Republicans, who were generally more supportive of the war and the incumbent president, Richard Nixon. And though the size of the partisanship gap in trusting the government varies from one election period to the next, and its *direct* effect is not as potent as the influence of presidential approval (cf. figures 6.2 and 6.3), the reader should not forget the very substantial *indirect* effect of partisanship through its influence on judgments of the president's performance. Together, partisanship and approval of the president make up much of what respondents evidently "have in mind" when they are asked about trusting the "government in Washington"—contrary to the intent of the standard NES question about the institutions of the "government in general."

Fast-forwarding to the period of George W. Bush's presidency (2002), we discover, to no one's great surprise, that two-thirds (67 percent) of "strong Republicans"—"strong Republicans," mind you—said they trusted the government in Washington to do what was right "just about always" or "most of the time" (figure 6.4). But less than half of "strong Democrats" (46 percent) felt the same way as of November 2002. One can only speculate about how much larger this partisanship gap in trusting the government might have been as the war with Iraq heated up in the winter of 2003. Suffice it to say that the partisanship gap in trusting the "government in Washington" during the war with Iraq would probably have been substantial, given what we now know about partisan differences in approval ratings for George W. Bush during this period (Newport 2002a).

Tom Smith (2003) has recently produced even more intriguing evidence for the partisanship artifact hypothesis. Using data from the NORC General Social Survey time series on confidence in U.S. institutions from 1973–2002, his analysis shows that the percentage of respondents expressing "a great deal" of confidence in the *executive branch of the federal government* varied much more among those identified with the Republican Party than among those identified with the Democratic Party. The meaning of trusting the government in Washington "to do what is right" has thus become confounded with partisanship and with approval of specific presidents in specific historical periods—an inseparable artifact of survey measurement.

A THOUGHT EXPERIMENT

Imagine for a moment that we had learned that the sharp rise in trusting the government in Washington during the first term of Reagan's presidency, 1980–1984 (see figure 6.1), or the upward spike in trust after September 11 (figure 5.2), was the result of a small change in the wording of the standard NES trust question, one that had been briefly footnoted at the bottom of a page from a poll report. Almost certainly, most public opinion analysts would seize upon this methodological detail to declare that the apparent change may well have been an artifact of a change in the wording of the question and that respondents were answering a somewhat *different* question because of this seemingly minor alteration. And they would probably be right because the change in wording would probably have altered the meaning of the question.

Here, I am basically saying the same thing. In this case, even though the wording of the standard NES question on trust in government has been essentially identical for the past forty-five years, a big chunk of its psychological meaning has shifted from one Democratic or Republican president to the next, and from one historical period to the next. In fact, it's not really clear what, if any, common meaning this question has, apart from partisan and personal evaluations of the incumbent president in specific historical situations and of particular Democratic- or Republican-dominated Congresses—not to mention the subtle alterations in the question's contextual meaning created by variations in question order and context within the NES interview schedules and questionnaires, which have varied noticeably across election periods (cf. the questionnaires in the NES, 1958–2002).

If nothing else, it should be crystal clear that the standard NES question on trust in government is measuring something partly or entirely different from what has been intended. By and large, for the past forty years or so, in measuring Americans' trust in the government in Washington, we have not been comparing an apple with an apple with an apple. Instead we have, in significant measure, been comparing a Johnson history card with a Nixon card, with a Ford card, with a Carter card, with a Reagan card, with a Bush card, with a Clinton card, and now with another Bush card. All that may have changed in the past forty years or so is how respondents of varying partisan persuasions have interpreted the question on trusting the government in Washington under different historical circumstances. And that means we have a pretty big measurement artifact on our hands.

What's to be done? Well, we certainly can't undo the damage by going back and rewriting the standard trust question, more specifically and concretely, to eliminate the artifacts of the past. Nor does it seem likely that the survey organizations using this question can be given sufficient incentives to incorporate, as a standard practice, open-ended, random probes to monitor how respondents are interpreting its meaning (cf. Schuman 1966; T. Smith 1989). Those in charge of the NES, as well as most pollsters, are also likely to continue asking the trust question in its present form, if for no other reason than that it's become a standard indicator that appears to still have some utility. But knowing what we now know about how contaminated this measure has become with presidential approval and its partisan associations in particular historical periods, we should make it a standard practice to present the trend lines and cross-tabulations for trusting the government in Washington separately for those who approve and disapprove of the president's performance, and for strong and weak partisans as well, while controlling for incumbency in the White House and the partisan character of the Congress. In so doing, we will be heeding the sage advice Howard Schuman gave in his presidential address to the American Association for Public Opinion Research (see Schuman 1986, 432–42), when he warned against the referendum point of view and its emphasis on the marginals in the interpretation of the results of public opinion polls: "Don't trust the marginals in any absolute sense is one of the first lessons a person should learn when working with survey data." For, as he keenly reminded us in his own research, the univariate marginal percentages that we routinely present to the public in the form of referendums—saying, for example, that a majority of Americans favor policy X rather than Y—are often too easily affected by the way a question is worded (or by the order and context in which it is presented) to have any absolute, unambiguous meaning. Indeed, he regarded the widespread practice in the field and the press to accept such numbers literally as a picture of public opinion as a naive form of "survey fundamentalism" (Schuman 1998, 441). Likewise, I would argue in the present case that the univariate marginal percentages showing the trend in trusting the government in Washington over the past forty to forty-five years are all too easily affected by changes in the meaning of the question because of changes, among other things, in who is occupying the White House. Naively accepting such trend data as an accurate, absolute measure of Americans' trust in their government is just another form of survey fundamentalism in a different guise. Given the data presented here and elsewhere, the meaning of the decline in trust in the "government in Washington" has become ambiguous at best. So too have many of the other canonical questions in our political attitude and public opinion surveys—presidential approval, the most important problem facing the country, consumer confidence, the mood of the nation, and the like. Ambiguity rules. Understanding how respondents answer survey questions has thus become the foremost theoretical quest in contemporary public opinion research.

A RIVAL THEORY OF THE SURVEY RESPONSE

Faced with multiple problems in the measurement and understanding of public opinion, political scientists John Zaller and Stanley Feldman (1992; also see Zaller 1992) have developed what they call "a simple theory of the survey response," which vigorously challenges the conventional wisdom of the pollsters and many other social scientists: that respondents are merely reporting preexisting "true" attitudes or opinions when they answer survey questions. Instead, they argue, citing evidence from a sizable literature on question form, wording, and context effects, that survey questions do not measure preexisting opinions but rather create them, and that respondents are essentially constructing their opinions at the time they are asked the questions (cf. the cognitive models of the survey response in Krosnick and Alwin 1987; Sudman, Bradburn, and Schwarz 1996; Tourangeau, Rips, and Rasinski 2000). They argue, moreover, that the problem of survey question effects and the well-demonstrated instability of individual responses to survey questions over time have proved to be intractable problems for previous theories such as Converse's (1964, 1970) black-and-white nonattitude model of mass belief systems and "measurement error" models that attempt to explain response instability as a function of the vague language of survey questions (Achen 1975; Erickson 1979). The challenge, as they see it, is to develop a theory that can parsimoniously account for both the phenomenon of apparently random response instability and the typically unpredictable effects of question form, wording, and context on responses to public opinion surveys.

As a solution, Zaller and Feldman propose an axiomatic model of the survey response. Their "ambivalence axiom" assumes, first of all, that "most people possess opposing considerations on most issues, that is, considerations that might lead them to decide the issue either way," where a consideration is defined as a "reason for favoring one side of an issue rather than another" (Zaller and Feldman 1992, 585). For example, a person might think of "government bureaucracy" as a consideration in deciding whether to favor or oppose health care reform legislation. In addition, they postulate two other axioms (586):

1. The "response axiom" assumes "individuals answer survey questions by averaging across the considerations that happen to be salient at the moment of response," where saliency is determined by the "accessibility axiom."
2. The "accessibility axiom" postulates that the "accessibility of any given consideration depends on a stochastic sampling process, where considerations that have been recently thought about are somewhat more likely to be sampled."

With these three basic assumptions they purport to explain a wide variety of findings on survey question effects and response instability in surveys, deducing multiple testable propositions about the nature of the survey response and public opinion. Their analysis, which is based primarily on data from an experiment in a two-wave panel study conducted as part of an NES pilot study, appears to corroborate their model, which has since become the dominant paradigm for most political scientists in understanding the nature of mass opinion (see Zaller 1992 for a full exposition).

An experimental replication by my associates and me (data not presented here; see Bishop et al. 1995), however, suggests that Zaller and Feldman's findings are largely an artifact of the inherent ambiguity and vagueness of the NES questions used in their experiment. For example, the greater the vagueness and ambiguity of such question phrases as "government services" or "increases in government spending," the more likely respondents were to interpret the NES questions in multiple ways and produce the illusion of what Zaller and Feldman (1992) call "opposing considerations." My colleagues and I (Bishop et al. 1995) have thus argued that the basic ambivalence axiom, which underpins Zaller and Feldman's theory of mass opinion and the survey response, is essentially untenable. As an alternative, we have proposed a more parsimonious explanation of survey question effects and response instability: the question ambiguity model. Though it has much in common with previous "measurement error" theories of the survey response, it differs in that it does not make the assumption that respondents have "true attitudes" upon which they base their self-reported opinions. Instead, we assume respondents construct their opinions on the spot, based on how they interpret the question at the moment. Once more, as Clark and Schober (1992, 27) put it, "Respondents . . . make the interpretability presumption: 'each question means what it is obvious to me here now that it means.'"

More formally, I would contend that the following set of propositions would account for much, if not most, of the survey question effects and response instability identified by Zaller and Feldman (1992), among many other investigators, as well as the many findings reported in this and the preceding chapters in this volume (e.g., the ephemeral opinions induced by September 11):

Ambiguity. The greater the ambiguity or vagueness of the meaning of a survey question, the greater will be the variability in interpretations of that question.

Variability. The greater the variability in interpretations of a given question, the greater will be the instability of responses to that question over time.

Susceptibility. The greater the vagueness or ambiguity of the question, the more susceptible respondents will be to variations in the wording and format of the question itself, such as the presence or absence of middle response categories, the order in which the response alternatives are presented, and the sequence and context in which the questions are asked.

Opinionation. The greater the vagueness or ambiguity of the question, the more likely respondents will be to give "no opinion," "don't know," "not sure," "undecided," and other nonsubstantive responses.

By systematically varying the ambiguity, specificity, or concreteness of any given survey question, an investigator can readily test all these propositions. Not only is it readily testable, but the question ambiguity model is also potentially far more useful to the public opinion practitioner since it locates the heart of the problem not so much in the minds of the respondents as in the language of the survey questions themselves—something pollsters can readily do something about.

NOTE

The choice of epigraph for this chapter was suggested by the title of an article by Joseph Tannenhaus and Mary Foley: "The Words of Things Entangle and Confuse," *International Political Science Association* 3, no.1 (1982): 107–29.

7

Spurious Impressions in the Press

> The concept of presidential popularity rating is in largest part an artifact of polling itself.
>
> —Irving Crespi, *Public Opinion, Polls, and Democracy*

Professional public opinion researchers have become increasingly dismayed by the endless proliferation of "pseudopolls" in the mass media, on the Internet, and over the phone. As Herbert Asher (2001) summarizes the abuse in his citizen consumer guide *Polling and the Public*, "pseudo-polls . . . give misleading portraits of public opinion because of loaded and unfair question wording, self-selection biases in the respondents, outright efforts to stack the results, or other deficiencies." Writing in the fiftieth-anniversary issue of *Public Opinion Quarterly*, guest editor Eleanor Singer (1987) bemoans the growing utilization of such polls in the mass media and the lack of quality control over their dissemination: "'Pseudo' Polls (phone-ins, write-ins, interviews with convenience samples) are reported as if they were *real*, discrepancies between polls are reported without explanation, and the newsworthiness of a finding takes precedence over the quality of the process by which it was arrived at" (emphasis added). The increasing prevalence of pseudopolls, I would argue, also reinforces the illusion of a public that is informed and opinionated on just about every topic under the sun. Furthermore, merely reporting the results of such polls in the mass media somehow makes the opinions seem more real and credible than they might otherwise be. Spurious impressions of public opinion occur, however, not just in pseudopolls, but also in a variety of ways in supposedly legitimate polls, ranging from the totally contrived to the unintended consequences of question design and misleading interpretations of the meaning of poll results. The data, as we like to say, don't speak for themselves. And sometimes there are no data at all.[1]

THE CONTRACT WITH AMERICA

One of the best-known examples of misrepresenting public opinion to the American people arose as part of the Republican Party's creation of the Contract with America during the 1994 congressional election campaign. Intended as a unifying campaign theme for GOP congressional candidates, the contract listed ten "common-sense" reforms such as a balanced budget amendment, welfare reform, a strong national defense, and congressional term limits. As part of a widespread media campaign, Republican pollster and strategist Frank Luntz claimed that at least 60 percent of the American public supported each of the ten commonsense reforms (Drinkard 1994, cited in Traugott and Powers 2000). But this claim of public support for the contract turned out to be misleading at best and specious at worst. As Traugott and Powers (2000) tell it in a critique of his claims, Luntz was censured by the American Association for Public Opinion Research for violation of its professional standards of disclosure for publicly reported polls because he refused to provide any data that would verify his claims of public support for the Contract with America. This suggested perhaps that no such data ever existed and that it was all an illusion. Using archival data on public opinion that was readily available, and that could have been used at the time by journalists as an independent check on claims of public support for the contract, Traugott and Powers (2000) show that with the exception of congressional term limits, for which there was evidently strong public support, Luntz's claims were either without foundation or at least subject to other plausible interpretations. For example, on the question of support for a "strong national defense . . . by restoring the essential parts of our national security funding," Traugott and Powers' analysis of data from the National Election Studies shows that public support for increased defense spending had actually declined since the Reagan-Bush era and that only about 25 percent of the American public still favored increasing spending for defense at the time of the 1994 congressional campaign. Data they examined from the National Opinion Research Center General Social Survey in the 1994 period also indicated that, in response to a differently worded question, only a very small percentage of Americans (16 percent) felt we were spending "too little" on military defense; a third (33 percent) actually thought we were spending "too much"; and almost half (47 percent) felt we were spending "about the right amount" (cited in Traugott and Powers 2000). So, contrary to Luntz's claims, they discovered that public support for increased defense spending was far from a supposed majority of "at least 60 percent."

Luntz's claims of public support for welfare reform were likewise misleading, at best. The Contract with America stipulated, "The government should encourage people to work, *not* to have children out of wedlock" (cited in Traugott and Powers 2000). Though most Americans (three out of four), as Traugott and Powers' analysis shows, favored the idea of replacing "welfare with a system of guaranteed public jobs," at the same time they opposed (by 51 percent to 42 percent) the idea of stopping "increases in welfare payments to women who give birth to children while on welfare." This, as Traugott and Powers note, was essentially the heart of what was called for in the contract's welfare reform article. Contrary to Luntz's claim, not only was it not supported by "at least 60 percent," but the majority of Americans on this issue in the *Time*/CNN poll cited by Traugott and Powers (2000) fell in the opposite direction. Public opinion on the welfare issue, they argue, was far too complex to be captured with a single survey question, and "it was not clear that a majority of Americans supported all modes of welfare reform and penalizing mothers and their children."

The myth of public support for the Contract with America, however, tells just part of the story. Polls conducted shortly after the contract was announced and extensively publicized in the mass media, and throughout the rest of the election campaign, revealed that the great majority of Americans knew little or nothing about it. A Gallup survey in early October of 1994 for CNN and *USA Today*, for example, found that three out of four American adults (75 percent) had not heard of the Contract with America. An NBC News/*Wall Street Journal* poll in mid-October discovered that only 12 percent of respondents had heard "a great deal" or a "fair amount" about it; 9 percent had heard "just some"; and the rest (79 percent) had heard "not that much" or nothing at all or were not sure if they had heard anything about it. A national poll carried out by the *Los Angeles Times* at almost exactly the same time reported that the vast bulk of its respondents (82 percent) had likewise not heard or read "anything about a set of proposals recently made by Republicans called 'The Contract with America'" and that just 6 percent had heard "a great deal" or a "good amount" about it. Two weeks before the election, in late October, a survey sponsored by the Times Mirror Center for the People and the Press showed that public awareness of the contract was still quite low: only 29 percent of Americans had heard about "Republican congressional candidates [in 1994] signing a Contract with America." A *Time*/CNN poll conducted two days later by Yankelovich, Inc., produced equally dismal numbers on public awareness: three out of four adults (75 percent) had not heard or read anything at all about the contract. Just one week before the election, seven out of ten respondents (70 percent) in a CBS News/*New York Times* poll still knew nothing about it.

As if that were not enough, two weeks after the electoral triumph of the GOP in the 1994 congressional election—which was regarded in large part as a national referendum on the Contract with America—a follow-up poll by CBS and the *New York Times* found that 70 percent of American adults had still not heard "anything about the Republican 'Contract with America,' which outlines proposals the Republicans in the U.S. House of Representatives promise to vote on in the first 100 days of the new Congress." But if such a small percentage of Americans knew anything about the contract, how could they have voted on it? Public opinion about the contract as a whole, for the most part, did not exist—no more than did public support for the various articles in the contract, contrary to the claims of GOP pollster Frank Luntz. Instead, public opinion about it became an elaborate fabrication foisted on journalists who failed to independently verify Luntz's claims (cf. Traugott and Powers 2000), leaving the broader public essentially unprotected from such a misleading impression.

DENIAL OF THE HOLOCAUST

The cautionary tale of the Holocaust poll controversy has become a classic illustration of how easily public opinion can be misread and misrepresented (Ladd 1994; T. Smith 1995). The tale begins with a survey conducted for the American Jewish Committee (AJC) in November of 1992 by the Roper Organization. Released in conjunction with the dedication of the Holocaust Memorial Museum in April of 1993, the results of the poll produced the shocking headline that perhaps as much as one-third (34 percent) of American adults believed that the Holocaust might never have happened, thus giving potential aid and comfort to the ever-present deniers of the Holocaust. But other public opinion researchers, who were equally stunned by the finding, quickly discovered that the wording of the question that generated these unsettling results was fundamentally flawed (T. Smith 1995). The question asked by the Roper Organization, they argued, confused respondents because it was constructed in a complicated "double negative" form, which read, "Does it seem possible or does it seem impossible to you that the Nazi extermination of the Jews never happened?" Those who believed that the Holocaust did happen, in other words, had to respond that it was "*impossible*" that it *never happened*, an ambiguous option that presumably decreased the percentage of respondents affirming the reality of the Holocaust.

Suspicious of the results produced by this question, the Gallup Organization designed an experiment about a year later (January 15–17, 1994) to assess how much of a difference the wording of the question might have made. All respondents were first asked, "Do you happen to know what the term 'The Holocaust' refers to or not?" Regardless of how they answered (82 percent said yes), they were then informed in the preface to the next question, "The term Holocaust usually refers to the killing of millions of Jews in Nazi death camps during World War II." One random half of the sample then received the double negative version of the question originally asked by the Roper Organization. The other half was read the same preface and then asked, "Do you *doubt* that the Holocaust actually happened, or *not?*" When asked in this way, only a small percentage (9 percent) of respondents expressed any doubt that the Holocaust had actually occurred; another 4 percent said they were not sure, which meant that just 13 percent could possibly be counted as Holocaust skeptics. But, confirming what the Gallup researchers (Moore and Newport 1994) had suspected, when posed in its original double negative form, the question produced almost exactly the same percentage of Holocaust doubters discovered in the Roper survey of November of 1992: 33 percent said it was possible it never happened, and another 2 percent said they were unsure, for a total of 35 percent. To make sure there was no doubt about it, all the respondents were also asked, "Just to clarify, in your opinion, did the Holocaust definitely happen, probably happen, probably *not* happen, or definitely *not* happen?" At this point, nearly everyone (95 percent or more), regardless of which version of the question they had previously been asked, said they thought the Holocaust had definitely or probably happened.

Presumably that settled the matter. The Gallup experiment had conclusively shown that the original double negative form of the question asked by the Roper Organization had unduly alarmed political and intellectual elites about the magnitude and potential of anti-Semitic denial of the Holocaust in America. Based on the follow-up questions it had asked, Gallup estimated that the percentage of true doubters was probably no more than 5 percent at worst (Moore and Newport 1994). The Roper Organization itself concurred. Having been burned by the controversy, Roper (with the consent of the American Jewish Committee) repeated the survey in March of 1994 with an improved version of the initially flawed question. It now read, "Does it seem possible to you that the Nazi extermination of the Jews never happened, or do you feel certain that it happened?" When the question was asked in this new and supposedly correct way, 91 percent felt certain that the Holocaust had happened; only 9 percent expressed any doubt about it, as compared to 34 percent in the original November 1992 Roper survey (see Ladd 1994). Once more, what appeared to be public opinion on a controversial issue—in this case, whether the Holocaust had actually happened—depended on how the question was asked.

The reader should not, however, get the false impression that any of these other ways of asking the question represents a "true" reading of the percentage of those in doubt about the reality of the Holocaust. Consider again the supposedly "right" way (cf. Ladd 1994) in which the Gallup Organization asked the question in its January 1994 experiment: "[As you know,] the term Holocaust usually refers to the killing of millions of Jews in Nazi death camps during World War II. Do you *doubt* that the Holocaust actually happened, or *not?*" To begin with, the question informs respondents, whether they already knew it or not, that there is something called the Holocaust and then defines it for them in a fairly specific way. Having told respondents that it exists, the question then asks them if they doubt it happened, as if to say (implicitly) to respondents, Do you doubt what I just told you to be the case? When the question is phrased in this way, it's a wonder that anyone would say they did doubt it. The framing of the question thus constructs the reality of the Holocaust for the respondent and then validates its existence. More than just another academic demonstration of how variations in the wording of questions affect poll results, this experiment illustrates how readily one illusion of public opinion, "Holocaust denial is a problem," can be replaced by perhaps another, "Holocaust poll is in error." Reality almost never sits so close to the surface.

THE PARADOX OF CLINTON'S APPROVAL RATINGS

In the case of President Bill Clinton, the reality underlying his paradoxically high approval ratings during the worst moments of his presidency became rather elusive, to say the least. Understanding what the standard presidential approval question is measuring, however, represents a big piece of the puzzle. "Do you approve or disapprove of the way [president's name] is handling his job as president?" Asked by the Gallup Organization for over fifty years, and replicated in one form or another by nearly every major polling organization in the United States, this question on presidential job approval has become one of the most frequently used barometers of the overall mood of the country. Conceived during the FDR era as an ongoing referendum on the public's support for keeping the incumbent president in office, it has—with the notable exception of the 2000 presidential election between George W. Bush and Al Gore—proved to be an outstanding predictor of the percentage of the popular vote received by the incumbent party. So it came as a surprise to a great many political scientists, pollsters, and pundits when this indicator failed so badly in forecasting the outcome of the 2000 presidential contest. But it came as an even greater surprise to many of the same prognosticators, in the years immediately preceding the election (1998–1999), when President Clinton's job approval ratings appeared to be impervious to all the adverse publicity he received during the Lewinsky scandal and impeachment episodes.

As the scandal unfolded, many pundits became convinced that Clinton was not long for this political world and that his approval ratings would surely plummet (Kagay 1999). But, paradoxically, his ratings rose rather than fell and remained fairly high throughout his personal and political crises. As Frank Newport (1999), editor in chief of the Gallup Poll, documents in an analysis published several months after the resolution of the impeachment crisis, Clinton's average job approval rating in 1998 (63.8 percent) was 5.7 percentage points higher than it was in 1997 and 12.5 points higher than his administration average during the five years preceding the 1998 crisis. Even more puzzling to many observers, his approval rating, as Newport notes, jumped an average of 5.6 points in the first quarter of 1998, just as the public became aware of the Clinton-Lewinsky liaison. And more baffling still, when the impeachment crisis came to a head in the final months of 1998 and the first quarter of 1999 (as it was debated in the House and Senate), Bill Clinton, as Newport tells it, received "the highest approval ratings of any of the 25 quarters of the Clinton administration to date" (Newport 1999)! Perhaps the most paradoxical and telling data point of all in the Gallup polls is that Clinton got the highest approval rating of his entire presidency (73 percent) at exactly the worst moment of the political crisis (December 19, 1998): when the House of Representatives voted to impeach him on charges of providing false and misleading testimony to a federal grand jury as well as obstruction of justice. None of this fit the standard understanding of how the public should have reacted (see, e.g., Erickson and Tedin 2001, 104–10).

Interpretations of what one scholar (Keeter 1999) called "the perplexing case of public opinion about the Clinton scandal" proliferated nonetheless. The late Everett Carll Ladd (1998) argued that the high approval ratings Clinton received did not measure what everyone thought they did and that the polls were consistently underestimating his real loss in public support. What he called "the 'approval score' trap" indicated merely that most Americans felt generally satisfied with the state of the nation, particularly the performance of the nation's economy. Rating the president highly represented just another way of expressing this satisfaction with the country as a whole. Analyzing the numerous presidential approval polls conducted by the Gallup Organization before, during, and after the Lewinsky/impeachment controversy, Newport (1999) concluded that Clinton's overall job approval ratings in 1998 had remained high because of the public's perception of how well he was handling the economy. He also argued, as did many other observers, that the public separated (some would say "compartmentalized") what it thought of his personal, moral, and ethical behavior in the sexual scandal and its cover-up, of which the public was rather disapproving, from what it thought of the way in which he was doing his public job as president.

Echoing many of the same arguments in his presidential address to the American Association for Public Opinion Research, Michael Kagay (1999), news survey editor at the *New York Times*, presented a pile of evidence from CBS/*New York Times* polls showing that while much of the public was highly critical of the moral values of Bill Clinton, the man, and believed that it was "probably true" that he had "committed perjury in his testimony before the Independent Counsel's grand jury," a majority continued to think he was still doing a pretty good job of handling his responsibilities as president and remained opposed throughout it all to his impeachment and removal from office. And, much like respondents to the Gallup surveys, the great majority of those responding to the CBS/*New York Times* polls in 1998 viewed Bill Clinton's relationship with Monica Lewinsky "more as a private matter having to do with Bill Clinton's personal life" than with "Bill Clinton's job as President." As a consequence, many, if not most, public opinion researchers have come to believe that the public's separation of Bill Clinton, the man, from Bill Clinton, the president, made it possible for a majority to continue approving of "the way he is handling his job as president." That is now the conventional wisdom (see, e.g., Brody 1998; Newport 2001a).

But the conventional wisdom, I would contend, may represent no more than another illusion generated by a misunderstanding of what the standard question on presidential approval was actually measuring during President Clinton's scandal-and-impeachment predicament. First, consider what it was not measuring. Contrary to what many may now believe, the *variations* in President Clinton's approval ratings during the period in question (January 1998 to the first quarter of 1999) bore little or no relationship to Americans' satisfaction with the way things were going in the country at the time, to how they thought the economy was doing, or even to how they thought he was handling the economy. Take, for example, the standard Gallup measure of the public's satisfaction with life in the United States: "In general, are you satisfied or dissatisfied with the way things are going in the United States at this time?" In January of 1998, shortly after the news of the sexual liaison with Monica Lewinsky broke in the *Washington Post* (January 21), a Gallup poll found that 63 percent of Americans were satisfied with the way things were going in the United States. As the data in figure 7.1 indicate, satisfaction with the state of the nation hovered around 60 percent for the next eight months; it then dropped precipitously to 50 percent in the period from late October to the end of December—precisely during the height of President Clinton's political crisis, after the House had begun impeachment proceedings (October 8) and, later, voted articles of impeachment (December 11–

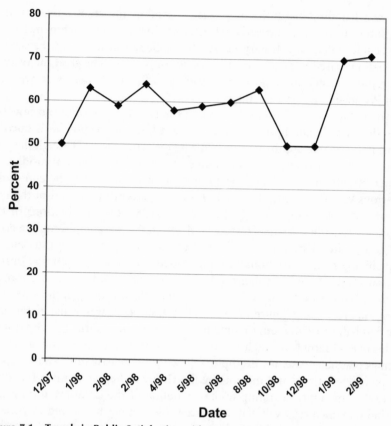

Figure 7.1 Trends in Public Satisfaction with State of Nation: 1997–1999

Response: Satisfied

Question: "In general, are you satisfied or dissatisfied with the way things are going in the United States at this time?"

Source: Gallup surveys archived in POLL database, Roper Center for Public Opinion Research, University of Connecticut.

12). But at the same time, Clinton's approval ratings were climbing to an all-time high of 73 percent (December 19–20).

So, contrary to Ladd's (1998) argument about "the 'approval score' trap," satisfaction with the state of the nation and the president's approval ratings were moving in opposite or, at best, unrelated directions; the approval ratings were definitely not tracking the satisfaction trends. If anything, it appears that many Americans were actually responding with evident dissatisfaction to what was happening in Washington in the final months of 1998 while at the same time registering their strong approval of the way Bill Clinton was handling his duties as president. And as the crisis moved toward resolution in January and early February of 1999 (the impeachment trial in the Senate ended on February 12, 1999), public satisfaction with the state of the nation soared to an all-time high of 70–71 percent. The great majority of Americans seemed to be saying they were glad the whole mess was over and that President Clinton was still in charge.

The public's evaluation of the state of the nation's economy and how the president was handling it also seem to have little connection with fluctuations in his overall approval ratings during the crisis period. Though the percentage of Americans rating "economic conditions in the country today" as either "good" or "excellent" had jumped from 48 percent at the end of the previous year (December 18–21, 1997) to 66 percent by the end of the first quarter in the Gallup poll (March 20–22, 1998), their evaluations of the economy remained relatively steady and within the margin of sampling error (plus or minus 3 percent) for the rest of the crisis period and thus cannot explain any of the variations in the president's overall job approval during the same time frame (see figure 7.2). Nor does the trend in public approval of the job the president was doing in handling the economy in the CBS/*New York Times* polls (see figure 7.3; the Gallup time series was available for only the first half of 1998) seem to quite mirror the nuances of the ups and downs in his overall ratings throughout the year of turmoil. As his overall approval ratings gradually rose, for example, following the release of the Starr report (September 9, 1998) and the vote by the House of Representatives (October 8, 1998), the approval rating for his handling of the economy during this period remained relatively flat: 71 percent (September 8–10) and 70 percent (October 12–13). And though his ratings shot up at the end of December 1998—reaching their highest point ever (73 percent for December 19–20)— and stayed close to the high point of his presidency throughout the month of January (1999), the public's rating of his handling of the economy in the CBS/*New York Times* polls did not budge from November 15, 1998 (76 percent) to January of 1999 (76 percent). So how could it possibly explain what happened? Clinton's overall approval ratings, in other words, were not tracking his handling of the nation's economy (cf. Newport 1999). Something else was going on.

An intriguing clue to what was going on came from a quasi-experimental before-and-after set of surveys conducted by the Gallup Organization during the early days of the scandal period. In the weeks just before the revelation of the scandal in the *Washington Post* (January 21, 1998), President Clinton's overall approval ratings hovered around 59–60 percent (see polls for January 6–7 and 16–18, 1998, in figure 7.4). Surprisingly, the polls conducted by Gallup immediately after the scandal hit the press (January 23–24, 24–25, 25–26,

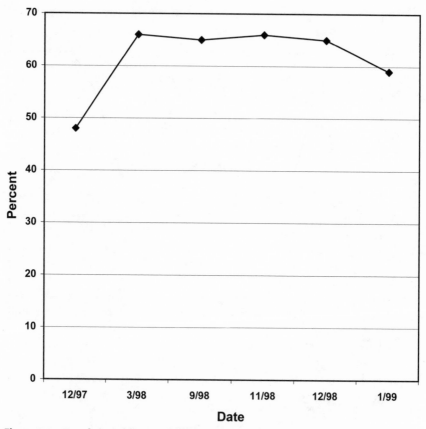

Figure 7.2   Trends in Public's Evaluation of Nation's Economy: 1997–1999

Response: Excellent and good
Question: "How would you rate economic conditions in this country today—excellent, good, only fair, or poor?"
Source: Gallup surveys archived in POLL database, Roper Center for Public Opinion Research, University of Connecticut.

1998) produced no evidence of any change whatsoever. Clinton's ratings continued to hover around 59 percent. But several days later, right after he gave his State of the Union address (January 27, 1998), his approval ratings shot up from 59 percent the previous weekend to 67 percent (January 28, 1998). Even more telling, as David Moore (1998) observes in his analysis of these poll numbers, the increase in Clinton's approval score occurred only among independents and Republicans. In both groups, Clinton's ratings jumped by about twelve percentage points, whereas among Democrats, who already rated him quite highly (88 percent), there was no change at all. The

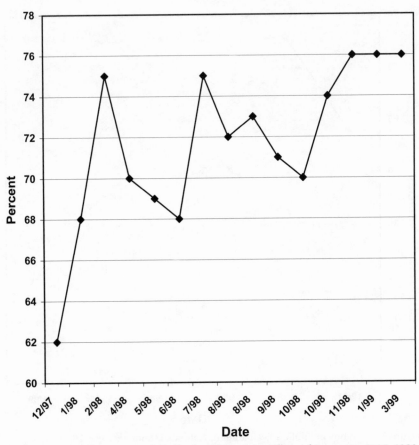

Date

Figure 7.3   Trends in Approval Rating for Clinton's Handling of Economy: 1997–1999

Response: Approve
Question: "How about the economy? Do you approve or disapprove of the way Bill Clinton is handling the economy?"
Source: CBS News/*New York Times* surveys archived in POLL database, Roper Center for Public Opinion Research, University of Connecticut.

same pattern, as Moore notes, turned up on other indicators of support for Clinton. Before-and-after favorable ratings of him as a person went up eight percentage points overall (55 percent to 63 percent), but the shift showed up only among independents (fifteen points) and Republicans (four points). Perhaps most telling of all, the biggest boost for Clinton, as Moore points out, "came in the number of Americans who have confidence in his ability to carry out his duties as president." The percentage saying they were either "very" or "somewhat" confident jumped from 63 percent before his State of

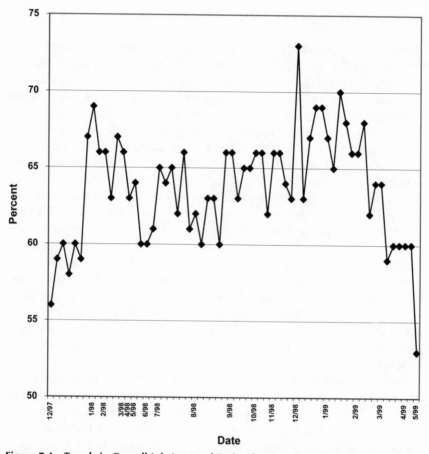

Date

Figure 7.4   Trends in Overall Job Approval Rating for President Clinton: 1997–1999

Response: Approve
Source: Gallup surveys archived in POLL database, Roper Center for Public Opinion Research, University of Connecticut.

the Union address to 76 percent afterward, with the largest increases coming, once again, among Republicans (19 percent) and independents (14 percent). In other words, despite the shocking revelation about his extramarital affair with Monica Lewinsky, his State of the Union address reassured the American people—particularly independents and Republicans—not so much about the state of the economy and other domestic and world affairs, but rather that he could still carry out his day-to-day duties as president under the extreme pressures now facing him. That, essentially, is what the Lewinsky crisis made salient to respondents as they interpreted the question, "Do you approve or disapprove of the way Bill Clinton is handling his job as president?"

Why is this so crucial to understanding the public's reaction? What becomes salient to the public in the press, as we now know from the work of presidential scholar George Edwards and his colleagues (Edwards, Mitchell, and Welch 1995), is what explains changes in presidential approval. When asked if they "approve or disapprove of the way [president's name] is handling his job as president," respondents will generally interpret the question by evaluating the president's performance in terms of whatever issue has been made salient to them by extensive coverage in the mass media—the well-established "media priming effect" (see Zaller 1992, chap. 5). To take one of the more conspicuous examples, the overall approval ratings of George H. W. Bush rose dramatically as the Persian Gulf War and his handling of foreign policy became highly salient to the American public (see Edwards, Mitchell, and Welch's 1995 analysis of "the Bush paradox") and then dropped precipitously once the war ended and the deteriorating condition of the economy moved to the top of the mass media's agenda. So too did Ronald Reagan's approval ratings plummet once the Iran-Contra affair became salient to the American public because of extensive coverage in the mass media (Brody 1991, cited in Edwards, Mitchell, and Welch 1995; also see King and Schudson 1995 on the press's illusion of public opinion about Ronald Reagan's popularity).

Similarly, for Bill Clinton, I would argue, what became salient to the American people in their evaluations of his performance, beginning in January of 1998 and continuing until the conclusion of the impeachment trial in the Senate in February of 1999, was not the economy or the state of the nation but rather his obvious struggle with the personal and political crises facing him. Their high approval ratings of the way he was "handling his job as president," particularly when the going got really rough at the time of his impeachment by the House (December 1998), became another way of saying that he was doing the best job that could be done under extremely trying circumstances. In this sense, contrary to what various polling analysts have argued (cf. Kagay 1999; Newport 1999), the public did consider the implications of the scandal-and-impeachment circumstances to be "job related"; they became a test of Clinton's ability to carry out his duties as president—as a man under fire. Once the crisis had passed, with his acquittal on all charges by the U.S. Senate, Clinton's approval ratings, as Newport (1999) observes, began to slide to one of their lowest levels ever (53 percent by May of 1999). His ability to carry out his duties under fire was, in other words, no longer a salient criterion for evaluating his day-to-day performance as president. A failure to understand this key element of what the question on approval of

President Clinton was measuring all along, then, generated a highly misleading impression of American public opinion and a historical myth about why his presidency survived: because of the way he was handling the economy.

CREATIONISM IN PUBLIC SCHOOLS

"Americans Support Teaching Creationism as Well as Evolution in Public Schools"—so proclaimed the Gallup poll release (Moore 1999) in the wake of the Kansas Board of Education's August 1999 decision to downgrade the teaching of evolution in public schools. Dating back to the days of the Scopes "monkey trial" (1925), the creation-evolution controversy emerged briefly as an issue in the 2000 presidential campaign, when candidates George W. Bush and Al Gore each said they supported the teaching of creationism along with evolution in public schools if that's what the citizens of Kansas wanted to do. Such is the power of religion in American politics. And such, I would argue, is the potential of polls, like the one released by Gallup on the heels of the Kansas decision, to mislead policy makers, politicians, and the public alike. For it gave the unmistakable impression that this was an issue to which the American public had given some thought—only 3 percent of the poll's respondents had "no opinion" on the subject—and on which it had therefore arrived at an informed opinion. Furthermore, Americans supposedly favored the educational policy of "teaching creationism ALONG WITH evolution in public schools" by a whopping margin of better than two to one (68 percent to 29 percent).

The Gallup poll release went on to say that a majority of Americans (55 percent) would, however, oppose replacing the teaching of evolution altogether with creationism, but that was neither the big story that the poll headline reported nor the news that was disseminated by the poll's cosponsors in the press: CNN and *USA Today*. The big news story was about Americans' support for creationism—not to mention, as the release did, that nearly half the American public (47 percent) also believed in the biblical version of creation that "God created human beings pretty much in their present form at one time within the last 10,000 years or so." Not unexpectedly, the evangelistic organization Answers in Genesis (AIG) took great pleasure in the results, announcing in its international newsletter that "AIG is encouraged to hear the results of a recent CNN poll that revealed that 68 percent of Americans believe creation should be taught in schools" (Answers in Genesis 2000). A creationist-sympathetic American public thus became the dominant image in the mass media.

But, once more, a press release by a reputable polling organization had created a highly misleading impression of American public opinion. Just a few months later (November 2000), a national survey commissioned by the People for the American Way and conducted by the Daniel Yankelovich Group (DYG 2000) turned up a startling piece of evidence: When asked, first of all, "Have you ever heard the term Creationism?" nearly half of American adults either said "no" (45 percent) or that they were "not sure" (2 percent). Interviewers then asked those who claimed they had heard of it (53 percent), "How familiar are you with Creationism? Are you very familiar, somewhat familiar, or not that familiar with it?" At this point, even by an ambiguous, self-defined standard, less than half of the respondents (41 percent) indicated they were "very familiar" with it; 39 percent said they were "somewhat familiar" (whatever that means); and 20 percent now acknowledged that they were "not that familiar" with it—meaning that well over half the sample (57 percent) had either never heard of the term *creationism* or was unfamiliar with it. Furthermore, among those who claimed to have heard of it, a sizable number (36 percent), even when explicitly given two alternative definitions of the term *creationism*, chose the incorrect response (DYG 2000). Much of the public, then, was poorly informed, at best, on the subject of creationism but was induced by the Gallup/CNN/*USA Today* poll into offering an opinion on the issue of teaching it along with evolution in the public schools.

Understanding how the Gallup poll induced such opinions about the creationism issue in this case provides an object lesson as to how an illusion of public opinion can be generated in public opinion surveys more generally. Consider the context in which the question about creationism was asked. The transition to the sequence of questions read, "Next I'm going to read a variety of proposals concerning *religion and public schools*. For each one, please tell me whether you would generally favor or oppose it. First, ... Next, . . ." (emphasis added). Respondents were then presented a set of proposals in either the following order or in the reverse order:

1. Making public school facilities available after school hours for use by student groups
2. Allowing public schools to display the Ten Commandments
3. Allowing students to say prayers at graduation ceremonies as part of the official program
4. Using the Bible in literature, history, and social studies classes
5. Allowing daily prayer to be spoken in the classroom
6. Teaching creationism ALONG WITH evolution in public schools
7. Teaching creationism INSTEAD OF evolution in public schools

Regardless of the sequence in which these proposals were presented, the question became fundamentally one about whether religion should have any place in the public schools. Whether respondents knew much, if anything, about creationism, they knew it has something to do with *religion and public schools*, as they were informed in the preface to the sequence of questions. For many respondents, saying they favored "teaching creationism ALONG WITH evolution in public schools" became just another way of expressing their general support for the idea of religion having a role to play in public education. The constitutional issue of separation of church and state and the policy implications of their answers, which are of significant substantive interest to elites who interpret poll results, probably had little or no bearing on how many of them responded to the question. So while many respondents may have answered the question on the basis of their general attitudes toward the idea of religion having some place in the public schools, that is neither the specific policy issue the question was meant to address, nor the one that journalists, policy makers, and politicians have in mind as they interpret poll results based on such questions. Because of the way it was constructed—with no explicit opportunity for respondents to say they didn't know much, if anything, about creationism—and the context in which it was presented, the question about teaching creationism ended up measuring a vague, generalized attitude toward religion in public schools, but created the illusion that it measured something more substantively specific than that. To that extent, the question represents an invalid measure of public opinion on the creation-evolution issue, not only in the usual sense of not measuring what it was intended to measure, but also in the sense that Schuman (1998) means when he talks about validity as understanding what one has measured, even if it is partly or completely different from what one intended to measure.

THE CASE OF "INTELLIGENT DESIGN"

Another equally misleading impression of public opinion showed up in a series of recent polls about what some would say is just creationism in another guise: "intelligent design." Despite a pile of previous evidence showing the American public to be inattentive and uninformed about numerous aspects of public affairs, such as creationism versus evolution, many national and regional polls often fail to screen out respondents who know little or nothing about the subjects of the questions they ask. Not only that, but polling organizations frequently encourage respondents to answer such questions by presuming they are familiar with the topic. Survey questions of this kind typically begin by saying to the respondent, "As you may know . . . ," or by providing some other informative preamble. Pollsters generally defend these practices by saying they're just a way to find out how respondents would think about the issue or topic if they did know more about it. But such practices can result in illusions of an informed public that seriously mislead the policy-making powers that be.

Recent public opinion polls in Ohio on the issue of intelligent design illustrate just how misleading such findings can be. In 2002, the idea that an intelligent designer or some supernatural force created the universe and guided the development of human life became the center of a heated controversy among Ohio educators. Throughout the year, the State Board of Education in Ohio wrestled with the policy issue of whether to teach intelligent design in public school science classes as an alternative to the scientific theory of evolution. In October, a committee of the Ohio Board of Education recommended "that science classes in the state emphasize both evolution and the debate over its validity . . . and left it up to individual school districts to decide whether to include in the debate the concept of 'intelligent design'" (Associated Press, October 14, 2002). As far as most college and university science professors in Ohio were concerned, however, the concept of intelligent design did not have a shred of scientific evidence to support it and was essentially a religious view that did not belong in the science curriculum of the public schools (table 7.1). Despite this expert opinion, "public opinion" polls on the issue played an important role in telling the powers that be that a seemingly informed public wanted them to do otherwise.

Consider some of the headlines and news stories about public opinion produced by polls on the intelligent design issue:

1. *"Ohioans Don't Want Evolution Only."* In an article for the *Columbus Dispatch* (May 10, 2002), Catherine Candisky cited a poll conducted by Zogby International for an intelligent design advocacy group, the Discovery Institute, claiming "nearly two-thirds of Ohioans support instruction about both Darwin's theory of evolution and any scientific evidence against it."
2. *"Poll: Teach More Than Evolution; A Majority of Those Surveyed Want Evolution, Intelligent Design to Get Equal Time in Schools."* Writing in the Cleveland *Plain Dealer* (June 9, 2002), Scott Stephens and John Mangels reported the results of a statewide poll commissioned by the *Plain Dealer* and conducted by the Mason-Dixon polling organization. It showed that "a clear majority of the state's residents—59 percent—favor teaching evolution in tandem with intelligent design in public school science classes."
3. *"Ohioans: Teach Darwin, Design."* Picking up on the drumbeat of the *Plain Dealer* poll, the Associated Press (June 2002) told Ohio and the rest of the world that "a majority of Ohioans want public schools to

Table 7.1.   Expert Opinions of Ohio Science Professors on Intelligent Design

"The concept of 'intelligent design' is that life and the universe are too complex to have developed without the intervention of a purposeful being or force to guide the development of life. Which of the following do you think best describes it?"

Strongly supported by scientific evidence	2%
Partly supported by scientific evidence	5
Not supported at all by scientific evidence	90
Not sure	3

"Do you think the concept of 'intelligent design' is primarily a religious view?"

Yes	91%
No	5
Not sure	4

"Do you think Ohio high school students should be tested on their understanding of the basic principles of the theory of evolution in order to graduate?"

Yes	92%
No	4
Not sure	3

"Do you think Ohio high school students should be tested on their knowledge of the concept of 'intelligent design' in order to graduate?"

Yes	6%
No	90
Not sure	4

Source: Web survey of 460 science professors in Ohio colleges and universities by the Internet Public Opinion Laboratory at the University of Cincinnati, September 26–October 9, 2002.

teach evolution and a concept called 'intelligent design' when they discuss how life originated and changed."

For better or for worse, these headlines and news accounts became the *reality* of public opinion for the Ohio Board of Education, editorial writers, various pundits, and, of course, the politicians. On the contrary, I would contend that public opinion on the intelligent design issue, as it was presented in the press, was mostly an illusion produced wittingly or unwittingly by those who commissioned and conducted the polls. Consider the following piece of evidence from an Ohio Poll conducted by the Institute for Policy Research at the University of Cincinnati in September 2002 (Rademacher 2002). A statewide sample of Ohioans was asked, "Do you happen to know anything about the concept of 'intelligent design'?"

Despite the significant coverage, editorials, and polls on the intelligent design issue that had been presented in Ohio's news media for several months, the vast majority of Ohioans (84 percent) said "no"; they knew little or nothing about it. Only 14 percent said "yes" (and who knows what they actually knew), and the rest (2 percent) were "not sure." In other words, the great majority of Ohioans did not know enough about the concept of intelligent design to have formed an opinion (table 7.2). The vast majority of Ohioans probably also knew little or nothing about the nature of scientific evidence or what a scientific theory of evolution actually means. And yet they had appeared to be quite informed about this policy issue, according to the polls conducted by Zogby for the Discovery Institute—an advocacy organization for the intelligent design movement based in Seattle—and by Mason-Dixon for the Cleveland *Plain Dealer*. How was this false and misleading impression created? In one instance, it was done with leading questions; in the other, by educating the respondents.

Leading and Misleading Questions

The poll conducted by Zogby International (May 2002) for the Discovery Institute offers a classic example of how to bring a respondent to a desired conclusion (table 7.3). Like many other advocacy polls, the Zogby survey generated the false impression of an informed and opinionated public by first educating respondents about the issue and then asking them whether they had an opinion on it. In fact, it didn't even ask respondents whether they had heard or read anything about the intelligent design controversy but instead informed them in a seemingly even-handed manner—the standard "fairness" tactic of intelligent design advocates—that "the Ohio State Board of

---

Table 7.2. Responses to Ohio Poll Questions on Intelligent Design

1. "Do you happen to know anything about the concept of 'intelligent design'?"

Yes	14%
No/don't know anything about it	84
Not sure	2

2. "The concept of 'intelligent design' is that life is too complex to have developed by chance, and that a purposeful being or force is guiding the development of life. What is your opinion—do you think the concept of 'intelligent design' is a valid scientific account of how human life developed, or is it basically a religious explanation of the development of human life?"

Valid scientific account	21%
Religious explanation	54
Both (volunteered)	7
Not sure/don't know	17

Source: Ohio Poll, September 2002, Institute for Policy Research, University of Cincinnati.

Table 7.3. Responses to Zogby Poll Questions on Intelligent Design

1. "The Ohio State Board of Education is currently trying to decide whether high school students should learn both evidence for and against Darwin's theory of evolution. Regarding teaching the theory of evolution, which of the following two statements comes closer to your own opinion?

    A. Biology teachers should teach only Darwin's theory of evolution and the scientific evidence that supports it.

    B. Biology teachers should teach Darwin's theory of evolution, but also the scientific evidence against it."

       Results:

Teach only Darwin and evidence *for* it	19%
Teach Darwin and evidence *against* it	65
Neither/not sure	16

2. "Do you strongly agree, somewhat agree, somewhat disagree, or strongly disagree with the following statement? When Darwin's theory of evolution is taught in school, students should also *be able to learn* about scientific evidence that points to an *intelligent design* of life."

       Results:

Strongly agree	55%	
		Total agree = 78%
Somewhat agree	23	
Somewhat disagree	3	
		Total disagree = 13
Strongly disagree	10	
Not sure	9	

Source: Zogby International poll of 702 Ohio adults conducted May 7–8, 2002.
Note: Emphasis added by author throughout.

Education is currently trying to decide whether high school students should learn *both* evidence *for* and *against* Darwin's theory of evolution" (emphasis added). Respondents were then asked, "Regarding teaching the theory of evolution, which of the following two statements comes closer to your own opinion? A: Biology teachers should teach only Darwin's theory of evolution and the scientific evidence that supports it. B: Biology teachers should teach Darwin's theory of evolution, but also the scientific evidence against it." Not surprisingly, nearly two-thirds of Ohioans (65 percent) picked alternative B, not because they understood anything about scientific evidence, rival scientific theories, or the policy implications of their answers for the controversial decision facing the State Board of Education, but most likely because they endorsed the democratic, fair-minded idea of presenting evidence for and against any theory. After all, there are two sides to every issue.

Having gotten them to express an opinion with the general "fairness" framing of the issue, the Zogby poll then led respondents to the psychological implications of their answer by asking them, "Do you strongly agree, some-what agree, somewhat disagree, or strongly disagree with the following state-ment? When Darwin's theory of evolution is taught in school, students should also *be able to learn* about scientific evidence that points to an *intelligent design* of life" (emphasis added). Even though most respondents had probably never heard or read a thing about the concept of intelligent design, by a margin of more than six to one, they were more likely to agree (78 percent) than disagree (13 percent) with this apparently even-handed proposition, and just 9 percent said they were "not sure" (Zogby International 2002). Ergo, the headline "Ohioans Don't Want Evolution Only" in the *Columbus Dispatch* (May 10, 2002) represented what appeared to be an example of a well-formed "public opinion" on a controversial issue confronting the State Board of Education.

Educating the Respondent

Nor was this the only example of a seemingly well-informed public on the intelligent design issue. Just several weeks later, a statewide poll on the topic of evolution and intelligent design commissioned by the Cleveland *Plain Dealer* and conducted by the Washington-based survey organization Mason-Dixon gave the exact same impression of a decided majority. Said the head-line in the *Plain Dealer* (Stephens and Mangels 2002), "A Majority of Those Surveyed Want Evolution, Intelligent Design to Get Equal Time in Schools." Disseminating the same poll story, the Associated Press (2002b) proclaimed, "Ohioans: Teach Darwin, Design." Though better designed, free of advocacy, and much more comprehensive than those in the Zogby poll, the questions asked in the Cleveland *Plain Dealer* survey created the same misleading impression of an informed public that understood the complexities of the intelligent design issue and had formed an opinion on it.

But when asked how familiar they were with the concept of intelligent design, fewer than one out of five (18 percent) said they were "very familiar" with the idea; 37 percent indicated they were just "somewhat familiar" with it; and close to half (45 percent) admitted they were "not that familiar" at all with the notion. Regardless of how familiar they were with the idea of intelligent design, the *Plain Dealer* poll educated respondents as to what it was about in a follow-up question and then asked them to pass judgment on its *validity*: "The concept of intelligent design is that life is too complex to have developed by chance, and a purposeful being or force is guiding the development of life. Which of the following best describes your view of intelligent design . . . ?" About a fourth (23 percent) considered it a "completely valid account of how humans were developed"; nearly half (48 percent) regarded it as a "somewhat valid account"; and just 22 percent thought it was "not a valid account." The rest said they were "not sure." But what could the public possibly understand *validity* to mean?

Furthermore, as *Plain Dealer* reporters Scott Stephens and John Mangels (2002) make clear in their analysis of the poll, the great majority of respondents understood the religious undertones of the question about "a purposeful being or force that is guiding the development of life": "Two-thirds of the poll respondents believe the unspecified 'designer' in intelligent design really is God. In fact, that's part of the attraction." For many respondents, then, the question on intelligent design was interpreted not so much as a question about how human life actually developed but rather as a test of whether they believed in God, making it much easier for them to generate an opinion on the concept of intelligent design. Having brought the respondents up to intellectual speed with prior explanations of intelligent design and questions about God's role in the development of life on earth, the poll then got to the heart of the "equal time" issue by asking them the following question on what should be taught about the concepts of evolution and intelligent design in public schools: "Currently, the Ohio Board of Education is debating new academic standards for public school science classes, including what to teach about the development of life on earth. Which position do you support—teach only evolution, teach only intelligent design, teach both, teach the evidence both for and against evolution, but not necessarily intelligent design, or teach nothing about human development?" Unsurprisingly, given the "fairness" framing of the issue, a sizable majority (59 percent) of those polled favored the even-handed position of "teach both." The Cleveland *Plain Dealer* (Stephens and Mangels 2002) could now characterize public opinion in Ohio on the issue as decisive: "A majority of those surveyed want evolution, intelligent design to get equal time in schools" (table 7.4). Case closed.

CONCLUSION

Far from an isolated example, the type of illusion of public opinion generated by the Zogby and *Plain Dealer* polls on the issue of intelligent design represents an all-too-common occurrence in contemporary survey research. As I have argued here and elsewhere, such illusions have become more ubiquitous than ever, not only because of the proliferation of "pseudopolls" in the mass media that give the false impression of a public that has opinions on nearly every topic under the sun, but also, as outlined at the outset (chapter 1), because of chronic problems in the practice of asking survey questions: (1)

Table 7.4. Ohio "Public Opinion" on Teaching Evolution vs. Intelligent Design

"Currently, the Ohio Board of Education is debating new academic standards for public school science classes, including what to teach about the development of life on earth. Which position do you support?"

Teach only evolution	
Teach only intelligent design	
Teach both	59%
Teach the evidence both for and against evolution, but not necessarily intelligent design	
Teach nothing about human development	

"Should the state Board of Education require that intelligent design be part of the curriculum, or should this decision be left to local school boards and teachers?"

State Board of Education	33%
Local school boards and teachers	50
Not sure	16

"When it comes to teaching public school students in science class about the development of life, is it more important to teach only theories for which there is scientific consensus or teach all alternative concepts out of respect for individuals' beliefs?"

Teach only theories for which there is scientific consensus	27%
Teach all alternative concepts out of respect for individuals' beliefs	60
Not sure	13

Source: Cleveland *Plain Dealer* poll of 1,507 Ohio adults conducted May 28–June 4, 2002, by Mason-Dixon Polling & Research.

widespread public ignorance of public affairs, (2) the inherent vagueness of the language used in most survey questions, and (3) the unpredictable influence of variations in question form, wording, and context.

The danger in all this, of course, is that because there is typically no peer review of such "direct to the media" polls, nor any sort of journalistic gatekeeping (Newport 1998), virtually no one can tell the difference once the poll results are released to the public. The prestige of the polling organization releasing the results and the statistical percentages, accompanied with the usual reassuring scientific statement about sampling error, gives the impression that it is all just as reality based as a standard preelection poll. Unlike preelection polls, however, there is no Wednesday morning reality check with behavioral evidence. The result is a misled and unprotected public.

Some pollsters may, of course, prefer to continue business as usual, manufacturing opinions with lead-in phrases like "As you may know . . ." and other preambles that educate the respondent. If, on the other hand, they were to use filter questions on a regular basis to screen out the less well informed, it would probably not make good copy to report, again and again, that large numbers of citizens, and in some cases majorities, have no opinions on issues of everyday discourse in elite political, journalistic, and academic circles. But I think we do the public and the powers that be a great disservice by continuing to manufacture artificial and illusory portraits of an informed public on issues like intelligent design when we could do so much better. In the case of intelligent design, the power of the pollsters did a great disservice to the scientific community as well. So it's not pseudopolls alone that generate spurious impressions of public opinion in the press.

NOTE

1. The poll findings cited throughout this chapter on American public opinion were, except as otherwise noted, compiled from the following sources: the Roper Center for Public Opinion Research's online Public Opinion Location Library (POLL), the Polling Report (www.pollingreport.com), and the Gallup Organization's online poll data archive (brain.gallup.com).

8

Illusions of Causality: Asking Why

Asked, "Why are you doing that?" a superstitious person is likely to invent an answer.

—B. F. Skinner, *About Behaviorism*

Poll numbers, as we say, don't speak for themselves. Indeed, ever since pollsters began asking survey questions in the 1930s, they have rarely been content with merely describing the raw statistical results of their polls: what they call "the marginals." Like most of their journalistic contemporaries, they usually want to interpret what the poll findings mean. In most instances, this involves making inferences about why the public thinks the way it does about a particular issue, why the electorate voted for one political candidate or party, and the like (cf. Bauman and Lavrakas 2000). Breaking the results down by various demographic variables (age, race, sex, income, religion, party identification, etc.) in the form of cross-tabulations, or "cross-tabs," typically provides pollsters with some clues about what might be driving public opinion. But for many public opinion analysts, cross-tabs do not go far enough. In addition, they often believe that it is both necessary and feasible, causally speaking, to ask respondents directly about the reasons why they think and behave the way they do. Much as his sociological contemporary Paul Lazarsfeld (1944) did, George Gallup (1947) believed early on that it was possible to get at the reasons behind an individual's views by asking a simple question like, "Why do you feel that way?" Questions like this were, in fact, a key element in his elaborate "quintamensional plan" for question design. Asking why had likewise become essential to many of Gallup's pollster peer group. Commenting on the frequent practice of asking open-ended follow-up questions in public opinion polls during this era, Stanley Payne (1951) described the many variations of the "reason why" question he had discovered—among them: "Why would you say that?" "Why would you vote this way?" "What makes you say that?" "What would you say are the reasons?" "What do you think may have been the main reasons for this?" "What caused you to change your mind?" Though most cognitively oriented psychologists today would regard these follow-up probes as naive, primitive attempts to establish the causal sources of an individual's opinions, attitudes, and behavior, the practice of asking such "why" questions, in ever newer and more varied forms, has remarkably persisted to the present time.

CAUSAL VERSUS PLAUSIBLE REASONS

Consider just some recent examples from major national and regional polling organizations in the United States.[1] As part of the bipartisan Battleground 2002 Survey, the Tarrance Group and its associates (June 9–11, 2002) asked a national sample of registered likely voters, "Being as specific as you can, what are one or two reasons why you approve of the way George W. Bush is handling his job as president?" Following up on its standard presidential popularity question—"Do you approve or disapprove of the way George W. Bush is handling his job as president?"—the Gallup Organization periodically asks respondents, "Why do you approve/disapprove of the way Bush is handling his job as president?" The Ohio Poll uses a very similar follow-up probe to its standard approval question: "And could you tell me why it is you approve/disapprove of the way President Bush is handling his job as president?" Respondents readily answer such questions and typically give an amazing variety of answers (see, e.g., Gallup News Service 2001a). But, except in a naive, folk-minded way, these self-reports of why respondents approve or disapprove of the president's performance tell us little or nothing about the multiple social, economic, and autobiographical causes of their opinions about the president. Instead, the answers given appear to represent mostly plausible reasons or justifications for why they approve or disapprove of the president, as illustrated by such verbatim reactions as (Gallup News Service 2001a), "He hasn't done any worse than Clinton," "He's conservative," "He's honest," "I'm a Republican and I voted for him and I just like his tax policy," "I feel like he's a good Christian on his views on abortion and everything," "I just like him," "Taking charge," and, "Things seem to be going fine." And while many pollsters and social scientists may be skeptical of such dubious, superficial self-reports, others treat them as if they provide some unique causal insight into the president's approval ratings.

A press release of the Ohio Poll (Rademacher and Shaw 2001) illustrates this widespread tendency to make implicit causal attributions about the president's approval ratings based simply on responses to open-ended follow-up questions that ask why. After reporting in the headline, "President's Approval Holds Steady at 60 Percent," the story then goes on to say in the next subheading, "Bush's Tax Cut and Tax Policies Top Reasons for Approval." Being especially interested in answering "why" questions (Bauman and Lavrakas 2000), journalists who read these poll releases and disseminate them will almost invariably reinforce the idea that the president's policies are somehow causally responsible for the rise and fall in his approval ratings. This naive way of thinking about "reasons" fits very well, of course, with the typical layperson's folk epistemology and illusions of conscious will (Wegner 2002) that attribute causation to individuals rather than situational, social, and historical forces. So when poll stories make such causal attributions about Americans approving or disapproving of the president because of what they say about his tax policy or some other thing, the stories only confirm the way most journalists, politicians, pundits, and policy makers reason about why people do what they do: because of conscious decisions by individual citizens.

The same kind of naive causal reasoning turns up again and again in numerous national polls with just different ways of asking the why question. An example from a recent national survey on the issue of stem cell research conducted by Princeton Survey Research and Associates for the Pew Forum on Religion and Public Life (Pew Research Center 2002c) asked respondents to make causal attributions about various sources of influence on their thinking: "Which one of the following has had the *biggest influence* on your thinking on this issue [the government should/should not fund stem cell research, or it depends]? A personal experience, the views of your friends and family, what you have seen or read in the media, your religious beliefs, your education, or something else?" (emphasis added). The results were as follows:

A personal experience	7%
The views of your friends and family	4
What you have seen or read in the media	34
Your religious beliefs	18
Your education	22
Something else	13
Don't know/refused	2

Scientifically speaking, respondents cannot be expected to give interviewers a multivariate, causal account of the sources of their opinions on the stem cell issue. Instead, as with responses to the follow-up probes of the presidential approval question, they tend to select what they regard as the most plausible influence on their thinking about the issue. In this case, the largest plurality thought it was something they had seen or read in the mass media; more than one out of five (22 percent) thought it must have something to do with their education; a little less than a fifth (18 percent) figured it was probably their religious beliefs, and so forth. Accepting such plausible justifications at face value, however, the Pew Center analyzed these findings and constructed a seemingly plausible causal account to explain why Americans think the way they do on the stem cell issue:

> The vast majority of those who support government funding of stem cell research are influenced by what they have seen in the media (42 percent) or their education (28 percent). Religion plays a relatively minor role in shaping the views of supporters—just 5 percent cite it as having the biggest influence on their thinking.
>
> By contrast, 37 percent of those who think the government should not fund stem cell research cite religious beliefs as the biggest influence. This is particularly the case among white evangelical Protestants, fully 55 percent of whom explain their opposition to stem cell research in terms of their religious beliefs. Just 31 percent and 27 percent of white mainline Protestants and white Catholics, respectively, cite religious beliefs in explaining their opposition to stem cell funding. (Pew Research Center 2002c)

But this plausible-sounding account, I would contend, represents no more than another mirage for mass media consumption, one that could seriously mislead policy makers and pundits about the multiple causal forces driving public opinion on the stem cell issue. And this is just one of many such examples of faulty causal inferences that could be drawn from the archives of public opinion polls today.

Box 8.1 shows a variety of other ways in which pollsters have asked questions that generate naive causal inferences, especially questions about what respondents think influences their voting preferences. Causally speaking, do respondents actually know what the *main reason* is for their opposition to cloning, or are they simply selecting what appears to be the *most plausible reason* from the list of alternatives presented to them? Do they really have any idea whatsoever as to *how much influence* Bush's and Clinton's positions on health care had on their voting decision, except as a plausible, after-the-fact rationalization? And how could they possibly know whether a political candidate's position on the abortion issue will be the *most important factor* in deciding whether or not to vote for that candidate, except as a plausible justification? Probably because pollsters, like many of their intellectual peers in democratic society, believe personally that a candidate's position on various issues should be an important factor in deciding how to vote, it only seems natural to them that respondents should think the same way and should also be able to tell interviewers what issues were important to them in making their voting decisions. This presumption of issue voting has become one of the more enduring myths in American politics, and was the subject of an experiment by my colleague and me (Bishop and Fisher 1995a, 1995b) to test the illusion of causal influence created by the way in which exit polls typically ask respondents about the reasons for their voting decision.

EXIT POLLS AND ISSUE VOTING

The belief that issues matter in deciding elections has become one of the more popular myths in the American political culture. Much of this myth stems from normative democratic theories about how voters should make their electoral decisions. The issue factor also occupies a central place in contemporary empirical theories of voting in which rational voters make

---

BOX 8.1
Examples of Survey Questions Eliciting Naive Causal Inferences in Opinion Polls

"What is the *main reason* you are against the cloning of human beings? Because of your religious beliefs, because cloning interferes with human distinctiveness and individuality, because cloning could be used for questionable purposes like breeding a superior race or clone armies, because the technology involved is dangerous." (Yankelovich Partners for *Time*/CNN, February 7–8, 2001)

"Please tell me *how much influence*, if any, each of the following have had on your own views toward gays and lesbians. What about . . . personal experience with gays and lesbians you know? Has this had a lot of influence, some, only a little, or no influence on your own views toward gays and lesbians?" (Princeton Survey Research Associates for Kaiser Family Foundation, February 7–September 4, 2000)

"When thinking about who you'll support for president, what is the *most important factor* on which you base your vote?" (Fox News/Opinion Dynamics, May 24–25, 2000)

"Generally speaking, do you think a political candidate's position on abortion—whatever it may be—is the *most important factor* to you in
(continued)

deciding whether or not to vote for that candidate, or an important factor, but not the most important one, or is it not an important factor to you in deciding whether or not to vote for a candidate?" (*Los Angeles Times*, June 8–13, 2000)

"Let me read you several factors some people say they will consider in deciding which candidate to vote for in this November's [2002] congressional election. For each one that I mention, please tell me whether this factor will be important enough to *determine* your vote, a significant consideration, or not a consideration at all. . . . The candidate has a strong record of delivering for your district." (Hart and Teeter Research Companies for NBC News/*Wall Street Journal*, January 18–21, 2002)

"*How much influence* did the [President George] Bush and [Bill] Clinton positions on health care *affect your voting* decisions last November [1992]?" (Gallup Organization for Employee Benefit Research Institute, February 1993)

"*How much influence* do you think decisions made by the U.S. [United States] Congress have on your daily life—a lot, some, not much, or no influence at all?" (CBS News, November 1998)

Source: Public Opinion Location Library, Roper Center for Public Opinion Research.
Note: Emphasis added throughout.

informed decisions, prospectively or retrospectively, mostly about the issue of the economy (see, e.g., Erickson and Tedin 2001, chap. 9; Neuman 1986). So the idea that issues matter or should matter comes naturally to those whose profession it is to describe, explain, and interpret what happens in elections: the academics, the journalists, the political pundits, and, of course, the pollsters. It should come as no surprise, then, to find this instinctive inclination toward the idea of "issue voting" showing up in the frequency with which exit pollsters and other public opinion researchers ask questions about why respondents voted for one candidate rather than the other. In addition to making election night projections of winners and losers, exit polls of voters have also become one of the principal ways in which the mass media interpret the meaning and mandates of elections.

Such interpretations are typically laden with issues that voters said were important to them in making up their minds. "Clinton Wins on Economy, Vision," said the headline in *Newsday* (Kessler 1992) following Bill Clinton's

1992 victory over George H. W. Bush. Citing data from a *Los Angeles Times* exit poll of roughly 15,000 voters from various polling places across the United States, staff writer Glenn Kessler notes that "nearly 60 percent of voters surveyed cited the economy as the most important issue in the election." Drawing from the same data source, Kessler goes on to say that "Clinton also attracted three-quarters of the votes of the people concerned about the soaring cost of health care. . . . Nearly 1 in 5 people said health care was an important issue." Four years later, in a postmortem on the presidential election, John Ritter, writing for *USA Today* (1996), analyzed the mood of the voters following Bill Clinton's defeat of Bob Dole in the bellwether swing state of Ohio. Pointing to exit polls as the evidence, he draws a typical journalistic inference about the issues that mattered most to Clinton and Dole supporters: "Dole got a lot more of the Ohio voters who thought taxes were the biggest issue in this election, while Clinton took the Lion's share of those who thought jobs and the economy were No. 1."

The bitterly contested presidential election of 2000 produced only more such reasoning. Despite the ambiguous outcome of the election, and perhaps encouraged by it, the same predilection for finding the issues that mattered most surfaced in journalistic interpretations of the minds of the voters. Trying to make sense of the electoral mood of Minnesota and the nation after the election, Bob von Sternberg, a staff writer for the *Minneapolis Star Tribune* (2000), looks to the national exit polls for much of the answer: "The exit poll indicated that Bush fared especially well among those who cared most about world affairs and taxes. Voters who cared most about Medicare and prescription drugs, Social Security, health care and the economy tended to favor Gore." Probably, as most journalists who interpret the outcome of elections do, von Sternberg assumes that voters interviewed as they leave their polling places on election day can actually tell us, in a true causal sense, why they voted for Bush rather than Gore, and vice versa. And while exit polls generally do an outstanding job of predicting the results of elections, they often perpetuate this illusion of causality by asking such naive inference questions.

Take, for example, the types of questions used in exit poll questionnaires in previous presidential elections (see Mitofsky and Edelman 1993, 1995; Merkle and Edelman 2000). In the 1992 Voter Research and Surveys (VRS) exit poll, near the beginning of the self-administered questionnaire, respondents were asked, "In Today's Election for President, Did You Just Vote For:

1. Bill Clinton (Dem)
2. George Bush (Rep)
3. Ross Perot (Ind)
4. Other: Who? _____

5. Didn't Vote For President

Next, they were asked, "Which 1 or 2 Issues Mattered Most in Deciding How You Voted?"

1. Health care
2. Federal budget deficit
3. Abortion
4. Education
5. Economy/jobs
6. Environment
7. Taxes
8. Foreign policy
9. Family values

The exit poll also varied the order in which these issues were listed on the questionnaire: some respondents, at random, saw them in the order listed above, whereas others saw them listed in the reverse order (family values, foreign policy, etc.). Not surprisingly, Mitofsky and Edelman (1993, 1995) discovered that the results depended in part on the order in which the issues had been presented (table 8.1). As would be expected from previous experiments with a list of response alternatives presented in the visual format of a self-administered questionnaire (see Bishop and Smith 2001 for a recent review of the literature; also see Sudman, Bradburn, and Schwarz 1996), the pattern of responses shows clear evidence of a "primacy effect." Respondents were more likely to indicate that an issue mattered most in deciding how to vote if it appeared at or near the beginning of the list than if it showed up later in the list. The issue of health care, for example, was chosen by 24 per-

Table 8.1. Percent Saying Issue Mattered Most in Deciding Vote

Issue	Listed order	Reverse order
Health care	24	15
Federal budget deficit	25	17
Abortion	13	11
Education	12	13
Economy/jobs	41	44
Environment	4	7
Taxes	12	17
Foreign policy	7	9
Family values	10	20

Source: Adapted from Mitofsky and Edelman 1993.
Note: Percentages total to more than 100% because of multiple responses.

cent of the respondents when it was listed first but by just 15 percent when it came last on the list. Similarly, a fourth of the respondents (25 percent) picked the federal budget deficit as the issue that mattered most to them when it was listed second, as compared to 17 percent when it appeared second to the last on the list. On the other hand, twice as many respondents (20 percent) chose family values as the critical issue when it showed up as the first item in the list (on the reverse order form) than when it turned up last (10 percent). In other words, which issue respondents *thought* mattered most in deciding how they voted depended in significant part on the order in which the choices were presented to them—a causal influence of which they could not possibly have been aware (see Nisbet and Wilson 1977; Wegner 2002). In capsule form, this response order effect demonstrates how easy it is to generate the illusion that respondents know what has influenced their voting decision.

Nor is this the only way in which exit polls can produce the illusion of issue voting. The closed-ended form in which the issue question is typically asked creates subtle psychological constraints of another kind. As experiments by Schuman and Presser (1981) and their colleagues (Schuman and Scott 1987) have repeatedly demonstrated, closed-ended questions can sharply limit a respondent's frame of reference by focusing his or her attention on just the list of alternatives presented. As a consequence, respondents may not feel free to volunteer answers outside the list, even when given an explicit opportunity to do so (e.g., with an explicit "other" response category). Follow-up experiments by Schuman and Scott (1987) have also shown that even if an issue or problem is only rarely mentioned spontaneously, in response, for example, to the standard open-ended question asked by the Gallup Organization about "the most important problem facing the country," respondents will nonetheless choose it in significant numbers if it is offered in a closed-ended list with other equally rare issues or problems (see, again, chapter 3). In this way, closed-ended questions powerfully constrain what many respondents *think* is "the most important problem facing the country." Open-ended questions, as Schuman and his associates would remind us, can likewise constrain a respondent's frame of reference, albeit more subtly (see Schuman and Scott 1987). In either case, the form in which the question is asked—open or closed—significantly determines what the respondent will decide is important.

OPEN VERSUS CLOSED UNIVERSES

The same considerations come into play with the standard closed-ended questions asked of respondents in exit polls: "Which 1 or 2 Issues Mattered

Most in Deciding How You Voted?" (Mitofsky and Edelman 1993, 1995); "Which one issue mattered most in deciding how you voted for president?" (Merkle and Edelman 2000). The question arises as to whether any of the issues listed in the standard exit poll questionnaire would have mattered to respondents in their voting decision if they had not been mentioned. What percentage of respondents, for example, would have spontaneously volunteered any of the issues listed in table 8.1 if the question had been asked in open-ended form? Is the "issue voting" generated by such exit polls merely an artifact of the form in which the question is asked?

One answer comes from a comparison with responses to an open-ended question about "the most important problem facing the country" asked by the Gallup Organization on Labor Day weekend at the beginning of the fall election campaign in 1992 (table 8.2). Even allowing for differences in sampling designs and changes between Labor Day and Election Day, with the exception of the "economy" and "unemployment," there is a conspicuous lack of congruence between the issues or problems spontaneously identified as important by the American public in table 8.2 and those listed in the closed-ended question used in the 1992 VRS exit poll (table 8.1). "Abortion" and "taxes," for example, appeared to be much more important in the VRS exit poll than they were in the national Gallup poll. "Family values," which appeared to be the second most important issue when it was listed first in the VRS exit poll question, did not even emerge as a separate category in the Gallup survey because it evidently was not mentioned by enough respondents. Even if we count "ethics/moral decline" as an indirect indicator of "family values" concerns, it was mentioned much less frequently in response to the open-ended question asked by Gallup (table 8.2) than "family values" was selected on the closed-ended form of the exit poll. Similarly, some problems, such as "poverty/hunger/homelessness," that seemed important to a noticeable percentage of Americans in the Gallup survey (7.3 percent for "poverty/hunger/homelessness") were not included at all on the closed list of issues in the 1992 VRS exit poll. Nor did the exit poll provide any explicit opportunity for respondents to volunteer such issues by offering an "other" category. Poverty, hunger, and homelessness did not exist as an issue in the election, in significant part because it simply wasn't listed on the exit poll questionnaire.

Furthermore, merely because such abstract issues or problems are listed on the questionnaire does not mean they exist as realities for respondents. In constructing their questionnaires, exit pollsters presume that the "issues" respondents typically volunteer when asked the "most important problem" question are also things that may actually matter in voters' decisions on Elec-

Table 8.2. Most Important Problem Facing the Country: Responses to Open-Ended Survey Question

	% of multiple responses
Economic problems	
Economy (general)	20.7
Unemployment	15.1
Federal budget deficit/failure to balance	5.0
Trade deficit	1.1
Cost of living/inflation	1.1
Recession/depression	0.5
Cost of borrowing/high interest rates	—
Other specific economic	1.7
Noneconomic problems	
Poverty/hunger/homelessness	7.3
Health care/hospitals/high cost of health care	6.7
Education/schools	5.6
Crime	3.9
Dissatisfaction with government	3.9
Ethics/moral decline	3.4
Drugs/drug abuse	3.4
Taxes	1.7
Environment/pollution	1.7
Too much time/money spent overseas	1.7
America first	1.7
Abortion	1.7
International problems	1.1
Medicare increases/senior citizens' insurance	1.1
Kuwait/Iraq/Middle East crisis/Gulf crisis/the war/Saddam Hussein	1.1
AIDS	0.5
Fear of war/nuclear war	0.5
Oil crisis/cost of oil	—
Other specific noneconomic	8.9

Source: Calculated from the *Gallup Poll Monthly,* September 1992, 11.

tion Day. But, as the late Everett Carll Ladd (1988) reminded us, such "problems aren't necessarily issues . . . a problem becomes an issue only when voters see the parties differing in their approach to it or their capacity to solve it" (cited in Bennett 1995). So it becomes questionable whether such so-called issues, especially in the vague, abstract form in which they are typically presented in exit poll questionnaires, even exist as meaningful factors in the decisions of voters, apart from their being forced to choose one or more of them in a canned, closed list of alternatives. Issue voting in exit polls may thus be largely an artifact of the question form.

AN EXIT POLL EXPERIMENT

To test the artifact hypothesis, my associates and I (Bishop and Fisher 1995a, 1995b) designed a split-sample experiment in which respondents were asked either an open- or closed-ended question about "the issue that mattered most" to them in deciding whether to vote for one congressional candidate or the other in the First Congressional District of Ohio. Carried out as part of a larger project on modes of data collection in exit polling, the experiment varied the order as well as the form of the questions. The response categories for the closed-ended version of the question listed seven issues that the congressional candidates, David Mann (Democrat) and Steve Chabot (Republican), had stressed in their fall 1994 campaign: abortion, crime, family values, gun control, health care reform, taxes and government spending, and welfare reform. Approximately half the respondents to the closed-ended form, at random, saw these alternatives in the order just listed; the other half received them in reverse alphabetical order (welfare reform, taxes and government spending, etc.). In each case, respondents, after indicating which congressional candidate they had voted for, were asked (using either the alphabetical or reverse alphabetical list of the seven response alternatives), "Which issue mattered most to you in deciding whether to vote for Mann or Chabot?" On the open-ended form of the question, respondents were simply asked (without a list of alternatives), "Which issue mattered most to you in deciding whether to vote for Mann or Chabot?" Interviewers were instructed to record verbatim whatever the respondent said was the most important issue in his or her decision. A random subsample of 30 percent of the respondents received this open-ended form; 70 percent received the closed-ended form, half of whom were given the list of alternatives in alphabetical order, half in reverse order (for a more detailed description of the research design, see Bishop and Fisher 1995a; see also Bishop and Fisher 1995b).

The results of the experiment, in table 8.3, look like two different worlds: a "closed world" of issue voting and an "open world" of other kinds of voting. On the closed form of the question, the vast majority of respondents selected one or more of the seven issue choices presented to them. But on the open form, less than 10 percent of the responses given spontaneously could be classified into one of these same seven categories, a finding that parallels those reported by Schuman and Scott (1987) in their experiments with open and closed question forms. Furthermore, only a small percentage of the responses volunteered on the open form contained any explicit issue content, such as references to NAFTA and Social Security. Instead, we find that the great majority of responses offered on the open form of the question had to do with other psychological dimensions, such as the candidates them-

Table 8.3.   Responses to Closed- and Open-Ended Questions about Which Issue Mattered Most in Deciding Congressional Vote

	Question form	
Issue responses	*Closed*	*Open*
Abortion	11.3%	3.0%
Crime	9.8	1.0
Family values	11.5	0.0
Gun control	6.5	0.5
Health care reform	9.4	0.5
Taxes and government spending	21.5	3.5
Welfare reform	9.2	0.0
All of these issues (volunteered)	4.4	—
Other (volunteered), e.g., NAFTA, Social Security	0.6	5.1
None/no issue	2.7	2.0
Candidate responses		
Vote record/views/performance	0.6	11.1
Experience/qualified/better man	0.4	6.6
Character/personal qualities, e.g., integrity	0.6	8.1
Like or dislike/positive or negative reaction	0.4	6.1
Friend/know him/personal contact	0.6	5.1
Other comments about candidate	0.6	0.5
Partisan Responses		
Democrat or anti-Republican	0.4	3.0
Republican or anti-Democrat	0.8	2.5
Anti-Clinton	0.0	1.0
Pro-Clinton	0.0	1.0
Other partisan comments	0.2	1.0
Campaign-related responses		
Negative ads/mudslinging/tone of campaign	1.3	9.6
Negative choice responses		
Lesser of two evils/didn't want either one/not much choice	0.6	4.1
Didn't vote for either one/neither/both bad choice	0.0	1.5
Other responses/no response		
Other responses not elsewhere classified	0.0	5.1
No response at all/refused	6.5	18.2
Total	99.9%	100.1%
Total responses	479	198
(N =)	(409)	(171)

Source: Exit poll conducted by Department of Political Science, University of Cincinnati, November 3, 1992 (see Bishop and Fisher 1995a, 1995b).
Note: Response totals include multiple responses.

selves, political partisanship, the tone of the campaign, and its "lesser of two evils" quality, suggesting that the word *issue* on the open-ended question form was interpreted rather loosely by respondents to mean anything that might have influenced their vote. Moreover, without the structure of an explicit list of response alternatives telling them what was meant by an "issue," a sizable percentage of respondents (18.2 percent) receiving the open form of the question could give no response at all. Such, then, is the constraining influence of the form of the question that a pollster would draw rather different conclusions from the different results about whether issues mattered at all in this 1994 congressional contest.

The contrast between these two parallel worlds looks even sharper when the responses to the open and closed forms are correlated with the respondents' reported votes for the two candidates for the House of Representatives in Cincinnati's First District. Table 8.4 presents a picture of what the world looks like when the question is asked in a closed universe of response options. It looks much like a world where issues really matter in the voting decision. Respondents who said they had voted for the Republican, Steve Chabot, were more likely than those who had voted for the Democrat, David Mann, to say that such issues as "abortion," "family values," and "taxes and government spending" mattered most in their voting decision. On the other hand, Mann's supporters were more likely to mention "crime" and "health care reform" as the issues that mattered most to them. Though these abstract issues are highly ambiguous in meaning, respondents interpreted them in a way that produced a relationship that not only was statistically significant,

Table 8.4. Issue Mattering Most in Voting Decision by Reported Congressional Vote: Closed-Ended Question Form

Issue	David Mann (Democrat)	Steve Chabot (Republican)
Abortion	11.7%	17.7%
Crime	13.3	7.5
Family values	13.3	17.7
Gun control	7.8	6.1
Health care reform	18.0	6.1
Taxes and govt. spending	25.8	35.4
Welfare reform	10.2	9.5
Total	100.1	100.0
(N =)	(128)	(147)

Source: Exit poll conducted by Department of Political Science, University of Cincinnati, November 3, 1992 (see Bishop and Fisher 1995a, 1995b).
Note: Chi squared = 15.34, df = 6, statistically significant at .05 level.

but also looked like a highly plausible pattern of how Democrat and Republican voters would differ. Any exit pollster or journalist looking at these data would surely conclude that issues played a significant role in deciding the outcome in this as well as many other congressional races in the historic election of 1994.

But the illusion of issue voting would vanish if the same pollster or journalist were to look at table 8.5. For when we attempt to correlate the same seven issue responses with the reported votes for the two candidates on the open form of the question, there is little or nothing to correlate. The cells of the table are essentially empty; a trivial demonstration, perhaps, but it drives home the point that much of what passes as voting on the issues in exit polls is largely an artifact of the closed-ended form in which the questions are typically asked. Given a limited list of issues, the great majority of respondents will oblige the exit poll interviewer by choosing one or more of them even though these issues may have had little or no relevance to how and why they voted for one candidate rather than the other. If you ask it, they will answer.

The Influence of Response Order

The results of the response order experiment summarized in table 8.6 indicate in yet another way that respondents really can't tell us what influences their voting behaviors. As would be predicted from previous experiments with response order in a visual format, the data show a pronounced primacy effect. With the exception of welfare reform, issues presented at or near the beginning of the list ("abortion" and "crime" on the alphabetical form and

Table 8.5. Issue Mattering Most in Voting Decision by Reported Congressional Vote: Open-Ended Question Form

Issue	David Mann (Democrat)	Steve Chabot (Republican)
Abortion	0	2
Crime	1	0
Family values	0	0
Gun control	0	0
Health care reform	0	1
Taxes and govt. spending	0	0
Welfare reform	0	0
(N =)	(1)	(3)

Source: Exit poll conducted by Department of Political Science, University of Cincinnati, November 3, 1992 (see Bishop and Fisher 1995a, 1995b).
Note: Entries are raw cell frequencies.

Table 8.6.   Issue Responses to Closed-Ended Form by Response Order

	Response order	
Issue	*Alphabetical*	*Reverse*
Abortion	15.2%	12.9%
Crime	15.8	8.6
Family values	14.7	14.5
Gun control	9.8	6.5
Health care reform	9.2	14.5
Taxes and govt. spending	23.9	31.7
Welfare reform	11.4	11.3
Total	100.0	100.0
Total Responses	184	186

Source: Exit poll conducted by Department of Political Science, University of Cincinnati, November 3, 1992 (see Bishop and Fisher 1995a, 1995b).
Note: Response totals include multiple responses.

"taxes and government spending" and "health care reform" on the reverse alphabetical form) were chosen noticeably more often than those near the middle or the end of the list. Though this demonstration represents perhaps a mere replication, it reinforces the point made earlier that what respondents *think* "mattered most" in their voting decision can be manipulated significantly by the sheer order in which the issue alternatives are presented to them, as well as by the form in which the question is asked: open or closed. Surely, no respondent would be likely to volunteer that the reason he or she chose issue X rather than Y was because of the order in which the response alternatives were presented to him or her. So much for what respondents *believe* are the influences on their behavior, and so much for their illusion of conscious will (Wegner 2002). For much of what happens in these experiments is no different from what happens in the rest of life. The causal influences on our behavior occur by and large outside of conscious awareness.

THE MEANING OF INVENTED REASONS

Methodologically speaking, these experiments represent yet another demonstration of the open versus closed question form effect. They show once more how powerfully the closed form of the question defines for respondents the frame of reference and what is meant by an issue, constraining their choices to the alternatives presented to them. Whereas the open form of the question allows them to interpret the question more broadly, as if the word *issue* meant "what [reason] mattered most to you in deciding how you voted?"

Respondents typically answer by suggesting a plausible reason that might have affected their voting decisions, such as the candidate's experience or character, his or her political party, or the mudslinging he or she is alleged to have engaged in during the campaign. Recognizing these other factors, exit pollsters (see Merkle and Edelman 2000) have done their best to include questions such as, "Which 1 or 2 Candidate Qualities Mattered Most in Deciding How You Voted for President?"

1. Has the right experience
2. Will bring about needed change
3. Is my party's candidate
4. Cares about people like me
5. Is honest and trustworthy
6. Has the best plan for the country
7. Would have good judgment in a crisis
8. His choice of Vice President
9. Has strong convictions

But I would contend that it is just another illusion that respondents can actually tell us what candidate quality mattered most in their voting decision, any more than they can tell us what issue mattered most. Theoretically speaking, the results presented here suggest that respondents, regardless of the form in which the question is asked—open or closed—give what they think is a plausible reason for their vote, rather than a causal reason. Indeed, respondents, as cognitive social psychologists would argue (Nisbet and Wilson 1977), cannot really tell us about the causes of their behavior except perhaps under highly unusual conditions (of "a gun to the head" variety). So our experimental demonstration of the profound influence of question form and response order on what respondents think affects their vote calls into question the implicit causal model of issue voting that has become so commonplace in the interpretation of exit poll reports on election night and in the days thereafter. Survey respondents cannot explain their actions or their opinions; they can only offer after-the-fact rationalizations and plausible justifications.

The same causal critique applies equally well to the many variations of the "why" question that have become so common in modern public opinion polling. Despite wishful thinking to the contrary, respondents cannot really tell us *why* they approve or disapprove of the way George W. Bush (or any other president) is handling his job as president; they don't know what had the *biggest influence* on their thinking on the stem cell research issue; they have no idea as to the *main reason* they're against the cloning of human beings; they're unaware of *how much influence* their personal experience with gays and lesbians has had on their attitudes toward them; and they're positively clueless when it comes to knowing whether a candidate's position on some issue was the *most important factor* in deciding their vote. After all, they're not multivariate, causal modeling machines, just naive human observers. And, as the ever-skeptical social psychologist Donald Campbell (1988, 347) reminds us in his essays on the epistemology of the social sciences, "Experience is naively realistic."

Epistemologically, this critique raises a question about the extent to which exit pollsters, public opinion researchers, and political scientists more generally construct social and political reality such as "issue voting" in elections. In this case, the *facts* of issue voting appear to be heavily laden with normative democratic theory and empirical theories of voting in which rational voters make decisions based on knowledge of the candidates' and parties' positions on the issues. As members of the academic, journalistic, and political elite that holds these rational democratic values, it should not be surprising that pollsters end up constructing survey questions about elections in a way that confirms those cognitive and normative biases. Such is the power of a semiconscious ideology. So much, cognitive social psychologists might say, for the rational voter, the rational public, and other rationalist illusions of people making conscious choices and presuming to tell us why. If only reality were so close to the surface.

NOTE

1. The poll findings cited throughout this chapter on American public opinion were, except as otherwise noted, compiled from the following sources: the Roper Center for Public Opinion Research's online Public Opinion Location Library (POLL), the Polling Report (www.pollingreport.com), and the Gallup Organization's online poll data archive (brain.gallup.com).

9

Improving the Measurement of Public Opinion

Measuring anything that exists.

—Earl Babbie, *The Practice of Social Research*

No reader should go away with the nonsensical notion that I am saying that most polls are just producing an illusion or that Americans have no real opinions on public affairs. To begin with, people probably have firm and well-grounded opinions on numerous everyday matters in the mass culture: whether they think one movie, football team, or wine is better than another; whether Pete Rose should be in the Hall of Fame, despite his gambling history; and whether some entertainer or celebrity is guilty as charged. They probably have strong opinions as well about familiar political figures such as Hillary Clinton, George W. Bush, Osama bin Laden, and Saddam Hussein. And some segments of the public—the politically attuned and well informed, which are far from a majority (see, e.g., Delli Carpini and Keeter 1996; Erickson and Tedin 2001, chap. 3)—have no doubt formed well-grounded opinions on multiple domestic and foreign affairs issues. But on numerous public affairs issues that have become the subject of the many vaguely worded questions in public opinion polls today, respondents are often generating illusory opinions, especially when they answer on the basis of being told, "As you may know. . . ." Just saying, "As you may know," or the like, doesn't make it so. It's not as though pollsters can psychologically simulate days, weeks, or months of what would happen to public knowledge and opinions as a consequence of a public policy debate on some issue by simply saying, "As you may know . . ." (cf. Fishkin 1992, 1995 on ordinary versus deliberative polls). Such survey questions construct no more than an illusion of public opinion.

In the same theoretical spirit, no reader should go away with the notion that measuring public opinion by merely asking survey questions somehow automatically tells us what is there. If you ask it, they will answer. But reality or its construction, as modern scientific instrumentation tells us, just doesn't sit so close to the surface. If we have learned nothing else from the empirical evidence and case studies presented here, it's that public opinion, like everything else in the universe, does not exist apart from the measurement process. In this case our measuring instrument, the social survey, is embedded in the inherent ambiguity and vagueness of the human language. How we ask the questions and the order and context in which we ask them can make a significant and typically unpredictable difference in the results of public opinion polls, and there is no way for the unprotected consumer to know, with the notable exception of election predictions, what is reliable and valid information and what is not. Add to this the problem of large segments of the mass public who are often uninformed about matters remote from their everyday lives but who will, in the absence of an explicit opportunity to say they "don't know," offer opinions on issues they know little or nothing about. As if that were not enough, we now know that identically worded survey questions can mean different things to different respondents and that the exact same question may mean different things over time, as we witnessed most transparently before and after the events of September 11, 2001. We also know now that mass media coverage and interpretations of poll results can generate rather spurious impressions about the nature and reality of public opinion, as when it tells us, for example, that the great majority of Americans support teaching creationism as well as evolution in the nation's public schools. And perhaps most discomforting of all, we must now shed the naive notion that pollsters, like alchemists, can somehow magically discover the influences, reasons, or causes underlying someone's opinion or voting preference simply by asking him or her why. The illusion of conscious will may persist in the polling establishment, but modern psychological research tells us that's all it is: mostly, if not entirely, an illusion.

All this said, polling as we know it is not likely to go away anytime soon. This social telescope, as Jean Converse (1987) referred to it, still has some time to run yet as an accepted scientific instrument for the measurement of what's going on in the human brain and its behavioral manifestations, including what we call "opinions." Nor should the reader go away without some practical suggestions for improving the measurement of public opinion. Just bashing the pollsters for some bad practices in measuring public opinion won't do much to change things. Having been highly critical for the bulk of this work, it behooves me to offer some constructive solutions. In that spirit, we first revisit a classic solution to the problems facing the field offered by pioneering pollster George Gallup (1947) in his "quintamensional plan for question design." Next we rediscover the value of Howard Schuman's (1966) greatly neglected random probe technique for measuring and monitoring the meaning of survey questions. We then take a look at Daniel Yankelovich's equally neglected attempt to measure public opinion with his "mushiness index" (Keene and Sackett 1981). After that we turn to the mainstream of modern survey research for a brief glance at the utility of a current practice for improving the measurement of public opinion: cognitive pretesting. I then smuggle in one other practical suggestion: routinely breaking down the results of public opinion polls released to the mass media, not only by the standard demographics, but also by the level of public attention or awareness to the issue. Finally, we struggle with the question, What are the pollsters' incentives for doing any of this? It's not without cost, and it may not be practical to measure public opinion with the same precision as we do in predictive preelection polls without any demands for a reality check from the gatekeepers—the policy makers, journalists, and public opinion analysts in the mass media—or from the public itself.

GALLUP'S QUINTAMENSIONAL SOLUTION

George Gallup thought he had an answer to the problem of measuring public opinion that might be more or less well informed. His conception of question design, as he recounted it (Gallup 1947), emerged from his organization's ongoing experience with the "split-ballot" technique, in which comparable samples of respondents would be given two different ballot forms ("A" and "B") as a way of testing the effects of different question variations (e.g., open versus closed, filter, dichotomous versus multiple choice, etc.). He called his question design plan "quintamensional" because it measured what he thought were the *five* key dimensions of an individual's opinion (Gallup 1976, 91):

1. The respondent's (R's) awareness and knowledge of an issue
2. R's spontaneous, overall views of the issue
3. R's opinion on the specifics of the issue or proposal
4. R's reasons for holding that opinion
5. R's intensity of feeling on the matter

The plan was an elaborate one. To probe these different aspects of opinion, Gallup developed five corresponding categories or types of questions. To measure whether a respondent had paid any attention to an issue, he recommended beginning with a filter question that he had found particularly useful over the years: "Have you heard or read about . . . ?" He had used it for the first time in a prewar poll conducted in January 1939, when he had asked a national sample in one form of a "split-ballot" experiment, "Have you heard or read about the Dies committee for investigating un-American activities?" (to which 58 percent replied "yes"). A more contemporary example from a July 1983 Gallup poll asked respondents, "Have you heard or read about a proposed Amendment to the U.S. Constitution that would allow voluntary prayer in public schools?" (to which 82 percent said "yes").[1] Unlike many of his modern polling descendants, Gallup believed that someone who had not heard or read about such a constitutional amendment, for example, was ill prepared to offer an opinion on it. He also thought that merely being able to say "yes" to such a minimal awareness question did not mean the respondent knew much about the issue. For that reason, he felt it was necessary to ask respondents follow-up questions to determine the depth of their knowledge and information about the topic—for example, what they might know about some of the details of a proposed constitutional amendment, what they thought were the major arguments in favor of, and against, the amendment, and so on. In this way he thought it would be possible to separate the opinions of those who had developed a more sophisticated grasp of the issue from those who were giving what he called "snap judgments," or what contemporary political psychologists would call "top-of-the-head" reactions to survey questions (cf. Zaller 1992, chap. 8).

Measuring knowledge and awareness was just the first step. Before asking respondents, with a more structured question, where they stood on a given issue or legislative proposal, Gallup felt it would be useful to find out how they thought about it in general, and more spontaneously, by asking them an open-ended or "free-answer" question, such as, "What do you think should be done about this proposed constitutional amendment?" Or, "How do you think this issue should be resolved?" (Gallup 1976, 93). This, he believed, would make it possible for the public opinion analyst to better understand the respondent's overall frame of reference in answering the questions and would perhaps uncover perspectives and interpretations of the issue that the investigator might have overlooked (cf. cognitive pretesting today).

The next step in Gallup's design was simply to ask respondents where they stood on a particular proposal or issue, typically with a dichotomous "yes" or "no" question form, such as, ""Do you favor or oppose this proposed amendment to the U.S. Constitution?" In some instances, Gallup thought it might be useful to explain the issue or proposal to respondents who had not heard or read about it, in as unbiased a fashion as possible, and then elicit their opinions for comparison with the opinions of those who were more aware of and better informed about the topic. By referring to respondents' answers to the initial filter and the open-ended questions about their overall frame of reference, Gallup thought it would be possible to better understand the meaning of the "no opinion" responses that are commonly recorded for survey questions, namely, by separating those who say they have "no opinion" because they don't know much about the issue from those who give a "don't know" response because they are undecided about which position they favor on the issue.

He also believed he could readily determine the influences on people's opinions. Though naive by contemporary cognitive psychological standards (see, e.g., Nisbet and Wilson 1977; Wegner 2002), Gallup thought he could gain some critical insights into the causal reasons behind an individual's opinion simply by asking him or her why he or she favored one side or the other on a given issue or proposal: "Why do you feel this way?" He followed this question with nondirective probes like, "Can you explain that in greater detail?" (Gallup 1947, 1976). In fact, he often found that respondents would spontaneously volunteer such "reasons why" in answering the open-ended question about their overall views on the issue.

Finally, as did other public opinion researchers of the time (see, e.g., Katz 1944), Gallup felt it was critical to assess the intensity of a respondent's feeling or the depth of his or her conviction on an issue by asking a question such as, "How strongly do you feel about this—very strongly, fairly strongly, or not at all strongly?" Knowing that respondents felt strongly about their position, he believed, would be useful in predicting what action they might be willing to take on behalf of that opinion (e.g., casting a vote, signing a petition, going on strike) and how likely they would be to change their opinion—a measure of its "crystallization," as it was called in those days. And when this information was combined with the other dimensions in his quintamensional design, he thought it would produce a relatively complete picture of public opinion on any given issue, once the individual opinions were aggregated. How different from the practice of modern public polling!

Table 9.1 gives an example of how Gallup's classic quintamensional plan for question design might be adapted today to a perennial issue in American society: the teaching of creationism versus evolution in public schools, an issue that has resurfaced in the guise of the concept called "intelligent design" (ID). By comparison with Gallup's multifaceted design, which would separate the opinions of the well informed from those of the less informed and the totally uninformed, the questions used in the recent poll conducted by Zogby International for an organization advocating intelligent design (Zogby International 2002), the Discovery Institute, generated the illusion that the great majority of citizens in Ohio had thought about this issue and formed a firm opinion that intelligent design should be taught in public schools (see the discussion of the Zogby and Cleveland *Plain Dealer*/Mason-Dixon polls

Table 9.1. Quintamensional Question Design for the Issue of Intelligent Design

1. Filter/knowledge questions	"Have you heard or read anything about a proposal to teach a concept called 'intelligent design' in Ohio public schools?"
	"What, exactly, have you heard or read about it? Anything else?"
	"What do you think are the major arguments in *favor* of teaching it? *Against* it?"
2. Open-ended question	"What is your own feeling as to what the State Board of Education should do about this issue?"
3. Closed-ended question	"Do you *favor* or *oppose* the teaching of the concept of 'intelligent design' in Ohio's public schools?"
4. Reasons question	"Why do you feel this way?"
5. Intensity question	"How strongly do you feel about this issue—very strongly, fairly strongly, or not at all strongly?"

Source: Adapted from examples in Gallup quintamensional plan (Gallup 1947, 391).

in chapter 7). As many other advocacy polls and pseudopolls do, the Zogby poll generated the impression of an opinionated public by first educating respondents about the issue and then asking them whether they had an opinion on it.

How different public opinion on this issue would have looked had the Zogby and Cleveland *Plain Dealer*/Mason-Dixon polls simply asked, as Gallup advocated in his quintamensional plan, "Have you ever heard or read anything about a proposal to teach a concept called 'intelligent design' in Ohio's public schools?" And, if so, "What exactly have you heard or read about it?" Even with the Ohio school clues provided in this wording of the filter question, it would not be surprising to find a majority, perhaps a sizable majority, saying they had not heard or read anything at all about such a proposal, as was confirmed by a subsequent Ohio Poll (September 2002), in which only 14 percent claimed to have heard or read about the ID concept. Nor, when asked what exactly they had heard or read about it, would it be surprising to discover many respondents volunteering things that had absolutely nothing at all to do with the evolution controversy—e.g., intelligence testing, artificial intelligence, interior design, and so forth. Much of the public was evidently unfamiliar with the concept of intelligent design and had yet to form an opinion on the issue of teaching evolution versus intelligent design in the schools, except when educated to do so by prior questions and explanatory preambles to questions, such as, "The concept of intelligent design is. . . ."

Practicality aside, would anyone seriously argue that Gallup's quintamensional plan would not have provided a far better measure of Ohioans' awareness and knowledge of the intelligent design issue; their unprompted views on it; the direction and intensity of their opinions on the specific proposal to teach ID in the public schools; and their reasons or justifications for holding such opinions? Would the Ohio State Board of Education not have been much better off knowing that the public was grossly uninformed about the concept of intelligent design and that perhaps far greater weight should be given to expert scientific opinion (see, again, table 7.1) in deciding what should be taught about the theory of evolution in Ohio public schools? Just because it is possible to educate the public into offering an opinion is hardly a justification for doing so. Gallup had a much better idea for understanding the meaning of public opinion.

THE RANDOM PROBE TECHNIQUE

So did Howard Schuman. Developed originally as a method for evaluating whether respondents understood the meaning of closed-ended survey questions in the same way intended by the investigator (Schuman 1966; also see T. Smith 1989), the random probe technique can readily be extended to measure whether questions mean the same thing to all respondents and the same thing the second time as they did the first time. The technique, as described by Schuman (1966) and later by Tom Smith (1989), looks relatively straightforward. The investigator first selects a set of questions from the survey questionnaire, either randomly or systematically, to be probed with an open-ended follow-up question that asks respondents to explain what they had in mind when they answered the question. They might, for example, be asked, "Could you tell me a little more about that?" Or they could be asked to give an example of "what you mean" (see Schuman 1966 and T. Smith 1989 for these and other illustrations of the technique). The investigator then randomly assigns respondents to be probed on some questions but not others. For example, in Smith's (1989) study of the meaning and validity of questions in the National Opinion Research Center General Social Survey (NORC GSS), interviewers asked each respondent to explain his or her answer to just one of twenty-five GSS questions selected at random. On average, approximately fifty-five to sixty-five respondents were randomly probed for each question.

Tom Smith (1989) gives a good example of how it worked for a question on whether a respondent approved of homosexuality. The GSS question read as follows: "What about sexual relations between two *adults* of the *same sex*—do you think it is always wrong, almost always wrong, wrong only sometimes, or not wrong at all?" After answering this question, respondents were asked, "Could you tell me a little more about that?" Among the variable, verbatim replies he received to the random probe were these (T. Smith 1989, 307): "I don't like it, but I do think people are entitled to their own preference," "I could not imagine another woman touching me. It's not natural," and, "Because in the Bible it states that all homosexuals would not go to heaven."

The results of Smith's random probes of the GSS questions were largely reassuring. As Schuman had discovered in his survey twenty years earlier, Smith found that about 87 percent of the time, on average, respondents would give an explanation of their answer that was relatively clear and that accurately predicted how they had originally replied to the initial closed-ended question. As might be expected, however, some questions proved to be highly ambiguous, and it was difficult for respondents to explain their answers to them. The worst case turned up for a question that has become a staple topic in many American public opinion surveys: political ideology. In the GSS, the standard question reads, "We hear a lot of talk these days about liberals and conservatives. I'm going to show you a seven-point scale on which the *political views* that people might hold are arranged from extremely liberal—point 1—to extremely conservative—point 7. Where would you place yourself on this scale?"

1. Extremely liberal
2. Liberal
3. Slightly liberal
4. Moderate, middle of the road
5. Slightly conservative
6. Conservative
7. Extremely conservative

Not surprisingly, given the vagueness and ambiguity of such abstract terms as "liberal," "moderate," and "conservative," only a little more than half the respondents (52 percent) in Smith's investigation could give an explanation of their answer to the question that was sufficiently clear to predict where they had placed themselves on the seven-point scale. As Smith recounts it, many respondents had great difficulty in explaining to the interviewers how and why they ended up calling themselves a liberal, moderate, or conservative. Furthermore, as Conover and Feldman (1981) had previously discovered, Smith found that the meaning of these terms varied across respondents, and in some cases their explanations became rather nebulous, to say the least. This suggests that many other standard questions in public opinion research probably suffer from some of the same ambiguity to varying degrees and could be improved with systematic random probing on a regular basis. The point would be simply to determine whether all or mostly all of the respondents were interpreting them in essentially the same way and whether the meaning of the questions was shifting over time in reaction to events such as those associated with September 11 or in response to long-term secular changes. Monitoring the changing meaning of the language of survey questions with random probes would become a central task of public opinion polling.

Box 9.1 presents some canonical candidates for random probing in regional and national polls. For starters, consider the standard Gallup Organization questions on presidential approval. Randomly probing subsamples of respondents—for example, on what they "mean" when they say they approve or disapprove of the way George W. Bush is handling the economy—would probably yield a great variety of interpretations of what *the economy* means, not to mention what is meant by *approve, disapprove,* and *handling* the economy. Ditto for *foreign affairs,* the *Middle East situation, education, health care policy,* and other abstract concepts that have become the objects of presidential approval and disapproval in regional and national polls. The same holds for the standard questions on the state of the nation, consumer confidence, and the like. Random probes of such questions would be likely to yield multiple meanings and interpretations. As a consequence, public opinion researchers would presumably recognize the need to make their questions much more specific and concrete. For example, instead of asking one or two general questions about how the president is handling the economy, they would need to ask multiple questions about how he is dealing with more specific aspects of American economic life, such as tax cuts for upper- versus middle- and lower-income families, reducing the federal budget deficit, creating jobs, and spending for prescription drugs, homeland security, and so forth.

Of course, there are practical limits as to how specifically and concretely such questions can be written and how many can be asked in a given survey. But more specific questions would nonetheless be less susceptible to multiple interpretations than abstractions like "the economy," "taxes," or the "federal budget" and, if combined into a multi-item index of presidential approval, far more satisfactory from a survey measurement perspective (see, e.g., Fowler 2002, chap. 5). The same approach of multiple specific measures on foreign affairs, national defense, terrorism, and other policy domains would likewise yield more reliable and valid measures of public opinion on how the

---

BOX 9.1
Examples of Ambiguous Canonical Questions in Public Opinion Polling

Presidential Approval

"Do you approve or disapprove of the way George W. Bush is handling his job as president?"

"Do you approve or disapprove of the way George W. Bush is handling the economy?"

"Do you approve or disapprove of the way George W. Bush is handling foreign affairs?"

State of the Nation

"What do you think is the most important problem facing this country today?"

"In general, are you satisfied or dissatisfied with the way things are going in the United States at this time?"

"All in all, do you think things in the nation are generally headed in the right direction, or do you feel that things are off on the wrong track?" (NBC News/*Wall Street Journal*)

Consumer Confidence

"How would you rate economic conditions in this country today—as excellent, good, only fair, or poor?"

"Right now, do you think economic conditions in this country are getting better or getting worse?"

"Now thinking about a year from now, do you expect economic conditions in this country will be very good, somewhat good, somewhat poor, or very poor?"

Note: Except as noted, the questions are those used recently by the Gallup Organization.

---

president is handling his job, not to mention the state of the nation and other staples of public opinion polling today. If nothing else, merely randomly probing these indicators periodically would let pollsters know when the meaning of such measures had been altered by events like those of September 11 or by broader secular trends impinging on the meaning of political party identification, ideological identification, trust in government, and other long-term indicators. To proceed otherwise is tantamount to the proverbial putting of one's head in the sand. For a modest investment of resources, pollsters can get a much better handle on the meaning of their questions in measuring public opinion.

THE "MUSHINESS INDEX"

Psychologist and pollster Daniel Yankelovich also thought he had a better way of measuring the meaning of public opinion. It became known popularly as the "mushiness index," a multi-item indicator of the firmness or mushiness with which individuals held their opinions on a variety of topics (see Keene and Sacket 1981; Yankelovich 1991, 36). Similar in some ways to Gallup's quintamensional plan, the index included questions about four different components of an individual's opinion on a given issue (I have added component labels):

Involvement: How much the respondent thought the issue affected him or her personally
Knowledge: How well informed the respondent felt on the issue
Engagement: How much the respondent discussed the issue with family and friends
Conviction: How likely the respondent thought it was that his or her views on the issue would change

As Yankelovich viewed it, the index was especially well designed to assess the volatility of respondents' views on issues they were not well informed about, but about which they were willing to offer opinions, especially foreign affairs and complex domestic policy issues such as energy policy or, say, global warming and stem cell research today. Public opinion could thus range from very mushy on issues remote from the day-to-day concerns of most people to relatively firm on topics closer to home (for some examples, see Asher 2001, 39–42; Yankelovich 1991, 34–36). It would certainly seem useful for policy makers to know whether public opinion was more or less volatile or mushy on such issues as U.S. policy in the various conflicts in the Middle East and elsewhere, stem cell research, partial-birth abortion, gay marriage, and whatever else might reach the front burner in today's society. But valuable as the volatility index might seem, like Gallup's quintamensional plan, it never caught on with the journalistic and polling subcultures, perhaps primarily because it appeared too costly to ask four more questions each time one polled the public on a given issue. Such precious interviewing time could be better allocated to asking questions on other topics that would become the subject of additional press releases (also see Yankelovich's account of why it did not catch on). Given, however, the numerous examples in previous chapters of how polls have generated highly spurious impressions of public opinion (e.g., the case of intelligent design), reviving Yankelovich's volatility index would do much to prevent the manufacture and dissemination of such illusions.

To be sure, some survey organizations often include follow-up questions designed to measure how important an issue is to respondents, how strongly they feel about it, or how much they have followed it in the news. In recent years, the Gallup Organization, for example, has frequently asked the following type of question to assess respondents' awareness of and familiarity with an emerging issue (Gallup, February 1–4, 2001): "How closely have you been following the news about President Bush's initiative that will encourage religious organizations to use public funds to provide social services—very closely, somewhat closely, not too closely, or not closely at all?" While press releases often include the overall results of such indicators, public opinion itself is rarely broken down by levels of awareness in a way that clearly separates the attentive from the inattentive public. Furthermore, the questions and response categories used in these types of measures are themselves rather vague and ambiguous. What does it mean, for example, to follow the news "very closely," "somewhat closely," or "not too closely"? One person's "very closely" might be psychologically equivalent to another's "somewhat closely." For that matter, what does "following the news" mean? Ambiguity appears rampant. Understanding what these and other ambiguous terms mean to respondents in the questions we ask them is obviously essential to improving the measurement of public opinion. That now has become one of the central reasons for doing what is today called cognitive laboratory testing of survey questions (see Fowler 2002, chap. 6, for an introduction).

COGNITIVE PRETESTING

Most reputable survey organizations carry out what is known as a field pretest of their interview schedule and questionnaire. Typically this involves interviewing thirty to fifty respondents selected in a random or systematic manner from the population to be surveyed, followed by a group debriefing session in which the interviewers provide feedback on which questions posed problems in comprehension and administration, on how the sequencing and flow of the questions could be improved, and on similar utilitarian matters (Fowler 2002, chap .6). In my experience, field pretests are often cognitively superficial since they are geared mostly toward identifying significant practical problems in getting the respondents to answer the questions. Such field pretests, however, do not necessarily tell the investigator much about whether respondents are interpreting the questions in the same way and in the way intended by the research objectives. To ascertain this requires a much more in-depth form of interviewing known today as cognitive pretesting, in which respondents are asked to do such things as "think aloud" as they answer a question, say in their own words what they think the question is trying to get at, and explain how they chose their answer (Fowler 2002, chap. 6). These techniques help the investigator to determine whether the questions are being correctly and consistently understood in the way intended. They often identify problems of question comprehension and other cognitive difficulties that are routinely missed by standard field pretests. Costly and labor intensive, as the tests are not usually done by regular interviewers (sometimes by cognitively trained psychologists), cognitive laboratory testing has largely been adopted by federal agencies and academic survey organizations responsible for conducting national surveys on crime, health, employment, and other vital government statistics. To my knowledge, cognitive laboratory testing of survey questions has not been used, or perhaps has rarely been used, by commercial polling organizations in the United States for conducting public opinion polls.

The failure of commercial polling organizations to do cognitive pretesting represents a missed opportunity. Virtually every question asked in public opinion polls today could benefit from some form of cognitive laboratory testing. Cognitive pretesting of questions on presidential approval, the state of the nation, and consumer confidence (see box 9.1), for example, would probably reveal rather different interpretations by different types of respondents. Working-class African Americans, for instance, might interpret the standard question on how the president is handling his job in a rather different way than upper-middle-class whites; men in a different way than women; and older people in a different manner than younger people. Such differences in interpretation, rather than substantive reasons, could account for apparent racial, gender, and generation gaps in presidential approval. In any event, as with random probing, the results of cognitive pretesting of standard questions in American public opinion polls would likely mean having to ask more specific and concrete questions about presidential approval, the state of the nation, consumer confidence, and perhaps even such staples as political party identification. The objective would be to write questions that would be understood and interpreted in essentially the same way by all or nearly all respondents. At the present time, to my knowledge, there is no such assurance available for any of the questions repeatedly asked in any of the national or regional public opinion polls. For that matter, with the singular exception of preelection voting preferences, there does not appear to be any information available about the measurement reliability or predictive validity of any of the standard or nonstandard questions so commonly used in public opinion polls today. And all this is missing for perhaps an obvious reason.

Pollsters don't have much incentive. Aside from predicting the outcome of elections and issue referendums, for which they are held accountable by the actual results the next day, and on which they generally do quite well, why should pollsters bother to invest the time and resources necessary to improve the psychometric reliability and validity of their questions with cognitive pretesting and random probing? If a majority of Americans (e.g., 56 percent) say they approve of the way George W. Bush is handling the economy or two-thirds indicate they are opposed to partial-birth abortion, how can this ever be checked? Unlike an election outcome, it can't be validated. Nor, as Frank Newport (1998) has reminded us, is there typically any professional peer review of polling results that go directly to the mass media or any sort of journalistic gatekeeping. At best, what gets reported is sampling error and a statement about how the results might also be affected by variations in question wording and the "practical difficulties" of conducting public opinion polls.

In fairness, most professional pollsters do their very best to write (and replicate) questions that they believe represent a good measure of what the public thinks about various issues and problems in American society today. And as long as such questions prove useful in generating plausible demographic differences and trends over time, they will persist as standard practice. Perhaps the best that can be expected realistically, as Howard Schuman (1998) has urged, is that we focus our energies on the validity of what our survey questions are measuring, not in the traditional, psychometric sense, but rather, as he says, on "knowing what one has measured even if it is partly or even entirely different than intended" and, as he emphasizes, on "understanding the limitations of one's measures." I would like to believe that at least some of the examples presented here—on the impact of the events of September 11, for example—have contributed to knowing what we have measured, even if it is partly or entirely different from what was intended, and that it's not all just an illusion. I would also like to think the many examples and cautionary tales presented throughout this volume have created some incentive for doing things differently.

STRATIFICATION BY KNOWLEDGE
AND ATTENTION

But there is at least one other simple, practical thing that pollsters can do routinely to improve the measurement and presentation of poll results: stratify them by how closely respondents are paying attention to the issue or, even better, by how much they know about it. Analogously to the way that preelection polling results are often specified separately for the adult population as a whole, registered voters, and likely voters, pollsters could include as part of the standard demographics (age, race, sex, etc.) a breakdown of respondents' opinions by their level of knowledge of, interest in, or attention to the issue (see table 9.2 for a hypothetical illustration). In recent years, the Gallup Organization has taken significant steps in this direction with periodic analy-

Table 9.2.   Opinion on U.S. Troops in Liberian Peacekeeping Force by Issue Attention and Standard Demographics

Follows issue	*Favor*	*Oppose*	*Don't know*
Very closely	76%	21%	3%
Somewhat closely	68	27	5
Not too closely	54	32	14
Not at all	47	37	16
Gender			
Male	70	25	5
Female	58	33	9
Race			
African American	56	38	6
White	72	24	4
Age Group			
18–29	60	29	11
30–45	64	32	4
46–64	66	31	3
65 and over	59	37	4
Education			
Less than high school	54	36	10
High school graduate	55	39	6
Some college	62	34	4
College graduate	65	33	2
Party Identification			
Democrat	46	51	3
Republican	66	30	4
Independent	54	39	7

ses of the relationship between public awareness of and public opinion on selected issues (see, e.g., Carlson 2003), but the practice is far from common. Though there would obviously be a cost to adding such follow-up questions, if only for carefully selected topics (e.g., new or emerging issues), the payoff would lie in getting journalistic and policy-making elites into the habit of analyzing and stratifying public opinion into more or less attentive segments of the public. In much the same way as we now focus our best measurement efforts on identifying "likely voters" to predict the outcome of an election, so too would we begin to improve ways of identifying "likely opinion hold-ers" to accurately model public opinion, especially on significant policy issues. The idea of stratifying American public opinion by levels of awareness, knowledge, or attention is hardly a new idea. In fact, it was essentially what George Gallup had in mind many years ago when he invented that whimsi-cally titled technique he called "the quintamensional plan for question design." It was a good idea then, and it is still a good idea. My methodologi-cal and epistemological concerns notwithstanding, the measurement of pub-lic opinion can produce more than just an illusion.

NOTE

1. The poll findings cited throughout this chapter on public opinion were, except as otherwise noted, compiled from the following sources: the Roper Center for Public Opin-ion Research's online Public Opinion Location Library (POLL), the Polling Report (www. pollingreport.com), and the Gallup Organization's online poll data archive (brain.gal-lup.com).

References

Abramson, Paul R. 1990. "The Decline of Over-Time Comparability in the National Election Studies." *Public Opinion Quarterly* 54, no. 2 (Summer): 177–90.

Abramson, Paul R., and Ada W. Finifter. 1981. "On the Meaning of Political Trust: New Evidence from Items Introduced in 1978." *American Journal of Political Science* 25, no. 2 (May): 297–307.

Abramson, Paul R., and Ronald Inglehart. 1995. *Value Change in Global Perspective.* Ann Arbor: University of Michigan Press.

Abramson, Paul R., and Charles W. Ostrom Jr. 1991. "Macropartisanship: An Empirical Reassessment." *American Political Science Review* 85, no. 1 (March): 181–92.

———. 1994. "Question Wording and Partisanship: Change and Continuity in Party Loyalties during the 1992 Election Campaign." *Public Opinion Quarterly* 58, no. 1 (Spring): 21–48.

Abramson, Paul R., Brian D. Silver, and Barbara A. Anderson. 1987. "The Effects of Question Order in Attitude Surveys: The Case of the SRC/CPS Citizen Duty Items." *American Journal of Political Science* 31, no. 4 (November): 900–8.

Achen, Christopher. 1975. "Mass Political Attitudes and the Survey Response." *American Political Science Review* 69: 1218–31.

Allport, Floyd H. 1924. "The Group Fallacy in Relation to Social Science." *American Journal of Sociology* 29, no. 6 (May): 688–706.

———. 1937. "Toward a Science of Public Opinion." *Public Opinion Quarterly* 1, no. 1 (January): 7–23.

Andersen, Kristi. 1997. "Gender and Public Opinion." In *Understanding Public Opinion*, ed. Barbara Norrander and Clyde Wilcox, 19–36. Washington, D.C.: CQ Press.

Answers in Genesis. 2000. "Poll: Americans Want Creation in Public Schools." www.answersingenesis.org/docs2/4245news3-15-2000.asp

Apple, R. W., Jr. 2001. "Big Government Is Back in Style." *New York Times*, November 23, sec. B, p. 2.

Asher, Herbert. 2001. *Polling and the Public.* 5th ed. Washington, D.C.: CQ Press.

Associated Press. 2002. "Ohioans: Teach Darwin, Design." June 10.

Babbie, Earl. 1986. *Observing Ourselves: Essays in Social Research.* Prospect Heights, Ill.: Waveland Press.

Bartels, Larry. 2002. "Question Order and Declining Faith in Public Elections." *Public Opinion Quarterly* 66, no. 1 (Spring): 67–79.

Bauman, Sandra, and Paul J. Lavrakas. 2000. "Reporters' Use of Causal Explanation in Interpreting Election Polls." In *Election Polls, the News Media, and Democracy*, ed. Paul J. Lavrakas and Michael W. Traugott, 162–81. New York: Chatham House.

Belson, William A. 1981. *The Design and Understanding of Survey Questions*. Aldershot, England: Gower Publishing Co.

Beniger, James R. 1992. "The Impact of Polling on Public Opinion: Reconciling Foucault, Habermas, and Bourdieu." *International Journal of Public Opinion Research* 4, no. 3 (Autumn): 204–19.

Bennett, Stephen Earl. 1988. "Trends in Americans' Political Information, 1967–1987." *American Politics Quarterly* 17: 422–35.

———. 1990. "The Dimensions of Americans' Political Information." Paper presented at the annual meeting of the American Political Science Association, San Francisco, August 29–September 2.

———. 1995. "Comparing Americans' Political Information in 1988 and 1992." *Journal of Politics* 57, no. 2 (May): 521–32.

———. 1996. "'Know Nothings' Revisited Again." *Political Behavior* 18, no. 3 (September): 219–33.

Bishop, George F. 1987. "Experiments with the Middle Response Alternative in Survey Questions." *Public Opinion Quarterly* 51, no. 2 (Summer): 220–32.

———. 1992. "Qualitative Analysis of Question-Order and Context Effects." In *Context Effects in Social and Psychological Research*, ed. Norbert Schwarz and Seymour Sudman, 149–62. New York: Springer-Verlag.

Bishop, George F., and Bonnie S. Fisher. 1995a. "Issue Voting in Exit Polls: Fact or Artifact?" Paper presented at the annual conference of the American Association for Public Opinion Research, Fort Lauderdale, Fla., May 18–21.

———. 1995b. "'Secret Ballots' and Self-Reports in an Exit Poll Experiment." *Public Opinion Quarterly* 59, no. 4 (Winter): 568–88.

Bishop, George F., John Gulliford, Behzad Jabbari, and Brent van Zwaluwenburg. 1995. "Question Ambiguity and Question Meaning: An Alternative Theory of the Survey Response." Paper presented at the annual meeting of the American Political Science Association, Chicago.

Bishop, George F., and B. J. Jabbari. 2001. "The Internet As a Public Opinion Laboratory: Experiments with Survey Questions." Paper presented at the annual conference of the American Association for Public Opinion Research, Montreal, Canada, May 17–20.

Bishop, George F., Robert W. Oldendick, and Alfred J. Tuchfarber. 1982. "Political Information Processing: Question Order and Context Effects." *Political Behavior* 4, no. 2: 177–200.

———. 1983. "Effects of Filter Questions in Public Opinion Surveys." *Public Opinion Quarterly* 47, no. 4 (Winter): 528–46.

———. 1984. "Interest in Political Campaigns: The Influence of Question Order and Electoral Context." *Political Behavior* 6, no. 2: 159–69.

———. 1985. "The Importance of Replicating a Failure to Replicate: Order Effects on Abortion Items." *Public Opinion Quarterly* 49, no. 1 (Spring): 105–14.

Bishop, George F., Robert W. Oldendick, Alfred J. Tuchfarber, and Stephen E. Bennett. 1978. "The Changing Structure of Mass Belief Systems: Fact or Artifact." *Journal of Politics* 40, no. 3 (August): 781–87.

———. 1980. "Pseudo-Opinions on Public Affairs." *Public Opinion Quarterly* 44, no. 2 (Summer): 198–209.

Bishop, George F., and Andrew E. Smith. 1991. "The Gallup Split-Ballot Experiments." *Public Perspective* 2, no. 5 (July/August): 25–27.

———. 2001. "Response-Order Effects and the Early Gallup Split-Ballots." *Public Opinion Quarterly* 65, no. 4 (Winter): 479–505.

Bishop, George F., Alfred J. Tuchfarber, and Robert W. Oldendick. 1978. "Change in the Structure of American Political Attitudes: The Nagging Question of Question Wording." *American Journal of Political Science* 22, no. 2 (May): 250–69.

———. 1986. "Opinions on Fictitious Issues: The Pressure to Answer Survey Questions." *Public Opinion Quarterly* 50, no. 2 (Summer): 240–250.

Bishop, George F., Alfred J. Tuchfarber, Robert W. Oldendick, and Stephen E. Bennett. 1979. "Questions about Question Wording: A Rejoinder to Revisting Mass Belief Systems Revisited." *American Journal of Political Science* 23, no. 1 (February): 187–92.

Bishop, George F., Alfred J. Tuchfarber, and Andrew E. Smith. 1994. "Question Form and Context Effects in the Measurement of Partisanship: Experimental Tests of the Artifact Hypothesis." *American Political Science Review* 88, no. 4 (December): 945–58.

Blumer, Herbert. 1948a. "Public Opinion and Public Opinion Polling." *American Sociological Review* 13, no. 5 (October): 542–49.

———. 1948b. "Rejoinder." *Public Opinion Quarterly* 13, no. 5 (October): 554.

———. 1972. *Silent Politics: Polls and the Awareness of Public Opinion*. New York: John Wiley & Sons.

Bogart, Leo. 1967. "No Opinion, Don't Know, and Maybe No Answer." *Public Opinion Quarterly* 31, no. 3 (Autumn): 331–45.

———. 1972. *Silent Politics: Polls and the Awareness of Public Opinion*. New York: Wiley & Sons.

Bourdieu, Pierre. 1979. "Public Opinion Does Not Exist." In *Communication and Class Struggle*. Vol. 1, *Capitalism, Imperialism*, ed. Armand Mattelart and Seth Sieglaub, 124–30. New York: International General.

Bradburn, Norman M., and Carrie Miles. 1979. "Vague Quantifiers." *Public Opinion Quarterly* 43, no. 1 (Spring): 92–101.

Brady, Henry E. 1985. "The Perils of Survey Research: Inter-Personally Incomparable Responses." *Political Methodology* 11, no. 3 (June): 269–90.

Brody, Richard A. 1998. "The Lewinsky Affair and Popular Support for President Clinton." Polling Report, November 16, www.pollingreport.com/brody.htm.

Campbell, Donald T. 1988. *Methodology and Epistemology for Social Science: Selected Papers*, ed. E. Samuel Overman. Chicago: University of Chicago Press.

Campbell, Angus, Philip E. Converse, Warren E. Miller, and Donald E. Stokes. 1960. *The American Voter*. New York: Wiley.

Candisky, Catherine. 2002. "Ohioans Don't Want Evolution Only." *Columbus Dispatch*, May 10, 13E.

Cantril, Hadley, and Edrita Fried. 1944. "The Meaning of Questions." In *Gauging Public Opinion*, ed. Hadley Cantril, 3–22. Princeton, N.J.: Princeton University Press.

Carlson, Darren K. 2003. "Should the U.S. Keep the Peace in Liberia?" Gallup Poll Tuesday Briefing, August 5.

Citrin, Jack, and Donald Philip Green. 1986. "Presidential Leadership and the Resurgence of Trust in Government." *British Journal of Political Science* 16, no. 4 (October): 431–53.

Clark, Herbert H., and Michael F. Schober. 1992. "Asking Questions and Influencing Answers." In *Questions about Questions: Inquiries into the Cognitive Bases of Surveys,* ed. Judith M. Tanur, 15–48. New York: Russell Sage.

Clymer, Adam. 2001. "The Unbearable Lightness of Public Opinion Polls." *New York Times,* July 22, sec. 4, p. 3.

Connelly, Marjorie. 2000. "Who Voted: A Portrait of American Politics, 1976–2000." *New York Times,* November 12, sec. 4, p. 4.

Conover, Pamela, and Stanley Feldman. 1981. "The Origins and Meanings of Liberal/ Conservative Self-Identifications." *American Journal of Political Science* 25, no. 4 (November): 617–45.

Converse, Jean. 1976–1977. "Predicting No Opinion in the Polls." *Public Opinion Quarterly* 40, no. 4 (Winter): 515–30.

Converse, Jean M. 1987. *Survey Research in the United States: Roots and Emergence 1890– 1960.* Berkeley: University of California Press.

Converse, Philip. 1964. "The Nature of Belief Systems in Mass Publics." In *Ideology and Discontent,* ed. David E. Apter, 206–61. New York: Free Press.

———. 1970. "Attitudes and Nonattitudes: Continuation of a Dialogue." In *The Quantitative Analysis of Social Problems,* ed. Edward R. Tufte, 168–89. Reading, Mass.: Addison-Wesley.

———. 1987. "Changing Conceptions of Public Opinion in the Political Process." *Public Opinion Quarterly* 51, no. 4 (Winter): S12–24.

Crespi, Irving. 1988. *Pre-election Polling: Sources of Accuracy and Error.* New York: Russell Sage Foundation.

———. 1989. *Public Opinion, Polls, and Democracy.* Boulder, Colo.: Westview Press.

Daniel Yankelovich Group (DYG). 2000. "Evolution and Creationism in Public Education: An In-Depth Reading of Public Opinion." March. Washington, D.C.: People for the American Way Foundation.

Davis, James A. 1987. "The Future Study of Public Opinion." *Public Opinion Quarterly* 51, no. 4, pt. 2 (Winter): S178–79.

———. 1992. "Changeable Weather in a Cooling Climate atop the Liberal Plateau." *Public Opinion Quarterly* 56, no. 3 (Autumn): 261–306.

Dearing, James W. 1989 "Setting the Polling Agenda for the Issue of AIDS." *Public Opinion Quarterly* 53, no. 3 (Autumn): 309–29.

Delli Carpini, Michael, and Scott Keeter. 1991. "Stability and Change in the U.S. Public's Knowledge of Politics." *Public Opinion Quarterly* 55, no. 4 (Winter): 583–612.

———. 1996. *What Americans Know about Politics and Why It Matters.* New Haven, Conn.: Yale University Press.

Edwards, George C., III, William Mitchell, and Reed Welch. 1995. "Explaining Presidential Approval: The Significance of Issue Salience." *American Journal of Political Science* 39, no. 1 (February): 108–34.

Eisinger, Robert M. 1999. "Cynical America? Misunderstanding the Public's Message." *Public Perspective* 10, no. 3 (April/May): 45–48.

Erickson, Robert S. 1979. "The SRC Panel Data and Mass Political Attitudes." *British Journal of Political Science* 9: 16–49.

Erickson, Robert S., and Kent L. Tedin. 2001. *American Public Opinion.* 6th ed. New York: Longman.

Erskine, Hazel Gaudet. 1962. "The Polls: The Informed Public." *Public Opinion Quarterly* 26, no. 4 (Winter): 669–77.

———. 1963a. "The Polls: Exposure to Domestic Information." *Public Opinion Quarterly* 27, no. 3 (Autumn): 491–500.

———. 1963b. "The Polls: Textbook Knowledge." *Public Opinion Quarterly* 27, no. 1 (Spring): 133–41.

Eubank, Robert B., and David J. Gow. 1983. "The Pro-Incumbent Bias in the 1976 and 1980 National Election Studies." *American Journal of Political Science* 27, no. 1 (February): 122–39.

Faulkenberry, G. David, and Robert Mason. 1978. "Characteristics of Nonopinion and No Opinion Response Groups." *Public Opinion Quarterly* 42, no. 4 (Winter): 533–43.

Fee, Joan. 1981. "Symbols in Survey Questions: Solving the Problem of Multiple Word Meanings." *Political Methodology* 7: 71–95.

Ferber, Robert. 1956. "The Effect of Respondent Ignorance on Survey Results." *Journal of the American Statistical Association* 51, no. 276 (December): 576–86.

Fishkin, James S. 1991. *Democracy and Deliberation: New Directions for Democratic Reform.* New Haven, Conn.: Yale University Press.

Fishkin, James S. 1992. "The Idea of a Deliberative Opinion Poll." *Public Perspective* 3, no. 2 (January/February): 26–27.

———. 1995. *The Voice of the People.* New Haven, Conn.: Yale University Press.

Foddy, William. 1993. *Constructing Questions for Interviews and Questionnaires.* Cambridge, U.K.: Cambridge University Press.

Foucault, Michel. 1979. *Discipline and Punish: The Birth of the Prison.* New York: Vintage.

———. 1980. *Power/Knowledge: Selected Interviews and Other Writings, 1972–1977.* New York: Pantheon.

Fowler, Floyd Jackson, Jr. 1992. "How Unclear Terms Affect Survey Data." *Public Opinion Quarterly* 56, no. 2 (Summer): 218–31.

———. 2002. *Survey Research Methods.* 3rd ed. Thousand Oaks, Calif.: Sage Publications.

Francis, Joe D., and Lawrence Busch. 1975. "What We Now Know about 'I Don't Knows'." *Public Opinion Quarterly* 39, no. 2 (Summer): 207–18.

Gallup, George H. 1947. "The Quintamensional Plan of Question Design." *Public Opinion Quarterly* 11, no. 3 (Autumn): 385–93.

———. 1976. *The Sophisticated Poll Watcher's Guide.* Princeton, N.J.: Princeton University Press.

Gallup, George H., and Saul F. Rae. 1940. *The Pulse of Democracy.* New York: Simon and Schuster.

Gallup News Service. 2001a. "In Their Own Words: Why Americans Approve or Disapprove of Bush." July 3.

———. 2001b. "Religion in the Aftermath of September 11." December 21.

Gill, Sam. 1947. "How Do You Stand on Sin?" *Tide*, March 14, 72.

Ginsberg, Benjamin. 1986. *The Captive Public: How Mass Opinion Promotes State Power.* New York: Basic Books.

Gollin, Albert E. 1987. "Polling and the News Media." *Public Opinion Quarterly* 51, no. 4, part 2 (Winter): S86–93.

Goodnight, G. Thomas. 1992. "Habermas, the Public Sphere, and Controversy." *International Journal of Public Opinion Research* 4, no. 3 (Autumn): 243–55.

Groves, Robert M. 1989. *Survey Errors and Survey Costs.* New York: Wiley.

Herbst, Susan. 1992. "Surveys in the Public Sphere: Applying Bourdieu's Critique of Opinion Polls." *International Journal of Public Opinion Research* 4, no. 3 (Autumn): 220–29.

―――. 1993. *Numbered Voices: How Opinion Polling Has Shaped American Politics*. Chicago: University of Chicago Press.

―――. 1998. *Reading Public Opinion: How Political Actors View the Democratic Process*. Chicago: University of Chicago Press.

Hetherington, Marc J. 1998. "The Effect of Political Trust on the Presidential Vote." *American Political Science Review* 93, no. 2 (December): 791–808.

Holbrook, Allyson, Jon A. Krosnick, David Moore, and Roger Tourangeau. 2003. "Response Order Effects in Categorical Questions Presented Orally: The Impact of Warnings to Wait and Illusory Endings." Paper presented at the annual conference of the American Association for Public Opinion Research, Nashville, Tenn., May 15–18.

Jacobe, Dennis. 2003. "Increased Consumer Confidence: Real or Illusory?" Gallup News Service, May 13.

Jones, Jeffrey M. 2001a. "Americans Rate Cheney Positively." Gallup News Service, June 7.

―――. 2001b. "Two-Thirds of Americans Support Death Penalty for Convicted Murderers." Gallup News Service, March 2.

―――. 2002. "Bush Averages Near-Record 86% Job Approval Rating in the Fourth Quarter." Gallup News Service, January 17.

―――. 2003. "Support for the Death Penalty Remains High at 74%." Gallup News Service, May 19.

Kagay, Michael R. 1999. "Public Opinion and Polling during the Presidential Scandal and Impeachment." *Public Opinion Quarterly* 63, no. 3 (Fall): 449–63.

Katz, Daniel. 1944. "The Measurement of Intensity." In *Gauging Public Opinion*, ed. Hadley Cantril, 51–65. Princeton, N.J.: Princeton University Press.

Keene, Karlyn H., and Victoria A. Sackett. 1981. "An Editors Report on the Yankelovich, Skelly, and White 'Mushiness Index'." *Public Opinion* 4 (April/May): 50–51.

Keeter, Scott. 1999. "The Perplexing Case of Public Opinion about the Clinton Scandal." Paper presented at the annual conference of the American Association for Public Opinion Research, St. Petersburg, Fla., May 13–16.

Kessler, Glenn. 1992. "Clinton Wins on Economy, Vision." *Newsday*, November 4, 28.

Kinder, Donald R. 1985. "Public Opinion and Political Action." In *The Handbook of Social Psychology*, vol. 2, ed. Gardner Lindzey and Elliot Aronson, 659–742.

―――. 1998. "Opinion and Action in the Realm of Politics." In *The Handbook of Social Psychology*, ed. Daniel T. Gilbert, Susan T. Fiske, and Gardner Lindzey, 778–867. New York: McGraw-Hill.

King, Elliot, and Michael Schudson. 1995. "The Press and the Illusion of Public Opinion: The Strange Case of Ronald Reagan's 'Popularity'." In *Public Opinion and the Communication of Consent*, ed. Theodore L. Glasser and Charles T. Salmon, 132–55. New York: Guilford Press.

Knight, Kathleen, and Robert S. Erickson. 1997. "Ideology in the 1990s." In *Understanding Public Opinion*, ed. Barbara Norrander and Clyde Wilcox, 91–110. Washington, D.C.: CQ Press.

Krosnick, Jon A., and Duane F. Alwin. 1987. "An Evaluation of a Cognitive Theory of Response Order Effects in Survey Measurement." *Public Opinion Quarterly* 52: 526–38.

Ladd, Everett Carll. 1994. "The Holocaust Poll Error: A Modern Cautionary Tale." *Public Perspective* 5, no. 5 (July/August): 3–5.

―――. 1998. "Why Reporting of the Polls Has Consistently Understated the Drop in Clinton's Support." *Public Perspective* 9, no. 6 (October/November): 35–37.

Langer, Gary. 2002a. "Responsible Polling in the Wake of 9/11." *Public Perspective* 13, no. 2 (March/April): 14–16.

———. 2002b. "Trust in Government . . . to Do What?" *Public Perspective* 13, no. 4 (July/August): 7–10.

Lazarsfeld, Paul F. 1944. "The Controversy over Detailed Interviews: An Offer for Negotiation." *Public Opinion Quarterly* 8, no. 1 (Spring): 38–60.

———. 1950–1951. "The Obligations of the 1950 Pollster to the 1984 Historian." *Public Opinion Quarterly* 14, no. 4 (Winter): 617–38.

Lewis, Justin. 2001. *Constructing Public Opinion.* New York: Columbia University Press.

Lewis-Beck, Michael S. 1985. "Pocketbook Voting in U.S. National Election Studies: Fact or Artifact?" *American Journal of Political Science* 29, no. 2 (May): 348–56.

Lippmann, Walter. 1922. *Public Opinion.* Repr., New York: Free Press, 1997.

———. 1925. *The Phantom Public.* New York: Harcourt, Brace.

Luttbeg, Norman. 1968. "The Structure of Belief among Leaders and the Public." *Public Opinion Quarterly* 32, no. 3 (Autumn): 398–409.

MacKuen, Michael B., Robert S. Erickson, and James A. Stimson. 1989. "Macropartisanship." *American Political Science Review* 83, no. 4 (December): 1125–42.

MacKuen, Michael B., Robert S. Erickson, James A. Stimson, Paul R. Abramson, and Charles W. Ostrom Jr. 1992. "Question Wording and Macropartisanship." *American Political Science Review* 86, no. 2 (June): 475–86.

McLean, Scott L. 2003. "Rally-Round-Religion." *Public Perspective* 14, no. 1 (January/February): 25–27, 37.

Merkle, Daniel M., and Murray Edelman. 2000. "A Review of the 1996 Voter News Service Exit Polls from a Total Error Perspective." In *Election Polls, the News Media, and Democracy,* ed. Paul J. Lavrakas and Michael W. Traugott, 68–92. New York: Chatham House.

Miller, Warren E., and J. Merrill Shanks. 1996. *The New American Voter.* Cambridge, Mass.: Harvard University Press.

Mitofsky, Warren J., and Murray Edelman. 1993. "A Review of the 1992 VRS Exit Polls." Paper presented at the annual conference of the American Association for Public Opinion Research, St. Charles, Ill., May 20–23.

———. 1995. "A Review of the 1992 VRS Exit Polls." In *Presidential Polls and the News Media,* ed. Paul J. Lavrakas, Michael W. Traugott, and Peter V. Miller, 81–100. Boulder, Colo.: Westview Press.

Moore, David W. 1998. "Republicans, Independents Boost Clinton's Approval Rating to Record High." Gallup News Service, January 31.

———. 1999. "Americans Support Teaching Creationism As Well As Evolution in Public Schools." Gallup News Service, August 30.

———. 2001a. "Public Supports Concept of Missile Defense." Gallup News Service, August 1.

———. 2001b. "Terrorism Most Important Problem, but Americans Remain Upbeat." Gallup News Service, October 18.

———. 2002a. "Defense Spending." Gallup News Service, Special report, September.

———. 2002b. "Just One Question: The Myth and Mythology of Trust in Government." *Public Perspective* 13, no. 1 (January/February): 7–11.

———. 2003. "Americans Favor U.S. Peacekeeping Force in Liberia." Gallup News Service, July 11.

Moore, David W., and Frank Newport. 1994. "Misreading the Public: The Case of the Holocaust Poll." *Public Perspective* 5, no. 3 (March/April): 28–29.

———. 1996. "Public Policy Questions and Response Order: Prevalence of the Recency Effect." Paper presented at the annual conference of the American Association for Public Opinion Research, Salt Lake City, Utah, May 16–19.

Morin, Richard. 1995. "What Informed Public Opinion?" *Washington Post*, national weekly edition, June 26–July 2, 34.

National Election Studies. 1995–2000. *The NES Guide to Public Opinion and Electoral Behavior*. Ann Arbor: University of Michigan, Center for Political Studies (producer and distributor). At www.umich.edu/~nes/nesguide/nesguide.htm.

Neuman, W. Russell. 1986. *The Paradox of Mass Politics*. Cambridge, Mass.: Harvard University Press.

Newport, Frank. 1998. "Reporting Poll Results Better." *Public Perspective* 9, no. 2 (February/March): 87.

———. 1999. "Presidential Job Approval: Bill Clinton's High Ratings in the Midst of Crisis." Gallup News Service, June 4.

———. 2000. "Americans Favor Social Security Investment Proposal." *Gallup News Service*, June 12.

———. 2001a. "Clinton's Job Approval Legacy." Gallup News Service, January 4.

———. 2001b. "What We Can Learn from Americans' Views about the Death Penalty." Gallup News Service, May 17.

———. 2002a. "Iraq, Demographic Differences in Support for the War, Bush Approval, Satisfaction with the Way Things Are Going, Media Coverage of the War." *Gallup News Service*, March 25.

———. 2002b. "What Were Sept. 11's Effects on Religion in America?" Gallup News Service, January 2.

Newport, Frank, and Joseph Carroll. 2001. "No Public Consensus Yet on School Voucher Programs." Gallup News Service, January 15.

Nie, Norman H., with Kristi Andersen. 1974. "Mass Belief Systems Revisited: Political Change and Attitude Structure." *Journal of Politics* 36, no. 3 (August): 540–91.

Nie, Norman H., Sidney Verba, and John R. Petrocik. 1976, 1979. *The Changing American Voter*, enlarged ed. Cambridge, Mass.: Harvard University Press.

Nisbet, Richard E., and Timothy Decamp Wilson. 1977. "Telling More Than We Can Know: Verbal Reports on Mental Processes." *Psychological Review* 84, no. 3 (May): 231–59.

Noelle-Neumann, Elisabeth. 1993. *The Spiral of Silence*. 2nd ed. Chicago: University of Chicago Press.

Nye, Joseph S., Jr., Philip D. Zelikov, and David C. King. 1997. *Why Americans Don't Trust Government*. Cambridge, Mass.: Harvard University Press.

Orren, Gary. 1997. "Fall from Grace: The Public's Loss of Faith in Government." In *Why Americans Don't Trust Government*, ed. Joseph S. Nye Jr., Philip D. Zelikov, and David C. King, 77–107. Cambridge, Mass.: Harvard University Press.

Page, Benjamin I., and Robert Y. Shapiro. 1992. *The Rational Public*. Chicago: University of Chicago Press.

Parker, Suzanne L. 1995. "Toward an Understanding of 'Rally' Effects: Public Opinion in the Persian Gulf War." *Public Opinion Quarterly* 59, no. 4 (Winter): 526–46.

Payne, Stanley L. 1950–1951. "Thoughts about Meaningless Questions." *Public Opinion Quarterly* 14, no. 4 (Winter): 687–96.

———. 1951. *The Art of Asking Questions*. Princeton, N.J.: Princeton University Press.

Peer, Limor. 1992. "The Practice of Opinion Polling As a Disciplinary Mechanism: A Foucauldian Perspective." *International Journal of Public Opinion Research* 4, no. 3 (Autumn): 230–42.

Pew Research Center. 2001. "Post-September 11 Attitudes." Survey report, December 6.

———. 2002a. "Americans Struggle with Religion's Role at Home and Abroad." Survey report, March 28.

———. 2002b. "One Year Later: New Yorkers More Troubled, Washingtonians More on Edge." Survey report, September 5.

———. 2002c. "Public Makes Distinctions on Genetic Research." Survey report, April 9.

Price, Vincent. 1992. *Public Opinion*. Newbury Park, Calif.: Sage Publications.

Rabjohn, James N. 1976. "The Effect of Question Wording in National Surveys." Unpublished MA paper, Department of Political Science, University of Chicago, Spring.

———. 1977. "Political Constraint: Report on an Experiment in Attitude Measurement." Paper presented at the annual conference of the Midwest Association for Public Opinion Research, Chicago, Ill., October 27–29.

Rademacher, Eric W. 2001. "Most Ohioans Approve of President Bush in Wake of September 11." Ohio Poll press release, November 17, Institute for Policy Research, University of Cincinnati.

———. 2002. Ohio Poll project report to the Internet Public Opinion Laboratory, Institute for Policy Research, University of Cincinnati, November.

Rademacher, Eric W., and Tom Shaw. 2001. "Presidential Approval Holds at 60 Percent." Ohio Poll press release, July 30, Institute for Policy Research, University of Cincinnati.

Rasinski, Kenneth A. 1989. "The Effects of Question Wording on Public Support for Government Spending." *Public Opinion Quarterly* 53, no. 3 (Autumn): 388–94.

Riesman, David, and Nathan Glazer. 1948–1949. "The Meaning of Opinion." *Public Opinion Quarterly* 12, no. 4 (Winter): 633–48.

Ritter, John. 1996. "Mood of the Voters Ohio: Swing State Was a Bellwether for Dole's Camp." *USA Today*, November 6, 17A.

Robinson, John P., and John A. Fleishman. 1988. "Ideological Identification: Trends and Interpretations of the Liberal-Conservative Balance." *Public Opinion Quarterly* 52, no. 1 (Spring): 134–45.

Rogers, Lindsay. 1949. *The Pollsters*. New York: Knopf.

Roper, Burns W. 1983. "Some Things That Concern Me." *Public Opinion Quarterly* 47, no. 3 (Autumn): 303–9.

Roper, Elmo. 1942. "So the Blind Shall Not Lead." *Fortune* 25, no. 2: 102.

Rosen, Jay. 1999. *What Are Journalists For?* New Haven, Conn.: Yale University Press.

Rugg, Donald, and Hadley Cantril. 1944. "The Wording of Questions." In *Gauging Public Opinion*, ed. Hadley Cantril, 23–50. Princeton, N.J.: Princeton University Press.

Saad, Lydia. 1999. "Americans Divided over Abortion Debate." Gallup News Service, May 18.

———. 2002. "Have Americans Changed? Effects of Sept. 11 Have Largely Faded." Gallup News Service, September 11.

———. 2003. "Abortion Views Hold Steady over Past Year." Gallup News Service, June 2.

Sapiro, Virginia. 2002. "It's the Context, Situation, and Question, Stupid: The Gender

Basis of Public Opinion." In *Understanding Public Opinion*, ed. Barbara Norrander and Clyde Wilcox, 21–41. Washington, D.C.: CQ Press.

Schuman, Howard. 1966. "The Random Probe: A Technique for Evaluating the Validity of Closed Questions." *American Sociological Review* 31, no. 2 (April): 218–22.

———. 1982. "Artifacts Are in the Mind of the Beholder." *American Sociologist* 17 (February): 21–28.

———. 1986. "Ordinary Questions, Survey Questions, and Policy Questions." *Public Opinion Quarterly* 50, no. 3 (Fall): 432–42.

———. 1998. "Interpreting Poll Results Better." *Public Perspective* 9, no. 1 (February/March): 87–88.

———. 2001. "The Fine Line between Fiction and Non-Fiction." Posting on aapornet@usc.edu, July 20.

Schuman, Howard, and Stanley Presser. 1980. "Public Opinion and Public Ignorance: The Fine Line between Attitudes and Nonattitudes." *American Journal of Sociology* 85, no. 5 (March): 1214–25.

———. 1981. *Questions and Answers in Attitude Surveys*. New York: Academic Press.

Schuman, Howard, Stanley Presser, and Jacob Ludwig. 1981. "Context Effects on Survey Responses to Survey Questions about Abortion." *Public Opinion Quarterly* 45, no. 2 (Summer): 216–23.

Schuman, Howard, and Jacqueline Scott. 1987. "Problems in the Use of Survey Questions to Measure Public Opinion." *Science* 236: 957–59.

Schwarz, Norbert. 1995. "What Respondents Learn from Questionnaires: The Survey Interview and the Logic of Conversation." Working Paper Series, Survey Methodology Program, University of Michigan, Institute for Social Research, Survey Research Center, January.

Sears, David O., and Richard R. Lau. 1983. "Inducing Apparently Self-Interested Political Preferences." *American Journal of Political Science* 27, no. 2 (May): 223–52.

Singer, Eleanor. 1987. "Editor's Introduction." *Public Opinion Quarterly* 51, no. 4, pt. 2 (Winter): S1–3.

Smith, Eric R. A. N. 1990. "The Effects of Prestige Names in Question Wording." Public Opinion Quarterly 54, no. 1 (Spring): 97–116.

Smith, Tom W. 1984. "Nonattitudes: A Review and Evaluation." In *Surveying Subjective Phenomena*, vol. 2, ed. Charles F. Turner and Elizabeth Martin, 215–55. New York: Russell Sage Foundation.

———. 1989. "Random Probes of GSS Questions." *International Journal of Public Opinion Research* 1, no. 1 (Winter): 305–25.

———. 1990. "Liberal and Conservative Trends in the United States Since World War II." *Public Opinion Quarterly* 54, no. 4 (Winter): 479–507.

———. 1995. "A Review: The Holocaust Denial Controversy." *Public Opinion Quarterly* 59, no. 2 (Summer): 269–95.

———. 2003. "Trust in People and Institutions: A 30-Year Trend from the GSS." Paper presented at the annual conference of the American Association for Public Opinion Research, Nashville, Tenn., May 15–18.

Splichal, Slavko. 1999. *Public Opinion: Developments and Controversies in the Twentieth Century*. Lanham, Md.: Rowman & Littlefield.

Stephens, Scott, and John Mangels. 2002. "Poll: Teach More Than Evolution; A Majority of Those Surveyed Want Evolution, Intelligent Design to Get Equal Time in Schools." *Plain Dealer*, June 9, A1.

Stille, Alexander. 2001. "Suddenly, Americans Trust Uncle Sam." *New York Times*, November 3, sec. A, p. 13.

Stimson, James. 1999. *Public Opinion in America: Moods, Cycles, and Swings*. Boulder, Colo.: Westview Press.

Suchman, Lucy, and Brigitte Jordan. 1992. "Validity and the Collaborative Construction of Meaning in Face-to-Face Surveys." In *Questions about Questions: Inquiries into the Cognitive Bases of Surveys*, ed. Judith M. Tanur, 241–67. New York: Russell Sage Foundation.

Sudman, Seymour, Norman M. Bradburn, and Norbert Schwarz. 1996. *Thinking about Answers*. San Francisco: Jossey-Bass.

Sullivan, John L., James E. Piereson, and George E. Marcus. 1978. "Ideological Constraint in the Mass Public." *American Journal of Political Science* 22, no. 2 (May): 233–49.

———. 1979. "An Alternative Conceptualization of Political Tolerance: Illusory Increases 1950s–1970s." *American Political Science Review* 73, no. 3 (September): 781–94.

Tannenhaus, Joseph, and Mary Foley. 1982. "The Words of Things Entangle and Confuse." *International Political Science Association* 3, no. 1: 107–29.

Tanur, Judith M., ed. 1992. *Questions about Questions: Inquiries into the Cognitive Bases of Surveys*. New York: Russell Sage.

Toner, Robin. 2001. "Now, Government Is the Solution, Not the Problem." *New York Times*, September 30, sec. 4, p. 14.

Tourangeau, Roger, Lance Rips, and Kenneth Rasinski. 2000. *The Psychology of Survey Response*. New York: Cambridge University Press.

Traugott, Michael W., and Elizabeth C. Powers. 2000. "Did Public Opinion Support the Contract with America?" In *Election Polls, the News Media, and Democracy*, ed. Paul J. Lavrakas and Michael W. Traugott, 93–110. New York: Chatham House.

Turner, Charles F. 1984. "Why Do Surveys Disagree? Some Preliminary Hypotheses and Some Disagreeable Examples." In *Surveying Subjective Phenomena*, vol. 2, ed. Charles F. Turner and Elizabeth Martin, 159–214. New York: Russell Sage Foundation.

von Sternberg, Bob. 2002. "President: Minnesota Rewards Democrats; But Our Historically Democratic State Wasn't As Good to Gore As It Was to Clinton in 1996; Bush Swayed Most Undecided Voters, and Nader Took Some Votes, Too." *Minneapolis Star Tribune*, November 8.

Warren, Kenneth F. 2001. *In Defense of Public Opinion Polling*. Boulder, Colo.: Westview Press.

Wegner, Daniel M. 2002. *The Illusion of Conscious Will*. Cambridge, Mass: MIT Press.

Weisberg, Herbert F. 1987. "The Demographics of a New Voting Gap: Marital Differences in American Voting." *Public Opinion Quarterly* 51, no. 3 (Autumn): 335–43.

Yankelovich, Daniel. 1991. *Coming to Public Judgment*. Syracuse, N.Y.: Syracuse University Press.

Zaller, John R. 1992. *The Nature and Origins of Mass Opinion*. Cambridge, U.K.: Cambridge University Press.

Zaller, John R., and Stanley Feldman. 1992. "A Simple Theory of the Survey Response." *American Journal of Political Science* 36: 579–616.

Zogby International. 2002. "Results from Ohio Poll on Darwin's Theory of Evolution, Public Schools." May 8.

Index

Note: Page numbers in *italic* type refer to tables, figures, or boxes.

Index

About the Author

George F. Bishop, a PhD from Michigan State University, is professor of political science and director of the Graduate Certificate Program in Public Opinion & Survey Research at the University of Cincinnati. He is also director of the Internet Public Opinion Laboratory in the Department of Political Science. Dr. Bishop has published numerous articles on survey methodology and public opinion in such journals and periodicals as *Public Opinion Quarterly, Public Perspective, Political Behavior,* the *American Journal of Political Science,* and the *American Political Science Review.* In addition to his professorial duties, he has held a joint appointment as senior research associate in the Institute for Policy Research at the University of Cincinnati, where he designed and directed countless survey research projects. He has also been a guest professor in several visits at the Center for Survey Research and Methodology (ZUMA) in Mannheim, Germany.